Your Official America Online® Guide to Powering Up the Internet

Your Official America Online® Guide to Powering Up the Internet

by John Kaufeld and
Steven Hunger

AOLPress

Dulles, VA

Your Official America Online® Guide to Powering Up the Internet

Published by

AOL Press

An imprint of IDG Books Worldwide, Inc.

An International Data Group Company

919 E. Hillsdale Blvd., Suite 400

Foster City, CA 94404

www.aol.com (America Online Web site)

Library of Congress Control Number: 00-105638

ISBN: 0-7645-3500-5

Printed in the United States of America

10 9 8 7 6

1B/QR/QS/QR/IN

Distributed in the United States by IDG Books Worldwide, Inc. and America Online, Inc.

For general information on IDG Books Worldwide's books in the U.S., please call our Consumer Customer Service department at 800-762-2974. For reseller information, including discounts and premium sales, please call our Reseller Customer Service department at 800-434-3422.

 is a trademark of America Online, Inc.

 is a registered trademark or trademark under exclusive license to IDG Books Worldwide, Inc. from International Data Group, Inc. in the United States and/or other countries.

Welcome to AOL Press™

AOL Press books provide timely guides to getting the most out of your online life. AOL Press was formed as part of the AOL family to create a complete series of official references for using America Online as well as the entire Internet — all designed to help you enjoy a fun, easy, and rewarding online experience.

AOL Press is an exciting partnership between two companies at the forefront of the knowledge and communications revolution — AOL and IDG Books Worldwide, Inc. AOL is committed to quality, ease of use, and value, and IDG Books excels at helping people understand technology.

To meet these high standards, all our books are authored by experts with the full participation of and exhaustive review by AOL's own development, technical, managerial, and marketing staff. Together, AOL and IDG Books have implemented an ambitious publishing program to develop new publications that serve every aspect of your online life.

We hope you enjoy reading this AOL Press title and find it useful. We welcome your feedback at AOL Keyword: **Contact Shop Direct** so we can keep providing information the way you want it.

AOLPress

About the Authors

John Kaufeld writes books because he can't find anyone to pay him for playing games (well, at least not *full-time* pay). Granted, John loves writing, so that makes his full-time authoring (or writing?) mission a pretty fun occupation. He's responsible for a wide variety of Dummies books, including bestsellers *America Online For Dummies,* 6th Edition, *Access 2000 For Windows For Dummies,* and *Access 97 For Windows For Dummies.* Look for him on the third Monday of each month at his "AOL For Dummies" online event in AOL Live (Keyword: **AOL LIVE**).

Steve Hunger looks at the world through rose-colored digital gadgets, which he says will replace eyeglasses someday (really, they will!). Steve owns Rhino Tech (www.rhino-tech. com), a startup Web-hosting and e-commerce development company. When not wandering through the Internet in search of still more goodies to download, he has co-authored and contributed to several books for Brady Books and Macmillan Computer Publishing.

Credits

America Online

Technical Editors
Rowena Adamson
Jennifer Canestraro
Caroline Curtin
Ben Eisendrath
Andy Erickson
Keith Fleming
Marta Grutka
Kelly Kemmerer
Jeff Kimball

Debra Lavoy
Jane Lennon
Sheila Leverone
Carlos Silva
Bradley Spannbauer
Scott Spelbring
Ginny Wydler

Cover Design
DKG Design, Inc.

IDG Books Worldwide

Project Editor
Paul Levesque

Acquisitions Editor
Kathy Yankton

Senior Copy Editor
Barry Childs-Helton

Proof Editor
Jill Mazurczyk

Technical Editor
Susan Glinert

Permissions Editor
Carmen Krikorian

Publishing Director
Andy Cummings

Editorial Manager
Leah Cameron

Media Development Manager
Heather Heath Dismore

Editorial Assistants
Candace Nicholson, Seth Kerney

Project Coordinator
Valery Bourke

Layout and Graphics
Joe Bucki, Brian Torwelle,
Erin Zeltner

Proofreaders
Laura Albert, Corey Bowen,
Vickie Broyles, John Greenough,
Arielle Carole Mennelle,
Susan Moritz, Marianne Santy

Indexer
Sharon Hilgenberg

Authors' Acknowledgments

From John: Wow — another one bites the dust. First, special congratulations to my co-author, Steve Hunger. I knew we could do it, Steve!

Thanks to Andy Cummings, who involved me in this unique project. Perhaps now that the book is done, your hair won't come out in clumps any more. (Single strands make the loss go farther, believe me.) Thanks also go to Kathy Yankton, who delightfully endured the arduous job of herding Steve and me through the book-creation process. An entire truckload of chocolate and other wonderful things goes to Paul Levesque, our beleaguered editor. Paul rose above and beyond the call of duty — up, up, and away! — in his masterful work with our text. If anyone deserves a restful month on the French Riviera far away from cell phones and Internet access, it's Paul. (Come to think of it, Steve and I could use that too...)

Of course, kudos go to the myriad production and editing folks behind the scenes as well, because you wouldn't hold this book without their help! Thanks and a bouquet of delightful flowers go to our America Online contact, Kathy Harper, as well as to the many AOL staffers who helped us along the way. Without your assistance, this book wouldn't be what it is.

Finally, my love and thanks to my beautiful wife Jenny, and to the Kaufeld chicklets — J.B. and the Pooz. Anybody up for a trip to Chuck E. Cheese?

From Steve: I'd like to thank the folks on the AOL and IDG staff for their support on this book, with special thanks to Paul Levesque for input and suggestions as I occasionally struggled to assemble a coherent sentence. Thanks also to Kathy Yankton for her prodding to keep us on schedule. They have been invaluable to this book.

Of course, I must thank the three most important people in my life who gave their support to me as I worked on this book — my wife Sandy (for her loving support), my friend John (who asked me to co-author this book with him), and my Father (who has always been there when I needed him). I'd also like to thank Cody, who offered so many times to willingly test these gadgets (mysteriously, I seemed to be able to test them myself — thanks anyway, Cody).

Contents at a Glance

Table of Contents

Part IV: Protecting Your Privacy, Your Kids, and the Computer — 137

Chapter 15: Privacy Settings and Parental Controls Inside AOL . . . 140

Chapter 16: Protecting Your Stuff 150

Chapter 17: The Question of Cookies 160

Part V: Tools for Taming the E-Mail Beast — 169

Chapter 18: Information Delivered to Your Digital Doorstep 172

Part VIII: Playing the Night Away   263

Part IX: Saving Money, Spending Money   291

Introduction

Cool. Hot. New. Ever-changing. Incredible. Nerve-wracking. Fascinating. Capturing the essence of the Internet takes more than a word or two — it takes the better part of a dictionary. The Net created a world of permanent change and constant flux, where new technologies burst into view like skyrockets during a fireworks finale (and sometimes disappear just as quickly).

Entertaining as it is, this endless parade of technical innovation can leave people feeling a bit overwhelmed. New hardware and software — and worse, new ways of doing things — entertain the technological elite, but what about those of us with real (as in "non-Internet") lives to live and work to do?

This book is your solution — your defense against the rising techno-tide. It introduces and explores a broad variety of new technologies, giving you the knowledge and insight that you need to pick the ones that work best for you. It explains the technologies, identifies the main companies involved, and points out resources (both online and offline) for learning more. It's your handbook for the coolest and newest goodies on the Net.

Who Should Read This Book

This book takes you on a grand tour of the online world's coolest technologies. Of course, the tour has to start somewhere, so take a look at the following bullet points to see whether this trip is for you:

▶ Are you familiar with Windows 95 or 98, including using Windows and Windows applications, and installing programs?

▶ Are you using America Online version 5 or 6 for Windows?

▶ Are you curious about all the new, cool things happening on the Net?

You don't need *expert*-level knowledge about all these things to enjoy this book. (If you're *that* good, you should help us write the book!)

If you use a Macintosh computer, this book still offers a lot of useful information. Most of the software and technologies discussed in here exist for the Macintosh as well as Windows, although the program and process details may differ.

How the Book Is Organized

No matter how good the information in a book is, the volume's real value depends on whether you can *find* what you want to know when you need to know it. The eleven parts of this book corral its contents into topical chunks, simplifying your quest for information.

Some books demand that you read them straight through, from cover to cover. Other books don't care where you start reading or where you stop. This book follows with the second view, although you *can* still read from cover to cover. (After all, it *is* your book.) On the other hand, if you need a topic that's in the middle of the book somewhere, just jump straight to it — don't worry about skipping anything in the middle. Each part and chapter stands by itself, and includes cross-references to other parts of the book as needed.

Here's a quick overview of what's waiting for you inside these covers.

Part I: AOL Here, AOL There — It's AOL Everywhere

America Online caught — some might even say *made* — the first big wave of interest in the Internet, and AOL never looked back. Now, as the Net moves into new worlds of wireless e-mail, high-speed connections, and computer-less browsing, America Online leads the way. Part I covers AOL's efforts to be everywhere you are, and everywhere you want them to be.

Part II: The Best of the New Technology

Computer technology never stops changing, although sometimes you almost wish it would take a breather for a month or two. Part II describes the changes in computer hardware, including both desktop computers and palmtop wonders. For good measure, the part also peeks at non-traditional Internet access, high-speed connectivity, and other technological wonders.

Part III: Home Is Where the Network Is

Years ago, personal computers appeared at the office, and then they migrated to the house. The same thing is happening today with computer networking — another office-based technology wends its way homeward. This chapter explores the history and overview of computer networking and then applies the theories to the problem of connecting multiple computers at home.

Part IV: Protecting Your Privacy, Your Kids, and the Computer

Worried about your kids online? Of course you are! Part IV offers insight into America Online's suite of online protection tools, as well as general Internet tools that shield you, your kids, and your computers from unwanted eyes.

Part V: Tools for Taming the E-Mail Beast

Everybody loves e-mail — well, maybe not — but at least most everybody uses it. Discover a wonderful collection of ways to put your mailbox to work in this cool part of the book. Part V also explains the hows and whys of unsolicited commercial e-mail (including some tips for getting the dratted stuff out of your mailbox), plus a great introduction to PowerMail, one of the coolest AOL add-ons available.

Part VI: Images in the Digital Age

The online world not only changed the way we think of mail, but it completely altered our concepts of still photography and video as well. In Part VI, take a tour of the software and hardware tools available for messing around with digital photography, Webcams, and home video.

Part VII: Music Makes the Online World Go Around

Digital music is taking the world by storm, and Part VII equips you to join in the fun! Starting with the incredible range of online music stations, and then moving into the wild realm of MP3 and digital music formats, these chapters truly change your view of music forever.

Part VIII: Playing the Night Away

There's nothing like a nice game of chess — particularly when it's against an opponent half a world away! The Internet puts a whole new light on multiplayer games and gaming, as these chapters point out. Whether it's free fun on the Web, the best in high-tech games on America Online, or high-stakes excitement on a home network, there's plenty to play in the online world.

Part IX: Saving Money, Spending Money

If you love garage sales, hidden bargains, and any other form of shopping, then take the phone off the hook, get out your credit card, and dive head-long into these chapters. Part IX gives you the low-down on shopping through the Net, discovering wonderful deals in on-line auctions, and more. It even includes a section on getting some of the action for yourself as an online seller through the Net's cool auction services.

Part X: Doing the Net in High-Tech Style

America Online builds most of the Net's best features (searching, Web access, and more) directly into its easy-to-use software, but sometimes you want raw power instead of ease-of-use. For moments like that, turn to the chapters in Part X. They cover alternative Web browsers, powerful Internet software, Instant Messaging programs, and more.

Part XI: We Can Rebuild It! Making Your PC Newer, Faster, and Better

Although you feel frustrated at its lack of speed today, just a couple years ago your computer was the coolest (and fastest) thing on the block. Get a few more years out of that machine with some carefully-selected upgrades. The chapters in Part XI cover all your bases — including computer speed, disk space, video, and more.

Navigating Through the Book

The parts and chapters form the first level of support for finding your way through the book, but each chapter contains even more help, in the form of "Coming Up Next" sections and icons in the margin. These two features work hand in hand, simplifying your informational journey.

Each chapter closes with a "Coming Up Next" section. This section briefly previews the next chapter's contents, giving you a quick idea of what's ahead. These sections pay the biggest dividends to readers working their way sequentially through the book, although the notes help jump-into-the-midst readers as well.

A more common sight in the chapters are the icons, which are sprinkled here and there throughout the book. Each icon item includes some extra text that's relevant to the chapter, plus a visual cue describing the kind of details it contains. This book uses several types of icons, as described in the following list:

What on Earth does that term mean? Technology delivers tons of odd, peculiar, and down-right mysterious terms, so this icon reveals what the mysteries mean.

Track down more resources on the Internet or through an AOL Keyword.

What an idea! These tidbits simplify your online life.

When something needs a bit more explaining or insight, these icons ride to the rescue.

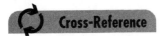

Each chapter can't be all things to all readers, so these icons point you to relevant informa-tion elsewhere in the book.

Watch out — this information steers you clear of trouble.

Chapter 1

AOLTV Makes the Tube Interactive

As more and more people go online and make the Internet and online interactivity a part of their everyday lives, many are doing so while they watch TV. Therefore, AOL has introduced a new interactive service to make it easier to combine these two activities into one; creating an even more rewarding experience. The new AOLTV[SM] service, an exciting addition to America Online's "AOL Anywhere" strategy, brings the most popular AOL features — and more — to the TV to enhance your viewing experience and to make TV more fun and entertaining. It's all designed to give you new and better ways to use and enjoy AOL *anywhere*.

What Is AOLTV?

AOLTV is the first interactive television service for mass-market consumers. AOLTV features a state-of-the-art AOLTV Program Guide[SM] and navigation features, which help you find what you want on TV faster and easier. In addition, AOLTV brings some of the most popular AOL features and services to the TV, enabling you to read and send e-mail, exchange instant messages, shop and chat online, and even access the Internet and browse the Web — anywhere you watch TV. You can also explore interesting online content about the program you are watching or its subject matter, set reminders and record your favorite TV shows, and more. With AOLTV, you're online, in tune, and in touch with the world like never before.

AOLTV enhances your television viewing experience by giving you fast, easy access to your favorite AOL features and services while you simultaneously tune in to your favorite TV programs. Plus, you get the added convenience of being able to use the AOL service on the computer and AOLTV at the same time — so two members on one account can enjoy an interactive experience from different devices at one time.

Revolutionizing the TV Experience

Imagine this scenario that occurs in many homes every day: While people settle down to watch television, they begin scrolling up and down a list of channels, passively looking for something to watch, or they surf endlessly through the whole channel line-up. Once they find a program they're interested in, they have to enter the channel number in order to see the program. Then they decide they want to watch something else, so they have to start scrolling, searching, and entering numbers all over again.

Find It Online

You can learn more about AOLTV online at www.aoltv.com or on AOL at AOL Keyword: **AOLTV.**

While watching a show they like, they think about how great it would be to talk to a friend, see how their stocks fared that day, get the score of a game, or check the weather forecast for the weekend. They also think about that one last e-mail that they forgot to send or read. They want to do all this, but they really want to keep watching the show, too. With AOLTV, you can. And you don't have to wait until a commercial break, miss one moment of a favorite program, or leave the comfort of the sofa.

Best of all, AOLTV gives you more control and makes navigating an array of TV channels simpler and easier — no scrolling through lists over and over.

The AOLTV Main Menu gives you one touch shortcuts to all the interactive features of the AOLTV service (see Figure 1-1). Among its features is the AOLTV Program Guide[SM], which simplifies navigation by organizing TV channels into 11 categories — such as networks, movies, news, kids and family, and others — so that you can find programs you want and change channels by clicking on words and graphics, as shown in Figure 1-2. You can view program summaries up to three days ahead of the broadcast date, and also customize a "Favorite Places" list of channels and shows for quick access. And, to ensure that you never miss your favorite programs, AOLTV makes it easy to set reminders and will notify you on-screen when a selected show is about to begin — AOLTV even records shows when you are away from your TV.

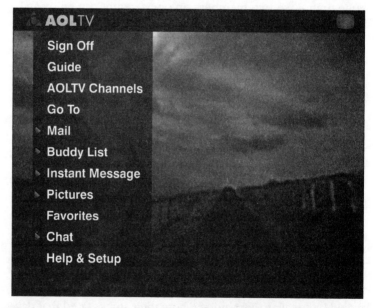

Figure 1-1. The AOLTV Main Menu is your gateway to all the features of AOLTV.

AOLTV is designed to allow for maximum enjoyment of both television programming and new interactive content. With its Picture-in-Picture (PIP) option, you can keep watching your favorite show while you check e-mail, get your stock quotes, and participate in a chat room discussion. At any time, you can go back to full picture viewing or simply sign-off of the AOLTV service. A special Notification Bar displays unobtrusive alerts to indicate when you have new e-mail messages or are receiving an instant message, and with a single click, you can again maximize the TV program to full screen size. The Buddy List feature is translucent, and fades or disappears when it's inactive. AOLTV's interactive features are always easily accessible whenever you want with one touch on the lightweight wireless remote keyboard.

AOLTV			
Networks	1	Interests	900
News	100	Music	1200
Money	300	Shopping	1500
Sports	400	Pay Per View	1600
Family	600	Local	2300
Movies	700		

Guides   Scheduler

AOLTV *Networks – Find out what's worth watching*

Mon 4:00p	7:30p		8:00p	8:30p
WJLA	4	Jeopardy!	Air Force One	
WUSA	6	Entertainment…	King of Queens	Ladies Man
WTTG	8	Seinfeld	That 70's Show	Titus
WRC	10	Access Hollywood	25 Years of Hits	
WMPT	12	Nightly Business	Secret of the Dead	
WDCA	15	Frasier	Moesha	The Parkers

Figure 1-2. The AOLTV Program Guide makes finding your favorite shows easy.

AOLTV makes it easy for everyone in the family to get the most out of their TV and have a personal, valuable interactive experience. AOLTV Channels offer interactive content and programming to complement TV shows. Sports fans, for example, watching a big game on TV can tune into the AOLTV Sports Channel to get immediate stats, scores, highlights, and additional coverage for other games and events. At any time, you can get instant weather forecasts for cities around the world, view local news updates, track stocks in your personal portfolio while watching business and market reports, join a chat community on a topic of interest, or participate in online polls and vote on different issues while watching headline news.

Parents will appreciate a built-in Parental Controls feature, which enables them to safeguard their children by limiting access to features such as chat, e-mail, instant messaging, and the Internet. AOLTV's "You've Got Pictures" SM feature is perfect for get-togethers — you can view photos with family and friends — right on the TV. And Shop@AOL offers TV viewers the most convenient one-stop shopping resource available online.

Putting It All Together

AOLTV is not a computer for the television. It's a new interactive service that delivers AOL's popular features, content, and services on the television through a small set-top box. The set-top box for the AOLTV service is easy to install and comes with a videotape explaining the setup process. The box plugs into the television through a cable port and connects online through a dial-up phone line.

You can watch your favorite TV shows and interact with the AOLTV service using a specially designed wireless keyboard and universal remote control, which are configured with special function keys that provide one-step access to key features such as the AOLTV Program Guide, E-mail, or the Buddy List feature. This design makes multitasking with AOLTV easy — from chatting about a show and exchanging instant messages with a friend to checking e-mail and even viewing Web content.

All you need to operate AOLTV is a television and a phone line; everything else is provided with the service, including membership to AOL and access to its global community of over 23 million people, and AOL's 24-hour customer service.

Find It Online

Check out how the different manufacturers come up with their own versions of AOLTV products at these manufacturers' Web sites: www.hns.com for Hughes Network Systems, www.philips.com for Philips Electronics, www.tivo.com for TiVo, and www.directv.com for DirecTV.

The Internet connection for AOLTV is presently based on AOL's nationwide dial-up network, but AOL is working with its manufacturing partners to support a number of high-speed options. In anticipation of such developments, all the AOLTV set-top boxes that are presently being manufactured come with a Universal Serial Bus (USB) port, which will allow for a Digital Subscriber Line (DSL), cable modem, or 56K-modem dial-up connection.

The AOLTV service is initially available with a Philips Electronics set-top box. A new platform also will soon be available through an AOLTV/DIRECTV set-top box manufactured by Hughes Network Systems that will combine AOLTV with digital television programming from DIRECTV. Additional platforms for accessing AOLTV are under development as well.

Text and figures courtesy of AOL.

Chapter 2

You've Got Mail —
In Your Hand

O f everything that the industry developed during the last decade, two computing technologies entered the new Millennium on the fast track. E-mail won our hearts and minds by keeping business running in the midst of impossible deadlines and far-flung co-workers, while handheld personal digital assistants (PDAs) tracked our busy day and fed a never-ending stream of vital phone numbers to our portable phone.

If they worked that well individually, imagine what they can accomplish together. With its new Palm and Windows CE (Windows for Consumer Electronics) e-mail clients, America Online marries the palmtop computing revolution to the world of online communication. This chapter explores this new world, and offers a peek into America Online's upcoming plans for even greater e-mail portability.

Reading Mail on Your Handheld

The tiny Palm Pilot fundamentally changed the way that busy people live and work. By compressing a person's entire collection of meetings, contacts, and notes into a single device, it prepared its users to face their hectic days. As Palm technology matured and Windows CE devices joined the fray, corporate computer departments took notice and integrated PDAs into the firm's data universe.

With so many of the devices on the market, it's no wonder that the developers at America Online took notice. As part of its ever-growing *AOL Anywhere* initiative, America Online developed e-mail software that meets the needs of busy, on-the-go people, while retaining America Online's hallmark ease of use. The resulting collaboration literally puts e-mail in your hand.

To use AOL Mail for Palm or Windows CE, you need one of the PDAs that the software supports. As of this writing, all Palm-manufactured organizers work with the program, as do many Windows CE devices. Palm-compatible devices like the Handspring Visor *may* work with the new e-mail application, but America Online doesn't guarantee full support yet.

In addition to the device itself, you need some kind of online connection. For the Palm devices, use the Palm modem, which is available at the AOL Shop Direct Store (AOL Keyword: **AOL Shop Direct**) or at most office supply and computer stores. Windows CE devices can use a direct network connection (connecting the device to your corporate or home network, then going to the Internet from there) or a dial-up link. Most palmtop Windows CE devices include a built-in modem, while handheld units usually require an add-on modem.

With the hardware pieces in place, it's time to download the software. For all palmtop and handheld e-mail programs, go to the AOL Anywhere area (AOL Keyword: **Anywhere,** shown in Figure 2-1), then follow the links for your specific device. Download and install the e-mail application according to your device's instructions. (The America Online e-mail program installs and works just like any other application for your palmtop or handheld device, so check your device's documentation for the details.)

Note

There's no extra fee to get e-mail through your Palm or Windows CE device, but the regular fees for your America Online account still apply. If you use an hourly usage plan, the time that you *connect* to America Online with your Palm or Windows CE device counts against your monthly total. Members using the Bring Your Own Access plan are charged per hour for local access number usage. All members pay a surcharge when using 800 number access.

Find It Online

Don't know if your Palm or Windows CE device works with the America Online e-mail client? Check the AOL Anywhere area (AOL Keyword: **Anywhere**) for a comprehensive list.

2

You've Got Mail — In Your Hand

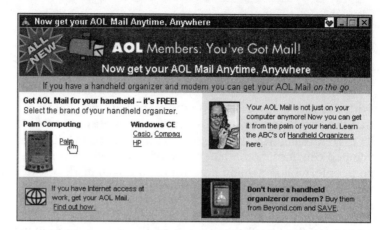

Figure 2-1. Whether you use a Palm or Windows CE digital assistant, your e-mail is only a few clicks away with AOL Mail for Palm or Windows CE.

Unlike the regular America Online software, AOL Mail for Palm and Windows CE doesn't offer a "guest" option. When you enter your screen name during the configuration process, AOL Mail for Palm and Windows CE permanently sets up for that account *only*. (Don't worry — it automatically detects new screen names for your account every time it checks for mail.) To use AOL Mail for these devices with a different America Online account, you must completely uninstall the program, then reinstall it.

Write your messages before connecting to the service, then use the AutoAOL feature to send and receive everything at once. It saves a lot of time and frustration!

After installing the program on your digital assistant, find a handy phone line, attach it to your device, and run the e-mail application. The first time you use the e-mail program, it runs through a series of configuration steps where it finds local access phone numbers and sets up for your screen names.

Once the phone numbers and screen names are in place, you're ready to send and receive mail. For new mail, the program signs onto America Online and then lists all your incoming messages. To save time, the program only shows the sender's address and part of the subject for each message — if you tap on a message entry in the list, the application goes back to the America Online service and downloads the whole message (up to 16,000 characters). It leaves file attachments on the service. Outbound mail that you wrote through the digital assistant lives in the Waiting section of the Personal Filing Cabinet until sent.

The Palm/Windows CE e-mail application includes a Personal Filing Cabinet for storing incoming and outbound messages and a full-featured phone book for storing local access numbers around the country. Like its big brother, the regular America Online software, the Palm/Windows CE program includes an AutoAOL feature that automates sending and collecting messages.

For in-depth help and information about the Palm/Windows CE e-mail program, visit the AOL Anywhere area (AOL Keyword: **Anywhere**). Make a habit of checking out the AOL Anywhere area frequently; that way you can keep up with up-coming features as well as new add-on applications.

There's Mail on Your Pager!

Accessing e-mail with your handy personal digital assistant adds a whole new dimension to your communication world, but there's still one big limitation: your e-mail is always a phone line away. No phone connection, no e-mail.

To overcome that problem, America Online is testing a wide variety of wireless e-mail options. In the coming year, you might get e-mail delivered straight to a pager or mobile phone. Who knows what cool possibilities a wireless future holds?

Coming Up Next

With the explosion of Internet connections cropping up everywhere from airports to libraries, Net-connected Web browsers are rarely out of reach. That's why America Online created the AOL Mail on the Web service, which puts your electronic mailbox as close as the nearest Web browser. Find out the details of this handy service in the next chapter!

Cross-Reference

Flip over to Chapter 8 for a look at taking the Internet with you everywhere through your mobile phone.

BROWSING YOUR
MESSAGES THROUGH
WEB-BASED AOL MAIL

Chapter 3

Browsing Your Messages through Web-based AOL Mail

E-mail rules the Internet. Sure, the Web looks flashier and offers tons of great stuff, but e-mail reigns as the undisputed King of Online Communication. Because it's an indispensable part of life these days, nobody wants to leave e-mail access at home or the office — but for a lot of people, lugging a laptop everywhere just isn't an option. What's a busy e-mail traveler to do? Turn to America Online's Web-based e-mail system, that's what!

Starting with a quick explanation of the whole Web-based mail concept, this chapter explores how America Online's Web-based mail keeps you in touch wherever you are. It includes tips for getting the most out of the system, plus a handy checklist of the similarities and differences between America Online's regular e-mail system and Web-based e-mail. Don't leave your e-mail without it!

Basics of AOL's Web-Based Mail

America Online's Web-based mail access looks something like one of the Web-only e-mail services, but its goals are quite different. The Web-only systems want to be your primary destination for all regular e-mail activities from this point onward. These systems not only set you up with an e-mail address, but they also offer all the tools you need to send, receive, and organize your mail on an ongoing basis.

AOL Mail on the Web (the official name of America Online's Web-based e-mail application) takes a different approach. It's not out to replace the America Online software as your primary mail program. Instead, it provides a set of tools for accessing your existing America Online e-mail box from almost any Internet-connected device on the planet. The Web-based system covers the e-mail basics (sending and receiving messages), but it doesn't replace the America Online software as your primary mail program. AOL Mail can't use fancy formatting in messages (as the AOL software can), but it does comprehend file attachments. The Web-based system exclusively serves as a mobile doorway into your existing America Online e-mail box, allowing you to access your AOL mail from "anywhere."

So how does AOL Mail compare to the e-mail features in the America Online software itself? Here's a quick overview:

> ▶ **Send, Receive, Forward, and Keep as New:** AOL Mail gives you all the simple e-mail tools you need, just like the full-tilt America Online software. Because AOL Mail works with your America Online e-mail box, you won't have to worry that you missed a message somewhere between the office and your current obscure location. If you saw it as an e-mail feature in the America Online software, you see it in AOL Mail.

> ▶ **File attachments:** Sending and receiving messages with attachments works just fine with AOL Mail. If you're on a borrowed computer (a machine in the public library or at an airport frequent-flier lounge, for example), don't download files from your e-mail messages to the machine. You might accidentally forget to delete the file, which could be a rather embarrassing mistake.

▶ **Address Book:** Because the Address Book lives inside the America Online software on your computer, there isn't much that AOL Mail can do for you. As smart as AOL Mail is, it can't wing its way through the Net and access something safely stored on your hard drive. That's why you should keep a copy of your most commonly used e-mail addresses in your planner or calendar (that simplifies moments like this).

▶ **Fonts, formatting, signatures, and spell checking:** The full America Online software really struts its stuff here. AOL Mail doesn't offer *any* of these options; you're stuck with basic, no-frills e-mail.

▶ **Return receipt service:** Just like the regular America Online software, AOL Mail includes return receipt service (so you know the e-mail arrived) for messages sent to America Online e-mail addresses. This service doesn't work for Internet addresses — sorry!

Be *very* careful when deleting messages through AOL Mail. Unlike the full America Online software, AOL Mail doesn't provide a way to recover accidentally deleted mail. The good news is that if you *do* delete a message through AOL Mail, you can restore the message through the America Online software (provided you do it within 24 hours of deleting the message).

Using AOL Mail on the Road

To get into AOL Mail, you don't need to take a laptop, personal digital assistant, or any other portable computing device along for the ride. Instead, all you need is an Internet-connected computer with a Web browser. AOL Mail also works with most alternative Internet-access devices (such as WebTV and AOLTV).

When you find an appropriate Internet-connected computer, you're mere moments away from checking your e-mail. Here's what to do:

Looking for a good place to check your mail while on the road? Try the Internet kiosks in airports and malls, cafés featuring Net connections (so-called *cybercafés*), and local public libraries.

1. With the computer linked to the Internet, start the Web browser.

   Although AOL Mail prefers either Internet Explorer or Netscape Navigator, it works with almost any browser.

2. Go to www.aol.com, the official America Online Web site.

   When the site appears, get your screen name and password ready.

3. Type your screen name and password into the Check Your AOL Mail boxes on the left side of the Web page (as in Figure 3-1), then press Enter.

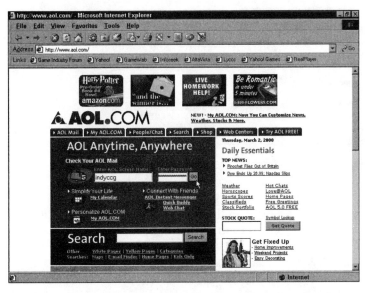

Figure 3-1. The screen name and password boxes sit prominently on the aol.com Web site.

Another window appears to tell you that your sign-on worked. Click the big Click Here to Continue button to keep heading toward your e-mail. You might also see a pair of dialog boxes that talk about going into and out of a *secure connection* to the Internet. Don't worry — America Online is protecting your account information. (Web browsers just worry about things like this.)

4. Your mailbox appears in the window, looking much like Figure 3-2.

Note

Along the way, you may see a dialog box asking if you want the Web browser to *helpfully* remember your password for next time. If that dialog box appears, click the No button to make it go away — you *do not* want this. (Saving the password means that anyone who sits down at this computer could easily access your mail. Bad idea!)

Figure 3-2. Congratulations — you have mail!

> To read a message, click its subject entry. The window
> clears and displays the message (see Figure 3-3). Click
> Close to return to the mailbox list.

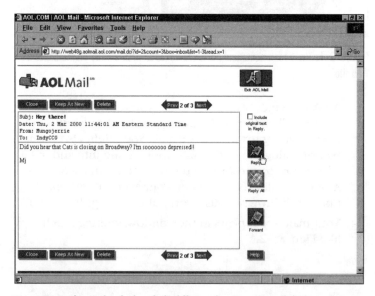

Figure 3-3. The window looks a little different, but it contains all the same buttons
you know and love.

The other buttons (Keep As New, Delete, Reply, Reply All, and Forward) work just as they do in the regular America Online software.

5. When it's time to say goodbye, click the Exit AOL Mail button.

 For security's sake, close the Web browser window. This forces the browser to forget everything it knew about your America Online account.

Tips for Staying Secure on the Road

Although AOL Mail uses the best security measures on the Web, you still need to think about your account's security while traveling. Follow these tips for a safe and happy on-the-road e-mailing experience:

▶ If the Web browser offers to "remember" your password, say no! It's a helpful feature at home, but on the road it's downright dangerous. Never, under any circumstances, store your password on a computer that you don't own. (For that matter, don't store your passwords on your own computer at home if several people have access to the computer.)

▶ Type your screen name and password yourself — don't dictate it to someone else. This may seem obvious, but I watched someone do this very thing in a crowded airport lounge one day. The person even belted out the screen name because the place was so noisy!

▶ When you finish, close the browser window. It only takes a moment, but this completes the security loop. It's *really* that important.

Coming Up Next

Life gets busier every day, but don't start pulling out your hair just yet. Thanks to the digital magic at America Online, the Internet can help you figure out where to go and what to do. The next chapter covers the amazing online calendar system. Stay tuned!

Tip

If one of your friends uses America Online, use his copy of the America Online software to access your account. To do that, select Guest from the sign on screen and a dialog box appears, asking for your screen name and password. Type in your information, press Enter, and you're online! Unfortunately, you *still* don't get access to your Address Book (it's on your computer back home or at the office), but that's a small price to pay for taking America Online on the road!

3

Browsing Your Messages through
Web-based AOL Mail

Chapter 4

Tracking Your Life Online

"**A**ll the world's a calendar, and our lives events thereupon." Well, it isn't Shakespeare, but the sentiment reflects life's hectic schedule these days. Between work, meetings, sports, lessons, and everything else going on in your world, tracking your family's day-to-day events makes a job in industrial logistics look like a piece of cake.

In hopes of simplifying your life, America Online built the ultimate online calendar and delivered it directly to a computer screen near you. The aptly named My Calendar system keeps you in command of your world, no matter where you are. If there's an Internet connection nearby, then your calendar awaits.

This chapter visits the My Calendar system, and gives you a good overview of its options and abilities, plus plenty of tips on making it work for you. Even if you already use one or more calendars, My Calendar delivers valuable information directly to your desktop — and this chapter tells you what you need to know about it.

The Info-When-You-Need-It Delivery Tool

Perhaps you use a hand-held electronic organizer. Maybe you meet your days armed with a classic paper calendar in a ring binder. You might even rely on a good ol' wall calendar hanging in the kitchen. With so many time-management tools at your disposal, why add yet *another* calendar to your world?

That question bothered me for a long time. As I looked at My Calendar, it seemed redundant at best, and terribly distracting at worst. As I explored it more, new light dawned in my mind: Something was different about My Calendar — something unique. This system does something that no other calendar in my life *can* do: It generates its own prospective entries.

Thanks to an extensive event database (more about that later in the chapter), My Calendar automatically points out all kinds of information important to your world: International holidays, movie and CD releases, concert dates, Initial Public Offering (IPO) dates — the list goes on and on.

The event database is the key to how My Calendar best fits into your life. Use it as an information delivery tool, not as a mundane appointment scheduling program. (Of course, if you don't already use any calendar at all, My Calendar is a great place to develop time-management skills.)

Setting Up the Calendar

Creating your online calendar involves a one-time setup step, followed by a lifetime of fiddling with events and appointments. Setup only takes a moment, so if you aren't paying close attention, you might miss it.

The first time you visit My Calendar, you and the My Calendar system spend a little bit of time getting to know each other by going through a couple of preference settings. After that, everything is ready and waiting — it's time to put My Calendar to work by adding appointments and events.

Tip

You can access your calendar from any Internet-connected computer with a good Web browser. Everything you do with My Calendar through the regular America Online software *also* works through the My Calendar link on the www.aol.com Web site. To use the Internet-based system, click the site's My Calendar link, and then enter your America Online screen name and password. Like magic, your calendar appears!

Figure 4-1 shows what to expect from your first trip into My Calendar. The system asks for your time zone and United States ZIP code. (Right now, My Calendar doesn't recognize Canadian postal codes or other international designations.) The calendar system uses this information to track entertainment events near your home.

Note

Leap into your online calendar by clicking the Calendar toolbar button, through AOL Keyword: **Calendar**, or by selecting My A̲OL⇨My Calen̲dar from the toolbar menu.

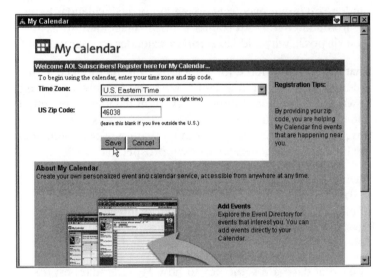

Figure 4-1. First on the agenda: Introduce yourself to My Calendar.

After you finish with the preference window, your newly-created calendar hops into view, as in Figure 4-2. A brand new calendar needs some decoration, so My Calendar offers to dress yours up with the daily weather forecast. To prove they have a sense of fun, the America Online programmers included a horoscope option as well (plus a big, helpful No Thanks button to make the horoscopes go away). To complete your calendar setup, click the weather forecast link, and then pick your city from the rather extensive list that My Calendar displays. After that, if you're feeling more brave than whimsical, you can click No Thanks to close the horoscope option.

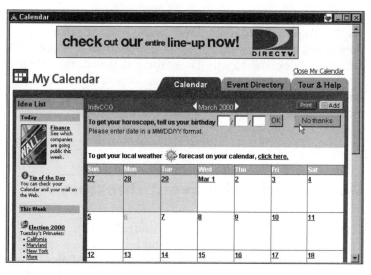

Figure 4-2. Your new calendar awaits!

Tabbing Through the Views

To make everything fit into a single window, the America Online programmers sprinkled several tabs at the top and bottom of the My Calendar window. Clicking the tabs changes how your calendar looks on-screen and what the calendar window itself shows.

The three tabs at the top of the window (as seen in Figure 4-2) control what you see on-screen:

▶ **The Calendar tab** displays the calendar itself. Use this tab to switch back to the calendar from any of the other displays.

▶ **The Event Directory tab** takes you to the main window of the Event Directory, a marvelous list of events you can include in the calendar. See the next section for more about this valuable tool.

▶ **The Tour and Help tab** opens the online calendar help system. Turn here when you need a quick answer to a specific question or want a walk-through of the calendar itself. It's a great resource.

Three more small tabs appear at the bottom of the calendar display. To find them, scroll down to the bottom of the window. Along the lower-left corner of the window sit three little tabs: Day, Week, and Month. These three tabs shift the calendar display, showing your appointment and event information in one of three views: full-month, by-the-week, or a detailed single-day listing. (By default, the calendar uses the Month view, in case you wondered.)

Dealing with the Event Directory

The Event Directory turbocharges your calendar with an incredible collection of happenings and holidays. Pick events important to your world and add them to your online calendar with only a few mouse clicks. America Online outdid itself here — My Calendar covers books, music, movies, art events, and sports, plus the requisite holiday lists and much more.

Note

Did you miss Submarine Day, Genius Day, or National Panic Day? Don't let that happen again! Remember all those holidays and many more with the *Celebrate the Day* listings in the Event Directory's Holiday area.

Start with the Event Directory's topic list to pick events for your calendar. To bring up the topic list, open your calendar, then click the Event Directory tab near the top of the window. The graphics flip around a bit, then the window lists the various event types that My Calendar tracks, organized by topic (as Figure 4-3 shows).

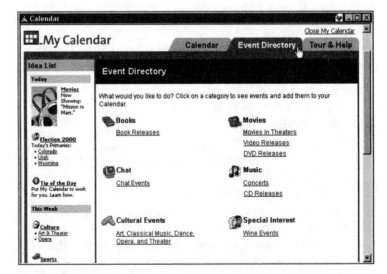

Figure 4-3. Click the Event Directory tab for a topical list of available events.

Adding events to your calendar is a quick four-step process.

1. Scroll through the list until you find a topic that looks interesting (such as new DVD releases, movies in theaters, pro sports events, online chats, television shows, and so on).

2. Click the underlined link next to the topic name, and follow the links to more detailed topic listings. Drilling through page after page of information about specific events may take some work, but the payoff (your online calendar filled with the information you want) makes the process worthwhile.

3. Mark one or more events on the list and add the events to your calendar. When you find an interesting event, mark it by clicking the checkbox next to the event listing.

4. After marking all the events you like on a particular page of the Event Directory, click the little Add button (at the top and bottom of the Event Directory page, as with Figure 4-4) This tells the software to add all the checked events to your calendar.

Note

If you click the wrong event type by accident, click the link marked "Top" at the beginning of each event list page to return to the Event Directory.

Figure 4-4. Check the events that you want, then click the Add button to include them in your calendar.

Using My Calendar with Your Calendar

As you cruise through the Entertainment channel (AOL Keyword: **Entertainment**), Moviefone (AOL Keyword: **Moviefone**), and other on-line areas on AOL, watch for links that say Add to Calendar. These links automatically add events to your online calendar with a single click.

What if you already solved the time organization crisis in your world with a Palm Pilot, a paper-based planner like the Franklin-Covey system, or a program like Microsoft Outlook? How does this new online calendar fit with the other time-management tools you already know and love?

In a word, it doesn't. At least not right now.

Currently, My Calendar stands alone in the time-management world. You can't send entries from your online calendar into a Palm Pilot or into a PC-based calendar program like Outlook, nor can you update your online calendar from your other software or devices. America Online's programmers share your pain about this, so they're actively solving the problem.

Coming Up Next

If you use a paper-based planner, you're ahead of the game (for once). You can print the entries in your on-line calendar and then carry them around with your main calendar. To print, pick the calendar view (Day, Week, or Month) that you want by clicking the appropriate tab at the bottom of the calendar, then click the Print button (also at the bottom of the cal-endar window) to do the deed. The printout may not be a true thing of beauty, but it beats transferring the information by hand.

Take a trip through the highly-connected world of Instant Messages in the next chapter. Thanks to America Online's Instant Messenger software, you're never out of touch with the ones you love (and the others you merely like). Find out the details next!

Chapter 5

Instant Messenger Everywhere

S tay in touch with AOL friends, catch up on the news, and check your e-mail even when you're away from your main computer. America Online's Instant Messenger, also known as AIM, allows you to use your screen name and chat with friends and colleagues via Instant Messages over the Net.

Instant Messenger is great for computers at work (when your main AOL software resides on your home computer), travel laptops, and even Windows CE devices. Because it requires a lot less memory than the full AOL software, you can squeeze it into small hard drive spaces.

AIM Overview

AIM uses an existing ISP connection to send Instant Messages over the Internet. With the advent of AIM version 4.0, it also does a lot more. While the software doesn't care whether you use a cable connection, a DSL line, or a traditional modem, it does run on top of a service provider. That means you need an Internet account of some kind in order to use AIM. Since many companies allow their computers online access these days, the easiest way to use AIM is generally from the office.

When you load AIM on your computer, a Mail alert window appears on-screen to tell you that e-mail awaits you (provided you have an AOL account or a POP 3 setup); a news ticker floats across the top of your screen, announcing the latest news stories, and a stock ticker scrolls along the bottom of the Buddy List window. Double-click the table icon next to the ticker, add your own stocks to the list, and keep an eye on your investments.

You don't have to create a new screen name to use the AIM software. Use your existing screen name so friends can find you when you're online. Of course, if you want to create a screen name just for AIM use, you can do that, too.

The AIM Buddy List window is your control center for the software (see Figure 5-1). From this window you can set preferences, open Instant Message windows, and set the software to alert you when you have incoming e-mail or one of your special buddies shows up.

Figure 5-1. Watch the stocks, add new buddies, or set your preferences in the Buddy Lists window.

You can find the AIM software at AOL Keyword: **Download AIM**. To download the software through your Internet connection, go to www.aol.com and click the AOL Instant

Caution

AIM privacy preferences work independently of the AOL software preferences. Screen names you blocked through AOL can find you when you use AIM unless you set the AIM preferences.

Messenger Link. Wherever you go, the download takes just a few minutes (or even less if you use a high-speed Internet connection). After downloading the software, install it with a quick double-click (don't worry — both download areas include all the installation instructions you need).

Not only does AIM give you access to all your AOL buddies via Instant Messaging, friends who don't have AOL can also use AIM to keep in touch with you. They can download the software from the AOL.com Web site and install it on their computers. Then you place their new screen names on your Buddy List so you know when they're online. AIM links into America Online's existing Instant Message system, so AIM works just like sending a regular IM through your America Online software.

Tips and Tricks

Version 4.0 brings all kinds of new cool features to your Internet connection. You can use your AIM software to send pictures to friends, share cool sounds — even drop a copy of the latest project blueprint into an Instant Message. With the addition of a microphone and your computer's sound card, you can actually talk to your buddy over the Net.

Alert Me

Use AIM's alert system to keep you notified of new e-mail, stock changes, and friends' comings and goings. Here's how to set up the various alerts:

1. My AIM⇨Mail Alert Window opens the Mail window. Resting near the bottom of your screen, it continually tells you whether you have mail.
2. Check your e-mail by clicking the highlighted e-mail address in the Mail window. It opens the AOL Mail section of AOL.com, and allows you to sign into the AOL mail system to retrieve your mail without signing on to AOL.
3. Highlight a buddy's screen name in the Buddy List window (or right-click a screen name), and then select People⇨Alert me when Screen Name signs on.

4. In the Edit Buddy Alert dialog box that appears, check one of the two boxes that tells the software how to notify you, and then click the OK button.

A bell appears next to your buddy's name in the Buddy List window.

Setting a Stock Alert is a bit more complicated. Here's how to do it:

1. Select <u>M</u>y AIM⇨Stock <u>T</u>icker Detail Window to open the Stocks window.

2. Highlight a stock name, and then select <u>S</u>ymbol⇨Edit Alerts <u>f</u>or the ticker symbol in the Stocks window. The Stock Alert List window opens.

3. Click the Add button to add an alert to the Stock Alert List window. A Stock Alert window opens, as shown in Figure 5-2.

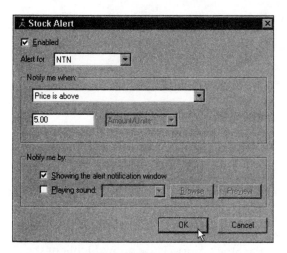

Figure 5-2. Set an alert and AIM tracks your stocks for you.

4. If the stock you want to place on alert doesn't already appear in the Stock Alert window's Alert For text box, select the correct stock.

5. In the Notify Me When section of the window, select the condition: options include Price is Above, Price is Below, and Price is Below 52 Week Low. Then enter a price or volume number into the empty text box beneath the condition line.

6. In the Notify Me By section, check the box that tells the software to show you an alert window, as seen in Figure 5-3, or play a sound. If you like, check both to be doubly notified.

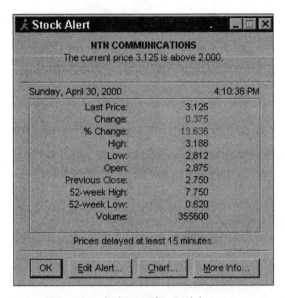

Figure 5-3. AIM Stock Alerts notify you of changes in your investments.

7. Click OK to set your changes and close the Stock Alert window.

8. Your new alert appears in the Stock Alert List window, complete with a bell to show you the alert is set. Click OK to close the Stock Alert List window.

When a stock alert trips, reset the alert so it will track the stock again. Open the Stock Alert List window, highlight the alert that tripped, and click the Reset button. When a Stock Alert trips, the bell turns yellow in the Stocks detail window. To quickly open the detail window, double-click the Stocks Table button next to the stocks ticker.

Share Yourself

Use the Instant Images and Talk features to let your buddies know a little more about you — or to catch Grandma up on everything happening at home. If you and your buddy both

use the 4.0 version of AIM, you can send and receive images, photos, sounds, and animated gifs. To send a picture or sound to a friend, click the picture icon in the Instant Message window. AIM asks your buddy whether she wants to connect directly; if your buddy clicks OK, then you see a Screen Name is Directly Connected message appear in the IM window. Click the picture icon again to insert an image or sound file; click the Send button and it wings its way to your buddy.

Add a microphone to your AIM software and you can actually talk to your buddy over the Internet. As long as you have an installed microphone and sound card, you can make a direct connection with your Buddy and chat the night away. To establish a direct connection, click the Talk button at the bottom of the Instant Message window (or highlight a screen name and/or click the Talk icon on the Buddy List). A Connect to Talk dialog box appears, containing Pause and Mute buttons so you can stop the conversation flow — as well as a sound meter (just like the level meters on a tape recorder or sound board) above each screen name to show you how well the sound is coming through.

Show your digital face to the world with an AIM Personality Profile. AIM Profiles work much like their AOL counterparts; you can enter as much or as little information as you like, and then people online can find you to chat. Select My AIM⇨Edit Profile to open the Create A Profile window. After the first window of information, you can select up to five interests that other AIM members can use to locate you online. Enter at least a first or last name if you want to click the Next button and select favorite interests. You can also include extra information that you want other AIM users to see while they chat with you.

Set Preferences

The AIM Preferences window (shown in Figure 5-4) allows you to set who sees you online (as well as who doesn't), how you want information displayed on-screen, the sounds that you hear when you use AIM, and more. Open Preferences by selecting My AIM⇨Edit Options⇨Edit Preferences from the Buddy Lists menu bar.

Definition

When AIM says that you're Directly Connecting with another AIM user, it means that your software is creating a direct link between your computer and your friend's machine. A direct connection works differently from a regular AIM (or Instant Message) conversation because the normal conversations use America Online's computers to relay messages back and forth. In a direct connection, the messages don't go through America Online at all — they bounce back and forth only between you and the other person. AIM uses a direct connection for voice communication, sharing pictures, and sending files to each other.

Tip

AIM Profiles can be seen by all AIM users, so refrain from entering information into the window that you actually want to keep private.

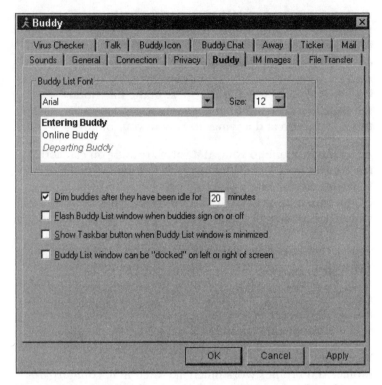

Figure 5-4. Use the AIM Preferences to make Instant Messenger work just the way you want.

The window opens with the Buddy preferences highlighted. From there, use the tabs at the top of the window to select the preference you want to alter:

> ▶ **Away:** Lets you write a message that responds automatically when you're away from your computer.

> ▶ **Buddy:** Sets fonts for the Buddy List window and lets you dock the Buddy List window permanently on the left or right side of your screen.

> ▶ **Buddy Chat:** Play sounds or announce on-screen when buddies enter or leave. Also use this section to block all incoming Buddy Chat invitations.

> ▶ **Buddy Icon:** Select an icon to use for yourself and your buddies.

> ▶ **Connection:** Contains server and proxy server information. Unless you have a specific reason to change this, it should work fine without resetting.

▶ **File Transfer:** Allows who may receive and send files. Also use this preference to set the file transfer speed.

▶ **General:** Look for Sign on, Instant Message, and default IM text settings here.

▶ **IM Images:** Set preferences for sending and receiving images.

▶ **Mail:** Here you can add e-mail addresses for Mail Alert to check. Also set your Mail Alert notification preferences in this box.

▶ **Privacy:** Use this setting to tell the software who you want contact from, the amount of information someone can unearth if they have your e-mail address, and whether or not users can see how long you've been on the system idle.

▶ **Sounds:** Set your Buddy List and Instant Message sounds.

▶ **Talk:** Select talk sounds and determine who you want to talk to online.

▶ **Ticker:** Select topics for the news ticker, symbols for the stock ticker, and change the ticker's speed.

▶ **Virus Checker:** Tells the AIM software where to locate your virus checker if you plan to accept files from other users.

Coming Up Next

They might look pretty strange, but the new USB devices open up a whole world of technology. Whether you're interested in physical add-ons or high speed networking, the next chapter takes a look at the devices and capabilities attached to those interesting-looking plugs.

Find It Online

If you think AIM is cool on your desktop, wait till you try it on your CE device or Palm Pilot. AOL Keyword: **Download AIM** takes you there. Check the download areas for the details of putting AIM in the palm of your hand.

FUNNY LOOKING PLUGS
THAT SIMPLIFY YOUR LIFE

Chapter 6

Funny Looking Plugs That Simplify Your Life

Recent advances in computer technology have gone beyond the internal workings of your computer console or monitor; some of the neatest advancements have involved the external devices (*peripherals*) you attach to your computer. The more we rely on such external devices (scanners, digital cameras, and Webcams, among others), the more we want them to connect easily — and communicate efficiently — with our computers. This chapter takes a look at two innovative ways to make that happen: Universal Serial Bus hubs and FireWire.

USB Hubs

In computer terminology, a *bus* isn't something your child might take to school every day, but rather an electronic pathway along which signals move from one part of the computer to another. Most buses are internal, meaning they carry information around inside the computer itself. A *Universal Serial Bus (USB)*, however, is an *external bus;* it brings information from external devices into your computer.

The USB standard for computer ports, developed in 1996, was a way to improve upon the performance of traditional serial and parallel ports (the other technology for giving information a path to follow between an external device and the inside of your computer). A USB port can handle transfer rates of up to 12 Mbps (as compared to serial at about 0.1 Mbps) and can communicate with 127 peripheral devices, such as USB mice, USB modems, USB printers, etc. USB is also *hot-pluggable* and *plug-and-play*, which means not only can you plug a device into the port without shutting the computer down first, you can also skip a bothersome configuration routine to tell Windows how to recognize the device. Windows discovers its new configuration instructions automatically.

Computer manufacturers quickly hopped on the USB-port bandwagon, recognizing its advantages. They duly started manufacturing computers with two handy USB ports. Consumers appreciated the new technology — including its ambitious promise of handling 127 different external devices — but soon realized that the USB had one sticking point. How could you actually *connect* 127 devices if the computer had only *two* USB ports?

The answer is (believe it or not) relatively simple: Add more ports. The Xircom PortStation and the Belkin USB Hub do precisely that.

Xircom PortStation

The Xircom (www.xircom.com) PortStation provides a fast and easy way to connect your external devices to your computer. With a Xircom Starter Kit, you simply connect all your external devices to the PortStation (as shown in Figure 6-1), and then connect the PortStation itself to an available USB port on your computer. If you discover that you want to add on even more devices farther down the road, you have a pleasant surprise in store: The rather solid-looking PortStation is actually a series of different modules that you can snap apart, add on to, and put back together. You can purchase and add individual modules (including 4-port USB modules, 7-port USB modules, Ethernet, modem, and modules for parallel and serial ports) as your computing needs change.

Tip

Keep in mind that since all the external USB devices share one bus, some devices may conflict with others. If you run into a problem with an external device, remove all other devices from the bus; then try the device again. If the remaining connected device works fine, you have a conflict. Contact the manufacturer of the problem device for help.

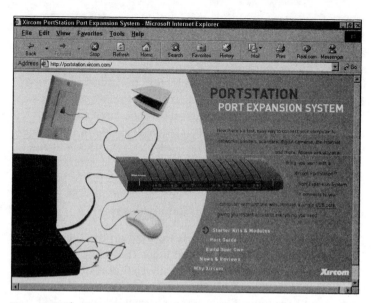

Figure 6-1. The Xircom PortStation makes assembling one for your needs easy.

Although the Xircom PortStation's modular features offer the computer user a great deal of flexibility, the product's design does have one drawback: The PortStation takes up a good piece of your desk real estate. You could conceivably stand it up on its end, but the more natural usage would have it lying flat on your desk. The Starter Kit, with its 7 USB ports, would take up the space of about two CD cases laying side by side. If you have a good-sized desk, that shouldn't be a problem — but if you are already feeling a bit crowded, you may want to consider the more vertically-inclined Belkin USB BusStation.

Belkin USB hub

The Belkin USB BusStation (shown in Figure 6-2) offers a modular design similar to the Xircom PortStation. The BusStation has four built-in USB ports, with the top three slots stacked vertically in the BusStation to let you change modules (including 1-port USB shown, 4-port USB, and serial ports) as you see fit. You can also use these changable modules independently of the station.

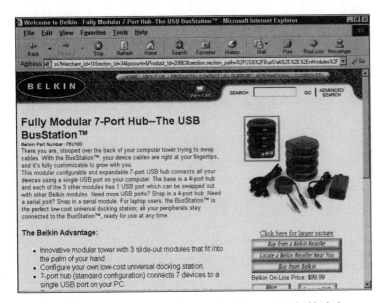

Figure 6-2. The Belkin BusStation hub's vertical stacking saves valuable desk space.

The modules interlock so you can stack them neatly together in the BusStation, saving some precious desk space by building upward.

FireWire

FireWire, developed by Apple Computer, is the newest set of official specs describing what the external bus should be and how it should perform. FireWire supports data-transfer speeds of up to 400 Mpbs, as compared to the 12 Mbps of USB. FireWire follows the same concept of USB, but it can only connect to 63 external devices (as compared to USB's 127). Although FireWire is extremely fast, it is also very expensive to make. Therefore, only those devices that need the speed incorporate this standard; video cameras are a prime example. Some video-capture programs (such as those mentioned in Chapter 24) come bundled with a FireWire card to handle the high-volume transfers of data from digital video cameras. Until this technology can be produced at a lower cost, however, I don't expect to see too many other devices adopt it.

Coming Up Next

Schedules, calendars, and e-mail are wonderful tools, but what happens when you can't access them? You could lose touch with people, miss meetings, and forget what to do next. Well, take heart; the next chapter shows you some tools that make your schedules, calendars, and e-mail portable. You *can* take it with you as you leave your desktop computer behind.

CARRYING THE WORLD IN
YOUR HANDHELD

Chapter 7

Carrying the World in Your Handheld

Long ago I started carrying a datebook in my pocket wherever I went. At the end of each year, I had to transfer all my addresses and appointments into the next year's calendar. Then I started keeping that information on my computer, but I found that sticking the computer in my pocket wasn't convenient. As soon as the handheld Personal Information Managers (PIMs) started to come on the market, I knew the PIM was my answer.

Today there are a number of gadgets all claiming to be PIMs. To me, in order to be a true Personal Information Manager, a handheld device must do more than merely keep a calendar, addresses, and a to-do list. I also expect a good PIM to handle some of the work you normally associate with your desktop computer. This chapter covers some of the top products that can actually assist you in doing such work when you are away from the computer.

Palm Pilot

The Palm Pilot is the top-selling handheld device on the market today. One reason for this popularity is the device's simplicity. It isn't cluttered with a plethora of menus, buttons, and options. Plus, it actually does fit in the palm of your hand.

The Palm's operating system (PalmOS) is the crucial component that makes it so successful. The applications built into the PalmOS include an address book, a calendar, a to-do list, an expenses tally, and an e-mail client. All its information updates with a special program on your computer, through a connection with the handheld device. A few third-party programs, such as Intellisync from Puma Technology, allow the Palm data to update with other applications, such as Microsoft Outlook, Lotus Notes, and ACT! (among others).

In addition to its built-in applications, the Palm Pilot has inspired the programming community to build numerous applications for it; these range from scientific calculators to doodle pads to board games. You can find some of these programs at www.pilotzone.com, www.pilotgear.com, and other sites.

The base model of the Palm Pilot is the Palm III, available in a variety of different versions, including Palm IIIs with 8MB of memory or outfitted with a new color display. The Palm V, as seen in Figure 7-1, comes with rechargeable batteries and an anodized aluminum finish. The Palm VII adds wireless connectivity to the Palm.net network for accessing the Internet from anywhere. The prices start at $149 for the Palm IIIe and go up to $449 for the Palm VII and Palm IIIc. And for $44.99 you can have unlimited access to the Palm.net Wireless Communication Service offered for the Palm VII.

Find It Online

You can find out more about the Palm Pilot from the Palm Web site at www.palm.com.

Tip

You can also get wireless Internet access for your Palm III with the help of the Novatel Wireless Minstrel III service (www.goamerica. net/html/showcase/ products/minstrel_ III). OmniSky (www. omnisky.com) offers a similar service for the Palm V.

7

Carrying the World in Your Handheld

Figure 7-1. The Palm V has an anodized aluminum case, giving it a professional look.

Find It Online

You can get your own Palm Pilot directly from AOL's Shop by using AOL Keyword: **Aol Shop Direct**. Select the Hardware button, and then click on Portable Computing. There is an entire selection of Palm merchandise for you to choose from.

Handspring Visor

One of the newest handhelds on the market, the Handspring Visor (see Figure 7-2) is in a position to challenge PalmPilot's dominance in the market. It uses the same operating system as the Pilot, so that any software that is available for the Palm Pilot will also work on the Visor. In fact, the Handspring even looks a little like a Palm Pilot, with its touch screen, power switch, and buttons. It comes in two versions — a 2MB version for $149 and an 8MB version for $249.

One major difference does exist between the Visor and the Palm Pilot — the Visor's expansion port. This expansion port, called the Springboard, has opened the way for the development of modules, expansions, and devices for the Handspring Visor. Already one can add the Tiger Woods PGA Tour Golf game, an 8MB memory expansion, modems, and a digital camera — with more to come.

Figure 7-2. The Handspring Visor is worthy of attention because of its plug-in modules.

Windows CE

Windows CE is not a handheld device as such, but rather an operating system created by Microsoft to function as a scaled-down version of the Windows desktop software that you have running on your personal computer. Microsoft designed this software in the image of Windows 95, but did so using much less memory so the operating system could fit in a handheld device. They then licensed the software for use in handhelds developed by other companies such as Casio, Compaq, and Hewlett-Packard. Microsoft later developed CE versions of their other popular programs (such as Word and Excel).

Some common features of Windows CE devices are similar to those of other handheld PIMs. These features include touch-screen-and-stylus for user input, quick-access buttons on graphical menus, updating information on the handheld through a connection with a desktop computer, and infrared data transfers. Some of the features unique to CE devices are color displays, voice-recording capability, and PCMCIA ports. These features are nice, but the additions begin to turn the simple handheld device into a scaled-down laptop. It appears that Microsoft is abandoning the Windows CE software for their new Pocket PC software, making the future of Windows

7

Carrying the World in Your Handheld

CE uncertain. Currently Compaq's Aero 8000, HP's Jornada 820, and Casio's Cassiopeia E-105 all still use the Windows CE operating system.

HP Jornada

There are other devices available besides the ones mentioned earlier. (In fact, they are so numerous that it is virtually impossible to mention every one. Instead, I recommend searching the CNet Web site (www.cnet.com), using Keyword: **Handheld,** to look up more information about these devices. For now, one product that has recently hit the market can serve to illustrate some of the current alternatives.

Point your browser at www
.microsoft.com/
pocketpc for more details
about Pocket PC software.

Jornada is not a new name from Hewlett-Packard (their Windows-CE-based handhelds used it), but some of their latest models are a new breed — such as the 540 series using Microsoft's new Pocket PC operating system. Its sleek new design (shown in Figure 7-3) gives people what they want in portability, functionality, and ease of use. The standard applications include Outlook, Word, Excel, Money, Internet Explorer, Windows Media Player, and an eBook reader. H-P has also packaged AOL Mail and Yahoo! Messenger for on-the-go communication.

To learn more about the
Jornada line of handheld
products, point your browser
at www.hp.com/jornada.

Figure 7-3. Jornada 540 — HP's first handheld device using the Pocket PC software from Microsoft.

For now, Hewlett-Packard provides options for wireless connectivity to the Internet by using selected compatable mobile phones with their handhelds. Their Web site can help you choose a suitable match. However, Hewlett-Packard plans to release, in the second half of 2000, a CompactFlash Type I Bluetooth module enabling wireless access to the Internet via Bluetooth enabled mobile phones (see Chapter 14 for more information on Bluetooth). The Jornada 540 series start at $499 for the 16MB version and $599 for the 32MB version. Both models come with the same wonderful capabilities, making the Jornada 540 Pocket PC an intriguing new kid on the block.

Coming Up Next

For the most part, handheld devices require a full-size computer as a "home base" from which to update their information; they simply can't carry as much info as their bigger ancestors. They're not always convenient when you need to stay on top of the latest news, business, and even e-mail. Wireless devices like phones or pagers can give you the edge you're looking for. You can find out more about this technology in the next chapter.

 **Cross-Reference**

Flip back to Chapter 2 for a look at how America Online, with its new Palm and Windows CE (Windows for Consumer Electronics) e-mail clients, is marrying the palmtop computing revolution to the world of online communication.

CHAPTER

8

WANDERING THE NET WITHOUT A PC

Chapter 8

Wandering the Net without a PC

IN THIS CHAPTER

Considering devices other than computers for connecting to the Internet

Using phones for more than talking

Putting the Internet in your hand with a wireless phone

Why pagers get a lot more than phone numbers these days

Will wandering the Net without a PC make your life easier? Who knows? The convenience of technology is often a trade-off; the more activity we have in our lives, the more tools we need to manage it all. But regardless of the tools, we still require communication. No, we *demand* it. The less time we waste in missed phone calls, meetings, and e-mails, the better we feel about our productive hours. Looking through this chapter, you can get a look at some newer technologies that can help out when a PC is not on hand and you have a use for one. This chapter answers questions you may have about keeping in touch while you are away from your computer.

Living in the Information Age

Computers have become so integrated into everyday life that many of us have become dependent on them to send and receive e-mail, check movie times, find stock prices, and get sports scores. Admittedly, the world may not come to an end if you can't access your e-mail right here and right now — but most people who use computers (and much of the existing technology out there) are used to having information they can summon at will, manage conveniently, and use efficiently.

Computers hooked up to the Internet are great tools for satisfying a wide range of individual information needs. For some, that crucial bit of information may concern an upcoming business transaction or the fall of a government in Venezuela; others may just want to see how the home team did last night.

But what happens if your computer, the tool that has made your life so much more convenient, is stuck back at home while you're stuck in traffic or waiting out a fog delay at the international airport? If the information you need depends on having a computer handy, then what do you do when the computer *isn't* handy? This basic question has spawned a solution: alternative devices that can do much of what a computer does.

Alternative devices

Have you ever wanted to contact someone you knew would be in a meeting? Or did you ever hang around for an important e-mail, but have to leave your computer before the message arrived? The next sections show how some new twists on some older technology (telephones, wireless phones, and pagers) can offer solutions to such problems — and make data communications without your computer easier to handle.

Phones

With the help of a high-tech version of Alexander Graham Bell's invention, you can access the Web without having to shell out big bucks for another computer. Take a look at the iPhone (see Figure 8-1), from Info Gear (`www.infogear.com`), a handy little device that not only makes regular telephone calls but also gives you dial-up access to the Internet.

Cross-Reference

Check out Chapter 1 for information about AOLTV as another alternative device for connecting to the Internet.

Tip

With the iPhone, you can connect to AOL's Web page at www.aol.com to access your e-mail and calendar.

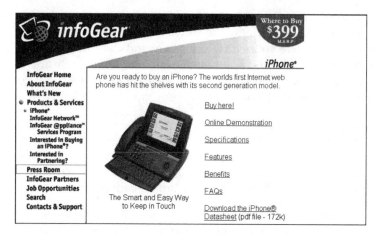

Figure 8-1. A phone that can access the Internet too. Talk to friends and then browse the Web.

Caution

The screen size of the iPhone is the same as that of a computer at the smallest possible setting (640 x 480). Therefore, some Web pages may appear too big for the screen; to see what's on the page (one little screenful at a time), simply scroll from side to side.

The iPhone is a full-featured speaker phone with a built-in digital answering machine. The phone comes with two-line access (one for voice, one for data), a built-in 56Kbps modem, and 12 programmable speed-dial keys. All these features are a plus on any normal phone. With a touch to the built-in display, the iPhone powers up to display its main viewing screen (see Figure 8-2) with a resolution of 640 x 480 pixels (the size of a computer screen). Because of the touch screen, the iPhone has no need of a mouse or any other pointing device. It comes with a stylus — a plastic stick to keep from scratching the touch-sensitive display. From this screen, you can access:

▶ **Your directory.** An address book of all the important names, phone numbers, and e-mail addresses that you create for this phone.

▶ **Call logs.** A built-in caller ID record of all the people that have tried to contact you while you were out, showing the name, number, and time of the call.

▶ **The Internet.** One touch dialup of the Internet to quickly start browsing.

▶ **E-mail.** Send, create, receive, and read e-mail directly through the phone.

▶ **Listings.** Search for a phone number of a person or business through online phone listings. Or look up movie times, maps, flights and much more.

▶ **Settings.** Adjust any of the preferences for the phone settings, like changing date, time, speed-dial numbers, and more.

Figure 8-2. Browsing the easy way with the iPhone touch screen.

Setting up the iPhone is simple. Just plug the phone lines into the appropriate connections and hook up the power supply. Then configuring the appliance to access the Internet is as easy as filling in a couple of on-screen entries so you can connect to any Internet Service Provider (ISP) capable of a PPP connection. It's just like setting up a computer for Internet access. When you press the Settings button on the phone screen, you get a set of tabs — each one offering options:

▶ **Time.** Use this tab to set the time and date for the phone; press the Set Data & Time button to keep your changes.

▶ **Dialing.** Use this tab to set any dialing prefixes, enter voice-mail information, or set speed-dial numbers.

▶ **Sound.** Use this tab to choose from a list of ringer sounds for incoming calls and turn on (or off) other sounds you hear from the phone.

▶ **Identity.** This tab shows your personal address information (name, street address, city, and so on).

▶ **Email.** Each person using the phone can have a personal profile for e-mail accounts up to four profiles. Press the Edit Profile button to add or change a profile. You will need to know Email Server Address, Email Address and Email password. You can also set up the phone to check for new e-mail messages at specified times — automatically.

▶ **Internet.** From this tab, you enter your account name (also known as *your logon ID*), password, and the

Definition

PPP stands for **point-to-point protocol.** Most ISPs use PPP for standard modem connections.

Note

You can get the latest news, sports, and weather by accessing the Wireless Web through your digital SprintPCS phone.

phone number of your Internet service provider (ISP). Your ISP must use a PPP connection for this option to work. If that's not a problem, you can press the TCP/IP button and tweak the settings required by your ISP (which they should provide when you call them).

▶ **Advanced.** This tab is for setting Parental Controls, adjusting the touch-screen settings, registering the iPhone online, and other such fine-tuning options.

If you are in need of a service provider, InfoGear Network™ offers nationwide access to the Internet. This service also provides a wide range of site content specially formatted to fit the iPhone screen.

Wireless phones

It's late afternoon on Friday, at the end of a long work week. Ah — family time at last! A picnic in the neighborhood park sounds perfect, but what about the weather? Are those rain clouds overhead? You pull out your Web-ready digital phone and pull up the local weather forecast. "Rats! Rain all evening. And tomorrow, too." Hmm . . . perhaps a movie instead? A couple of quick taps on your wireless phone's keypad brings up a complete listing for the local cineplex. Tap, tap, tap, and an evening at the cinema replaces a soggy twilight among the trees. And you did it all from the palm of your hand — thanks to your wireless, Web-ready phone.

In the hundred-plus years since the invention of the telephone, improvements on its design and advancements in what it can do have radically changed everyday life. Then mobile-phone usage exploded in the 1990s, and did it all over again. It's now rare to walk down the street or enter a store without seeing someone carrying or talking on a mobile phone. Is it any surprise that you can now access the Internet with one?

The digital phone service provided by SprintPCS Wireless Web (www.sprintpcs.com) gives you access to the Web from a Web-ready phone. The SprintPCS TouchPoint is one such phone that can access a wide range of information:

▶ Access your SprintPCS phone account information.

▶ Communicate by e-mail through a yahoo.com e-mail account.

▶ Buy books, music, and more through amazon.com.

> ▶ Buy, sell, and check your stocks through
> `ameritrade.com`.

> ▶ Keep up on the latest business information through
> `bloomberg.com`.

> ▶ Get the latest sports scores from FOX Sports at
> `foxsports.com`.

> ▶ Go2 wherever you like with precise directions from
> `go2online.com`.

> ▶ Set bookmarks to your favorite, most-frequented sites.

With such access to the Internet, you may no longer need to sit for hours in front of a computer — or even own a computer. The information age is still flooding in at full force, spilling over into all forms of technology. Phones are no longer limited to voice communication; e-mail over the phone is poised to take its place in our society, offering more options, power, and flexibility — provided we can improve on typing out a verbose message on a 9-button keypad.

Granted, a phone is a far cry from a computer (not much information can fit on the small screen of a mobile phone) — but for those on the go, the convienence of a phone may be all you need. A leading news story, for instance, shows up on the phone summarized in two or three sentences (no pictures). If the story continues to interest you, then you can get further details as snack-size bits of info (or find the whole story again with your computer, later). Otherwise, get the rest of the news headlines. Maybe the best way to think about the Web-ready phone is as a portable extension of your computer — with a fraction of the Internet power of a computer, but a good way to gather useful tidbits.

Note

Web-site companies are working with these providers of alternative Internet devices to format the text content so it fits the small screen sizes.

Pagers

Information technology continues to mutate, multiply, and crop up everywhere — or at least the electronic devices do. After strapping on, pocketing, or picking up the devices you carry around — electronic organizer, laptop computer, cell phone, pager — maybe you tried not to laugh the last time you looked in the mirror. (The Batman-utility-belt look has to go.) The question arises: *How can I meet my basic communication and information requirements without lugging all this stuff around?*

To find out more about two-way paging, go to AOL's Computing Channel and search for "pager" in "Find a product."

With service for the pager provided by SkyTel (www.skytel.com), you get two-way communications across the country.

Using AOL Keyword: **SendPage**, you can access services that send text messages to a pager — provided you know that the pager is signed up with a paging service such as MobileComm (www.mobilecomm.com) or MetroCall (www.metrocall.com) and you have the pager's ID available.

You might consider looking into Motorola's (www.motorola.com) new line of "Web W/O Wires" devices (see Figure 8-3). The PageWriter 2000X Two-way Pager is one of those got-to-have-it devices. This critter is chock-full of features that enable you to communicate in ways that ordinary pagers could never approach. In addition to receiving messages (whether phone numbers or text) you can send messages to other pagers, Internet e-mail, telephones, and fax machines. This pager can interface with a PC to synchronize stored data, and organize data itself with its built-in software (which has scheduler, to-do list, memo, and alert features, as well as a notepad).

Figure 8-3. Get connected to the Web with Motorola's Web without Wires.

The two-way pager offers you the option of responding immediately to urgent e-mail. It also stops the annoyance of phone-tag messages — and gives you quick access to stock prices, sports scores, or news. If you need to stay in touch with others on a voice system, you can send text messages that convert to voice messages (depending on the specific paging services available for the PagerWriter).

Coming Up Next

Have you ever wanted to talk to your computer just the way they do in the movies? Turn to the next chapter to find out how you can *say the word and make it so* on your computer. The magic recipe is voice-recognition software; the next chapter shows how you can use it to make your computer life more productive.

Chapter 9

Hello, Computer — Talking to Your Machine

IN THIS CHAPTER

Putting voice messages in e-mail

Software that lets you talk to your computer

I n science fiction movies like *2001: A Space Odyssey, Star Trek* (pick one), and others, we see people nonchalantly talking to computers as a way of accomplishing routine tasks. Although talking to computers is (for most of us) not yet part of our reality, voice does have a part to play in present-day computer reality. This chapter takes a look at what computers can do with our human voices.

If your computer did not come with a microphone, the AOL Shop (AOL Keyword: AOL Shop Direct) or your local computer store should have one. Inexpensive models (which may be all you need for basic audio) normally cost under $10.

Recording Your Voice

When it comes to human voices, the easiest process a computer can handle is simply recording them. If you have a sound card and a microphone, you can record your voice to a file. Windows comes with a program called Sound Recorder. You can find the program by clicking the Start button on the Windows task bar, selecting Programs, then Accessories, and then Entertainment (95/98) or Multimedia (NT), to reveal the Sound Recorder.

With your sound card installed, microphone plugged into the correct port, and your voice warmed up, you are ready to start recording messages. Access the Sound Recorder program as mentioned earlier. You will see a red button on the Sound

9

Recorder's Control Panel, as seen in Figure 9-1, which you click to start the recording. Speak into the mic, then click Stop (the button with the square) when you are finished. All you have left to do is save the recording to a file and you've done it — recorded your voice on the computer.

Figure 9-1. Ready to start recording a message with Sound Recorder.

When you have recorded a message you want to keep, click File from the menu and click Save As to give it a name. These files will be saved in .WAV format, the standard audio-file format on Windows-based computers. Later, you can open the file to listen to the message again.

Sending Voice Notes Through E-mail

After you get some practice recording messages, you can use that skill to attach voice messages to e-mail as you would any other file attachment. First, record the message you want to send using the Sound Recorder and then save the message as a sound file. Then open your regular e-mail program, compose your letter, and use the program's Attachment feature to send your verbal greeting along with your e-mail. When the recipient opens your message, a double-click on the icon that stands for the attached sound file opens the file and plays your message. It's as easy as 1-2-3.

For folks who want it even easier than 1-2-3, there is the VoicePod from Altec Lansing (www.alteclansing.com), a new bit of hardware that attaches to your computer and allows you to click a button, record a message, then click another button to instantly attach the message to an e-mail. When your recipient opens your e-mail, your message plays automatically.

If you're having trouble getting your voice recorded, double check that the microphone is plugged into the correct mic port of the sound card. In Windows, you can also double click the little speaker in the system tray (on the task bar) to make sure that none of the inputs are muted.

The Sound Recorder only records for 60 seconds at a time; however, each time the recorder starts, it gives you an additional 60 seconds to record. That means you can record 60 seconds, stop the recorder, and then start recording another 60 seconds all into the same file. Also, remember that every 60 seconds of recorded sound uses approximately 1.2 MB of disk space, which can add up over time.

The VoicePod comes with its own microphone and speaker built into the desktop unit, as well as a set of jacks for headphones. (See Figure 9-2.) Installation is simple: Just plug the speaker and mic cords into the computer sound card and connect the USB cable to a USB port. Then insert the VoicePod CD into your computer's CD drive and follow the on-screen setup instructions. That's all. You are ready to record and send voice messages.

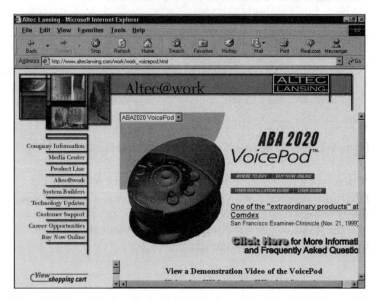

Figure 9-2. Record and send voice e-mails automatically with the VoicePod.

Speech Recognition

 **Find It Online**

You can see a quick demo of Altec Lansing's VoicePod at `www.alteclansing.com/work/work_voicepod.html`.

The next step toward the sci-fi scenario of humans conversing with computers is *speech recognition*, a process whereby a software program interprets commands spoken into a microphone — and then (in theory, at least) executes them.

Given the idiosyncrasies of each individual's speech patterns, you can imagine the difficulties involved in getting rather rigid software programs to recognize the subtle differences in human voices. When I first looked into the available software for speech recognition (also called *voice recognition*) some years ago, you had to spend a great deal of time training the software to recognize certain words — and always use precisely the same intonation whenever you used those words.

Otherwise, the software could not recognize the word you so painstaking "taught" it. With the development of more flexible software, speech-recognition programs are less likely to stumble over a word you inflect a bit differently today than you did two months ago. This progress has led to a speech-recognition rate of close to 75% in newer software.

The ultimate goal of voice recognition is to allow a person to communicate verbally to the computer using natural language, as easily as with another person and be understood. Don't misunderstand me, the computer may never respond as another person, but certainly can understand what is said. Currently, however, the available software is still a *long* way from understanding the nuances of meaning in the spoken word. Therefore, speech-recognition programs are limited to dictating letters, creating e-mails, and issuing specific commands to the computer. The following section gives a better idea of what is involved in setting up and using the currently available programs.

Speech-Recognition Software Programs

Applying speech recognition to computers can be helpful, educational and fun. Dragon Systems (www.dragonsystems.com), a leader in the speech-recognition field, has a number of products. Dragon's flagship program, NaturallySpeaking, is already a useful tool for the medical and legal professions, primarily for dictation. AOL's Point & Speak, also produced by Dragon Systems specifically for AOL, provides the lay person with easy voice-activated control for all the features of the AOL client software. The Point & Speak software lets your voice do the typing within the AOL client. It allows you to verbally type in e-mail, chats, Instant Messages, documents, and much more.

IBM (www.ibm.com/software/speech) also produces a speech-recognition program called ViaVoice. All the products enable integration with desktop applications, control computer fuctions with voice, and can be used by novice and expert alike (but, only ViaVoice is available with a downloadable demo).

Getting a speech-recognition program up and running involves a bit more than simply turning on the computer and installing the software. You have to train the software to recognize your own particular voice so that it can distinguish the way you say particular words. To see how this works, take a look at the AOL Point & Speak program.

Find It Online

AOL's Point & Speak is available from the AOL Shop (AOL Keyword: **AOL Shop Direct**) under **software** and **voice recognition**, as well as some of the other Dragon System products.

After installation, you can start up the program and have the handy wizard configure the software for you, asking for your name, adjusting speaker volume, and microphone volume. Next, you train the software to recognize your voice patterns by reading one of the provided stories into the computer's mic, a process that can take up to 30 minutes. You may feel a bit sheepish reading a bedtime story to a computer, but it is important to complete the training for the software to become more accurate. When you finish training the software, you can start using Point & Speak to open programs, issue commands, and dictate letters. If you find that the accuracy levels you get are not quite what you expected, you can beef up the program's ability to recognize words with the Vocabulary Builder, a feature you can use to create a custom vocabulary from text files and increase the program's range of recognized words.

A picture of a microphone appears on the system tray of your task bar. Use the mouse to turn on the mic. From here on, you can speak your commands to the computer. Speaking the command, "Click Start," for example, opens the Start menu on the task bar; "Click Programs" opens the Programs menu, and so on. You can control programs in a similar manner. The booklet that comes with Point & Speak is invaluable for helping learn the commands to control your computer — so read it.

You can get help through AOL for Point & Speak by using AOL Keyword: **P&S Tech Support.**

The key to using speech-recognition software is to speak clearly, consistently, and concisely. The software is designed to recognize the words as you speak them normally. The more slurred or choppy your speech, the more errors creep into the software's interpretation of what you're saying. It may take some time to adjust to this new technology; it did for me. In the mean time, hang onto your keyboard and mouse a while longer — I still use mine.

Coming Up Next

Do you ever feel like it takes forever to download Web pages, files, and even e-mail? Then you don't want to miss the next chapter. It covers the technologies you need to put the zoom back in the Internet, allowing you faster Internet access.

Chapter 10

Broadband Makes the Net Go Zoom

Years ago, accessing a computer bulletin board with a 300-baud modem was considered an outstanding feat. With today's technology, anybody would find a download speed of 300 baud humorously slow. In this chapter, you discover some of these new and not-so-new technologies, the pros and cons of each one, and how to determine what is best for you. You also see how a fast Internet connection can work with AOL to give you the best of both worlds.

Terms and Technologies

What do folks mean by *broadband?* The term gets bandied about a lot these days, so it may help to get a basic definition out of the way. *Broadband* is a high-speed, high-capacity connection from your computer to another computer on a network (usually a server). Broadband connections have the capability to carry video, voice, and data simultaneously. Conventional telephone wires, on the other hand, are limited by how much of a particular type of signal they can carry — and how fast they can carry it.

ISDN

Broadband technology comes in a variety of different forms. An old broadband standby has been *ISDN* (short for *I*ntegrated *S*ervices *D*igital *N*etwork), a set of communications standards allowing a single wire or optical fiber to carry voice, data, and video.

Consumer ISDN comes with two lines called B-Channels. Each channel can carry a signal at 64 Kbps (as compared to the fastest 56 Kbps modem). ISDN allows you to add the two lines together to get a connection of 128 Kbps.

ISDN technology has existed for a while — but its availability, expense, and hardware needs have prevented many people from using it for access to the Internet. In recent years, ISDN has become more affordable, its accessibility has increased, and the equipment has become simpler to install and set up. Besides raw speed, ISDN offers the capability of carrying voice signals; in fact, many external ISDN routers (which serve as an interface between the computer and the digital service) come with phone ports. It's an advantage that no other technology discussed in this chapter can offer.

Cable

Cable modems, the hot new form of broadband technology, are sweeping the country. The same line that provides your cable TV can also provide you with a lighting-fast entrance to the Internet. Cable modems share a 30MB (that's three-*mega*bit) connection to the Internet. You should know, however, that they aren't that fast all the time; cable modems *share* a connection. The more modems in your neighborhood (connected and in use, at least), the slower your access. Normally you wouldn't experience the effect of this shared connection until evening, when everyone returns home from the day and turns to the joys of browsing.

DSL

Digital Subscriber Line (DSL), one of the newest broadband technologies, provides a range of connection speeds. There are two types of DSL: synchronous and asynchronous. *Synchronous DSL (SDSL)* transmits and receives data at the same rate, while *asynchronous DSL (ADSL)* has two different

Note

Typically, the same company that offers a broadband service also includes a connection to the Internet as part of the deal.

Note

ISDN connections are solid digital signals that transfer at 64 Kbps with minimal noise. Analog telephone lines, on the other hand, often have static on the line, which can cause a modem to connect at a slower rate.

Tip

ISDN modems, like analog modems, install as a card inside a single computer. *ISDN routers* are external devices that plug into your network to share an Internet connection.

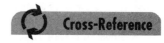

Cross-Reference

Look at Chapter 14 to learn more about integrating a cable modem with a home network.

rates. DSL speeds start at 128 Kbps and can exceed 7 Mbps. Location determines the maximum speed you can obtain; the farther you are from the DSL switch, the lower the transfer speed at which you can receive data. Figure 10-1 shows a re-markable difference in speed when downloading a 320K file. Best of all, America Online offers its own DSL service — AOL Plus (more about that in a minute).

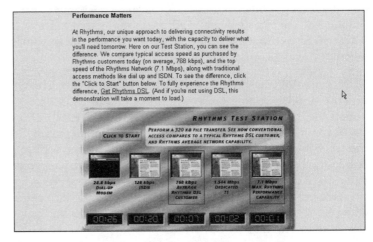

Figure 10-1. This simulation shows the speed difference visually.

DSL service is not yet available in all parts of the country. Even if the service is up and running in your area, your maximum speed might be less than you could get with other technologies. Bottom line: If you can get service, it blows the doors off any modem.

AOL Plus — Powered by DSL

If you are looking for a fast, broadband Internet connection, you may want to check out AOL Plus, the new DSL service from AOL that gives you everything you need to make it happen. With AOL Plus, you receive all the regular AOL services — *plus* the advantages of a high-speed connection (CD-quality streamed music, full-motion movies, and much more).

Signing up for AOL Plus gives you what you need to get your computer communicating with the DSL modem — DSL modem software, AOL Plus software, and a handy set of *phone filters*

Find It Online

As of mid-2000, AOL Plus was working in the Bell Atlantic and the SBC territo-ries — and becoming avail-able in more areas all the time. Use AOL Keywords: **DSL** or **AOL Plus** to find out whether the service has be-come available in your area— and to receive information when it does. National DSL providers with competitive rates are Rhythms (www.rhythms .net) and DSLNetwork (www.dslnetworks.com). You can try out the DSL simu-lation shown in Figure 10-1 at the Rhythms site.

designed to let you use the same phone lines to send and receive voice calls, faxes, and DSL data. This means you won't need to install additional phone lines to take advantage of this service. Everything works on your existing (single) phone line.

Though not yet available in all areas of the country, AOL Plus is steadily gaining ground. To find out whether this service is available to you, use the AOL Keyword: **AOL Plus** to get to the AOL Plus site — and then click the button that says *Yes! I want superfast AOL* (as seen in Figure 10-2). To find out whether your area provides this service, double-click the name of the state you live in, enter your 10-digit phone number, and click Next. If the service is not currently available, you can ask to be placed on a notification list to be contacted when the service becomes available.

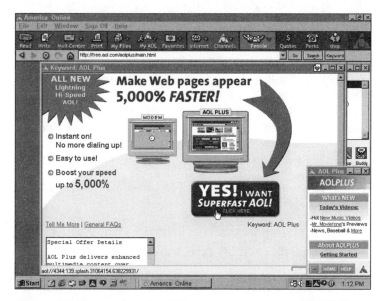

Figure 10-2. When you have the AOL Plus service running, you see the AOL Plus window in the lower-right corner of the client. This is your source for all broadband multimedia.

Satellite

The word *satellite* calls up notions of high-speed, high-tech connectivity. True, satellite technology does give you Internet data through a high-speed dish pointed at a high-tech satellite orbiting high about the earth. You do not, however, transmit data (such as Web-site requests) through the dish. The transmission

Find It Online

Look up AOL Keyword: **AOL Plus** to get the full story on this exciting new service offered by AOL.

is sent over a normal analog modem to the provider, who then processes the request and bounces the information off a satellite — and back to you at a rate of approximately 400 Kbps.

With the advancement of the satellite technology, you can now watch your favorite television programs *and* browse the Internet using the same satellite dish.

Find It Online

DirecPC is one satellite service available. You can find more information at www .digitalsat.com/ direcpc970323c.html. AOL's plans call for a mid-to-late-2000 release of a DirecPC version of AOL Plus to provide broadband-enhanced content. Use AOL Keyword: **AOL Plus** to get more details.

Picking the Right System for You

If you've already decided that faster is better when it comes to Internet access, then some form of broadband technology is definitely the thing for you. The next step is choosing the broadband technology that best fits your needs.

Each high-speed technology has its advantages and disadvantages. You may want to do some research (and some pointed questioning of salespeople) before deciding which system works best for you. Some of these systems have existed for years in certain parts of the country, while other parts are just now getting access. If you're living in a larger metropolitan area, you have an advantage over the rest of the country; more of these high-speed services will already be up and running.

To help you with your research, here are some questions and tips to consider:

▶ What services are available in my area?
▶ What are the monthly costs and setup fees for these services?
▶ Do I need additional equipment to set up a particular service?
▶ Will I have more fun with the Internet after I have a broadband service installed? Will the increase in speed significantly increase my enjoyment of the Internet by lessening my frustration with slow downloads? Will the benefits outweigh the costs (both initial and ongoing)?

Once you have narrowed down the choices, determined your costs, and justified getting the high-speed broadband connection, then get signed up to take advantage of your new, high-speed connection to the Internet.

AOL Plus delivers the content and features of enhanced multi-media over any high-speed connection — TCP/IP, DSL, cable, or satellite — to AOL members who use AOL version 5.0. The Speed Detect feature available in AOL 5.0 automatically downloads the technology that enables full-motion video and streaming audio (via the AOL Plus Tower, which appears in the lower-right corner of the screen whenever members sign on with high-speed broadband connections).

AOL Plus provides broadband-enhanced news and entertainment from industry-leading providers of programming — including AthletesDirect, CBS SportsLine, CBS MarketWatch.com, CNET Networks Inc., CNN, FOXNews.com, FOXSports.com, House of Blues, Launch.com, Max Broadcasting Network, Travelocity.com, and weather.com, as well as such exclusive America Online brands as MovieFone and Spinner.

Tip

When you inquire about a broadband service, ask the salesperson about special promotions. Sometimes you can get deals, rebates, and such on the service or equipment you've chosen when you sign up.

10

Broadband Makes the Net Go Zoom

AOL and a High-Speed Internet Service Provider

Having a high-speed connection to the Internet through an Internet service provider (ISP) other than AOL may have you thinking *Do I still have to use my slowpoke of a modem to access AOL?* The answer is a resounding *No.* The AOL 5.0 Client software makes provision for a dedicated LAN/Internet connection — which allows you to use your own ISP, rather than an AOL dial-up connection. If the newly installed AOL 5.0 software detects such a dedicated connection, that's the one it uses — automatically.

If you already have an existing AOL dial-up (modem) connection, you can convert it to a high-speed connection. The following steps show how:

1. Establish the communication to your new high-speed ISP.
2. Start the AOL software.
3. From the sign-on screen, click the Setup button.
4. Choose the last of the four options, labeled *Create a location for use with new access phone numbers or an ISP* (see Figure 10-3); then click Next.

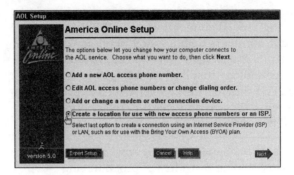

Figure 10-3. Selecting location at sign-on.

5. Select *Add a custom connection*; then click Next.

    The AOL software adds a new connection type and notifies you with a dialog box.

6. Click the OK button to continue.

7. Choose your new connection method from the list; then sign on to AOL.

From now on, you will be able to immediately access your AOL account using your new high-speed connection, giving you the best of both worlds. (Isn't technology wonderful?)

Setting AOL as Your Default Mail and Browser Client

The Windows operating system uses a built-in scheme of *associating* files and resources with applications. When you've set up an association, you can click a file icon to make the corresponding application open, showing the file you chose.

Associations also mean that specific e-mail and newsgroup programs, as well as Internet browsers, get set up as your default applications. Since you (as a faithful AOL patriot) will no doubt want to continue using AOL services as your default to access e-mail, newsgroups, and Internet browsing, you'll have to let Windows know that. Broadband Internet services come with their own e-mail/newsgroups programs and such, so you will have to set up an association to get AOL software recognized as the default. The following steps show you how that's done:

1. Start the AOL software and sign on using your existing account.

   Once you have logged onto the AOL system, you can make the changes you want.

2. Select My AOL⇨Preferences from the Main menu.

   The Preferences window appears, as shown in Figure 10-4. This window shows all the preference settings available to you for personalizing your AOL session.

Figure 10-4. There are a number of preference settings to choose from.

3. Click the Associations icon from the window.

   A dialog box will appear, as seen in Figure 10-5, giving you the option of making AOL your preferred application for Web browsing, e-mail and newsgroups.

4. Click the OK button if you are sure that you want to set up AOL as your default application.

   The AOL software registers with Windows to be the default e-mail, news and Internet browser.

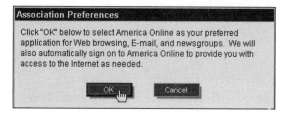

Figure 10-5. Setting up AOL as the default mail, news, and browser.

Changing Back the Default

If you discover later that you would rather not have AOL as your default e-mail/ newsgroup program, it is possible to change these settings back. Here is how you make those changes:

Set the default to the service you intend to use the most. If your primary Internet service was AOL before you had a broadband connection, then set the default to

1. Select Start⇨Settings⇨Control Panel from the Windows taskbar to bring up the Control Panel options.

2. From the Control Panel window, double-click the Internet Options icon to open the Internet Properties dialog box.

3. Click the Programs tab. The Programs tab controls the Internet applications and the associated functions.

4. Scroll through your options for e-mail and newsgroups by clicking the down arrow at the end of the respective text fields and select the application you want to act as your default (See Figure 10-6). Any application you've used previously will be available to you.

When setting up a default internet browser, you will notice a checkbox in the lower left corner of the dialog box. Once the check is removed, the question will not be asked again, so you will not be able to change the default browser.

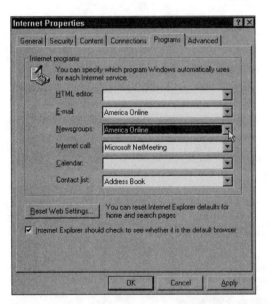

Figure 10-6. You can change e-mail and newsgroup defaults in Internet Options.

If you want to change your default Internet browser, you have to take a different route. Here's how:

1. Open the browser that you would like to use. A dialog box opens to inform you that another browser is acting as the default browser and to ask you whether you want this browser to become the default.

2. Click the Yes button to set up this browser as default. This sets the current browser as your default browser.

You can always change the defaults for your Internet functions. If you are using other applications and decide that the AOL software is what you want, then you can set the default to AOL and vice versa.

Coming Up Next

You've just discovered the world of high-speed Internet. What could be better than that? How about a home network? In the next section, you can find out what a home network is, what it can do for you, how to set one up, and what new devices exist for it. I start you off in the first chapter of the section by introducing you to some networking terms and definitions, listing some of the advantages to having a network at home, and letting you know what is needed for a network.

Chapter 11

Networking Isn't Just for Offices Anymore

Welcome to the networking chapter — your introduction to the wonderful world of networking, where computers do all the work and you get to sit back and enjoy the ride. Well, okay, that may happen *someday*, but don't hold your breath. In the meantime, this chapter explains what networks are all about, why they're useful, and why you may have uses of your own for them. Consider this chapter your Introduction to Networking 101. The other chapters in this section go into more depth of specific areas. Chapters 12 and 13 work together to assist you in assembling the hardware and configuring the software needed to run a home network; Chapter 14 covers alternate technologies you may want to use in your home network.

Terms and Tech Talk

The following list of common networking terms (and their meanings) gives you a sense of what people are actually saying when they throw around networking lingo. Although it isn't exhaustive, it should get you up to speed without too much fuss. These terms crop up throughout this section, so you might want to keep a finger here as you read on.

Network	A joining of two or more computers into a connected system for the purpose of communication and sharing files, data, or printing.
Local Area Network (LAN)	A collection of networked computers sharing information (and often resources such as printers) in relatively close proximity, as in a single building or a room. Any computer connected to such a network is part of that LAN.
Wide Area Network (WAN)	Two or more computers or LANs, located in different geographical areas but sharing information as one system, usually connected by phone lines.
Ethernet	A standard that requires a LAN to transfer data at a rate of 10 Mbps (megabits per second) between networked computers connected in a line or through a hub.
Wireless Ethernet	An Ethernet LAN that uses radio waves instead of wires for communicating between computers, but still transfers data at a rate of 10 Mbps.
Fast Ethernet	The next generation of the Ethernet LAN concept, similar in most ways except it can communicate ten times faster (at a rate of 100 Mbps).

Find It Online

If you come across a networking term that gives you no clue to what it means, look it up on the Web at www.netlingo.com, use it casually at the next office party, and watch the reaction.

11

Networking Isn't Just
for Offices Anymore

Note

To give you an idea of how quicker data transfer improves the performance of a network, imagine the data packets as couriers on bicycles. If a 10 Mbps network speed is like sending the couriers over a system of streets at 10 miles an hour, imagine how much faster a big report would get to its destination at 100 Mbps. Traveling over the same routes at 100 miles an hour, the couriers could deliver 10 times as much data in the same amount of time — entirely possible when the "street" is a wire and the "couriers" are electrical impulses.

Protocol	An agreed-upon standard that determines how the computers are going to talk to each other. Before exchanging data, the computers agree to use the same language and to handle data according to the same network etiquette. The process works like the "protocol" of sending a letter to a friend. The U.S. Postal Service will send only those letters that have postage in the upper right corner of the envelope, the address you are sending the letter to in the middle of the envelope, and the return address in the upper left corner. Similarly, a computer protocol includes information about the sender and the receiver that helps to route the message through the network of intermediary computers.
Transmission Control Protocol/ Internet Protocol (TCP/IP)	The basic protocol used on the Internet. Using TCP/IP, computers on different networks can communicate via e-mail, telnet, FTP, or other Internet applications.
IP Address	A unique number that identifies each computer on a network and serves as an online address that a computer using TCP/IP can recognize. An IP Address is required for communication on the Internet; an Internet service provider assigns one when someone makes a dial-up connection.
Internetwork Packet eXchange (IPX)	A simple protocol that tells local networks how to exchange information packets, without requiring any unique numbers or settings.

NetBIOS Enhanced User Interface (NetBEUI)	Protocol that gives a networked computer a standard way to communicate with other machines on the network, using its Network Basic Input/Output System (NetBIOS). NetBEUI is a fundamental protocol for networks.
Network Interface Card (NIC)	Network hardware installed inside a networked computer, usually a card with the electronics to send and receive signals to and from other computers on the network.
10BaseT	A common type of *Twisted-Pair cable* used in Ethernet networks. (*10Base* is a generic professional name for Ethernet cable; the other letters or numbers in the name specify what type — for example, *T* means Twisted-Pair and *F* means fiber-optic.) It has an *RJ-45 plug* on each end, using 4 of the 8 contacts available on the plug.
100BaseT	Twisted-Pair wiring used for Fast Ethernet networks. The cable uses all 8 contacts on its RJ-45 connectors.
CAT5 (Category 5)	CAT (for *category*) refers to quality standards set for network cable. This cable uses twisted pairs of wires that have to meet certain manufacturing specifications.
Twisted-Pair	Street name for CAT5 cable, which is made of 8 wires twisted into 4 pairs during manufacturing. Twisting the wires together reduces noise or static, which improves communication over the cable.
Cross-over cable	A cable that works much like Twisted-Pair cable, with one major exception: Switching the paired wires to each other's connecting pins at one end of the cable makes a direct connection possible. No network *hub* or other device is necessary for this simple, short-range connection.

RJ-45   The type of plug most commonly used
            with Ethernet wiring. An RJ-45 plug looks
            like the plug at the end of a phone wire,
            only larger. The phone plug has 4 or 6
            contacts; the RJ-45 has 8.

Hub   A device that provides ports for connect-
            ing several Ethernet cables, giving net-
            worked computers a common place to
            send the information they exchange. On
            many networks, hubs are like busy inter-
            sections for information.

Switch   Device that functions as a "policeman" at
            the intersection provided by the hub, di-
            recting traffic between different con-
            nected devices. The result is a better flow
            of information.

Gateway   The device that directs communication
            traffic to another network or to the
            Internet. The gateway allows only the traf-
            fic not meant for the local network to
            pass through.

Firewall   A device that uses encryption to provide
            a wall of protection that keeps outsiders
            from accessing a private network —
            while still maintaining connections to
            other networks and allowing the private
            network to access the Internet. A firewall
            is a security measure designed to isolate a
            network from unauthorized entry via the
            Internet.

Server   The part of a network whose sole pur-
            pose is to hold and offer information to
            the computers on the network. The term
            server can refer to hardware (the com-
            puter that does this job) *or* to the soft-
            ware used to provide the requested
            information. (For instance, a *Web server* is
            software that responds to incoming
            queries from Internet sources and pro-
            vides the requested information.)

How a Network Actually Works

Brushing up on networking terms isn't just a weird word game; it's a necessary first step in setting up your network. These terms are really just individual pieces of the network puzzle. Putting that puzzle together is the next step; you can use the rest of this chapter (along with Chapters 12 through 15) to navigate that step.

Fortunately, the networking puzzle has two big pieces that make good starting places:

> ▶ **The physical layer of the network.** This encompasses everything in the network that has a physical existence — wires, computers, plugs, NICs, and perhaps hubs and switches, depending on how many computers you want to connect to your network.

> ▶ **The communication layer.** This part of the network is composed of the protocols that actually allow the transfer of data across a network — in effect, special computer instructions that enable networked machines to agree on how to do the transferring. This layer may not be tangible, but it's just as important as the physical.

A Network's Physical Layer

The physical layer of a network is tangible enough that you could stub your toe on some of its bigger parts — yet this layer is also supposed to be nearly "invisible" to its users. Consider the phone as a familiar analogy: Most of us have used it more times than we care to count, without having to think too hard about how it works. But to talk on the phone, you must first *have* a phone, have it plugged into the wall outlet, and have wiring in your house that connects to other phones. And there you have it — the physical layer of the phone network — seemingly obvious because its users normally don't think about it.

The physical layer of your computer network has a similar relationship to its users. To "talk" with other computers, you need the computers themselves, the wiring, the outlets, and the plugs to connect everything together. Figure 11-1 shows a typical example — networked computers in different rooms, sharing one printer.

Find It Online

Plenty of individuals in the AOL community have already taken the step and set up their own home computer networks. Not only that, many are also willing to share their experiences and expertise. For help from experienced home networkers on AOL, use AOL Keyword: **Networking** and look up more information about "Setting up Networks."

11

Networking Isn't Just for Offices Anymore

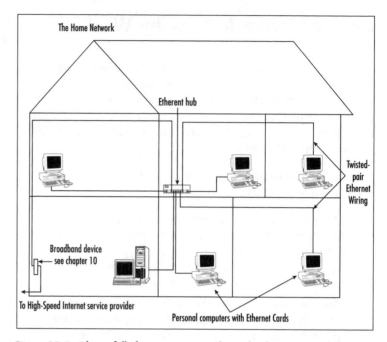

The Home Network

Etherent hub

Twisted-pair Ethernet Wiring

Broadband device — see chapter 10

To High-Speed Internet service provider

Personal computers with Ethernet Cards

Figure 11-1. A house full of computers can work together for printing and sharing files.

The Communication Layer

Wires with nothing running over them can't do much for you, so one important piece of the networking puzzle involves setting up the software on your various computers in such a way that data can flow across the physical wires of your network. Although software on your computer takes care of the details of the communication between computers, each computer on the network must use the same protocol to communicate. The analogy of the phone in your house may help again to make this clear. When someone makes a phone call, a certain protocol takes place: The phone rings and you answer it with a greeting. "Hello, this is Bob." Then a response on the other end. "Hello Bob. This is Jim. I was wondering . . ." A conversation breaks out; each person takes turns talking and listening. The protocol that a computer uses for communication works much like the sequence of verbal exchange in this example. Computer protocols are, however, a bit more complicated — a number of protocols are available out there, and they are all mutually exclusive. A computer that runs a particular protocol can only communicate with other computers that run the same protocol.

In practical terms, every computer on a network must have the same protocol installed in order to communicate with the others. Two common examples are the *IPX* and *TCP/IP* protocols; they work fine by themselves, but refuse to speak to each other. Networks connected to the Internet have to use TCP/IP. The IPX protocol, on the other hand, was not designed for the Internet; its heyday was with older computer games that could run on a small local network. Today, however, TCP/IP is the protocol of choice for computer games — many of which have live, online, multiplayer versions (as some game aficionados on AOL can tell you).

You may not need TCP/IP if you simply want to share that printer in the den. A third, much less used protocol — NetBEUI — may offer exactly the no-nonsense connection you need. The primary mission for NetBEUI is to help Windows machines communicate and share resources — which makes it an excellent choice for a small home network.

The Bare Essentials for a Network

What do you need for a network? The minimum requirements are simple: two computers, two NIC boards, and a wire, nothing more. If you are only interested in connecting two computers that are in close proximity, you may be pleasantly surprised to discover how easy it actually is. Normally, complications only arise when you want to connect more than two computers — or want to set them farther apart. The more computers — and the farther apart — the more complexity (hubs, switches, different wiring methods). All of which makes a great reason to start simple — say, with two computers in easy walking distance of each other.

Another essential element for a home computer network is a good networking plan. Even before you start checking out the local computer stores for networking hardware, sit down with a piece of paper and sketch out what you want your network to do for you. Keep the following questions in mind as you draw up your networking plan; they may help you come up with a feasible plan:

▶ **How many computers am I planning to network?**
The number of computers involved may have an impact on the kind of networking technology you can

Note

Although a computer may have to use more than one protocol on a network — which means it can have more than one installed — it can't use more than one at a time. The computer has to manage its protocols and choose the right one to use.

Cross-Reference

NetBEUI makes its debut appearance in the "Terms and Tech Talk" section of this chapter.

11

Networking Isn't Just
for Offices Anymore

Cross-Reference

If you have to check out alternative wiring methods or invest in a hub or switch, Chapters 13 and 14 can give you some tips on the best ways to explore such options.

use. Networking more than two computers, for example, means using a hub or switch. Keep in mind any future expansion.

▶ **How much networking hardware can I afford?**
You can acquire the minimum components for a two-computer network (a cable and two NIC boards), for around $100. If you add more computers, don't forget that each computer needs its own NIC card — and that a network of more than two computers also needs more cabling and a hub or switch.

▶ **What networking technology is best for me?**
Computer networks can use your house's phone lines, or use new cables laid down in your house for that purpose, or even go cutting-edge with wireless technologies that use transmitters and receivers. Each technology has its pluses and minuses; read on to get familiar with some of these pros and cons.

▶ **What is it I want to do with my network?** This is probably the most important question of all, which is why I devote the entire next section to it.

Why a Network Is Worth the Work

Keeping all these considerations in mind, and as you become more familiar with how a network operates, you might wonder how important a home network might be to your lifestyle. You are about to see four compelling reasons and a fifth "must-have" reason.

The first compelling reason to have a network is accessing a single piece of equipment — the printer. Some small offices will only have one to share between several computers. The printer must be available and moving the printer from computer to computer gets old, it's dangerous, and it even jeopardizes damaging the printer. Purchasing additional printers is far too expensive, especially when laser printers are the printer of choice. Sharing the printer on a network solves the roaming printer dilemma. Printer sharing is definitely one of the huge benefits of having a home network.

The second compelling reason — access to the Internet — is probably one of the major factors in considering a network. Everyone has heard of the Internet, and so most everyone in the house will want his or her turn browsing and surfing. What would be the point of having all your home's computers networked if only one of the computers could access the Internet? It is much more convenient to have one computer dial and connect to the Internet with the other computers sharing access to the Internet through the one connection, than to have multiple phone lines, modems and dial-up accounts. Most home network kits have features that address the problem of everyone having access to the Internet at the same time.

The third compelling reason is a need to back up near-sacred files. If you have ever lost data as a result of a problem with your computer, a network can help prevent a repeat loss. Backups are probably the most neglected activity in the world of computers. Using a network, you can create copies of files on other computers on the network — or archive the files on a special drive like a Zip, tape, or Jaz drive shared from another computer.

Backups bring us to the fourth compelling reason for having a network — sharing files. Although sharing files is not as glamorous a function as accessing the Internet (nor, perhaps, as compelling as backups), but it has its own advantages. Big corporate networks depend on file sharing to keep the work flowing among hundreds of people who need to share information with each other. To share files on a network simply means that every computer on the network can access any folders on any other computer hooked up to the same network, as long as those files are set up to make that access possible. You may not need a network as large as a corporate network, but the advantages remain the same regardless of size.

And last, but not least, the number-one reason, to have a network (drum roll, please) — to play games. Most games today are multiplayer; you can play other people, and the game is more fun that way — especially over a network. Today, small groups of hard-core gamers bring their computers together in one location to connect them onto a network to play computer games. Although it's a lot of fun, it does mean carting all that equipment around. Having a network at home allows you to have the fun of playing computer games with your family and friends without the hassle of carting the equipment.

See Chapter 12 in this part for details on home network kits.

Backups are critical for keeping your valuable data safe. People lose jobs, money, work, and opportunities because of lost data. Millions of dollars in fines are charged because of lost data. Although most home computer users will never be faced with these extremes, everyone can benefit from the peace of mind that backed-up data provides.

To learn more about protecting your data, go to Chapter 37 for the details on tape drives, backup software, and other assorted goodies.

Coming Up Next

Networks in the home allow you to utilize all the computer equipment you have in your house — printers, drives and Internet hookups — by sharing these resources. Networks allow the sharing of information and the peace of mind that comes from backing up critical files. Networks also help provide entertainment for multiple game players at once. If these advantages have won you over to the idea of home networks, look to the next chapter for details of how to set one up.

Chapter 12
Wiring Your Home Network

Chapter 11 gave you the big picture view of home computer networking; the next step involves the actual building of your own network. This section covers some of the building basics, with more to come in Chapters 13 and 14. You still have to do the work, but at least now you know where to start.

Before You Begin

Setting up a home network can be rewarding (if you're not sure how rewarding, re-read Chapter 11). However, because a home network can take shape in a variety of different ways, you need to make some decisions on your network before you begin purchasing parts and installing anything. You can pick out the best setup for you and your computer by deciding on which ways you want a home network to fit into your lifestyle. Following are some things to consider when deciding which type of network is best for you:

▶ **Decide where (approximately) you want to keep the computers.** The location of the computers for the network affects the type of equipment you will need. If all of the computers are in the same room or are in adjacent rooms, then any of the networks described in this chapter will work. On the other hand, if the computers are spread around the house, you may opt to choose one of the alternative networking options described in Chapter 14.

▶ **Determine how many computers you want to connect to your network.** The number of computers connected to the network will affect the quantity of equipment needed for your network. For the kind of simple Ethernet networks described in Chapter 11, you need to know the number of computers for your network to total the amount of equipment (number of cables, number of available ports on a hub, and number of NICs) you will need. In simple Ethernet networks, adding a new computer means just adding a twisted-pair cable and NIC, while other network technologies require additional hardware (see Chapter 14).

▶ **Investigate the kinds of networking technologies capable of working with your computers and your environment.** The most common network technology is a standard Ethernet with cables and a hub. Other network technologies include wireless technology, connecting the computers using household electrical and phone line wiring (see Chapter 14 for details).

▶ **Determine how much you are willing to spend.** Overall, a home-network setup using standard Ethernet technology can cost from $70 to $400, but don't forget: Standard Ethernet may not be the most feasible technology for your particular environment. No one can determine what fits your budget except you. Use the ideas and principles listed in this section to determine your choices, then do a little research on the products.

Note

Printers shared on a Home network don't need to be considered as a separate network connection. The printers will be shared from a computer that is connected to the network. See how to set up sharing a printer in Chapter 13.

12

Wiring Your Home Network

Doing It Yourself

Some people prefer the "do-it-yourself" kind approach to big projects. You may be one of those people — not at all daunted

Cross-Reference

For alternatives to traditional network wiring, see Chapter 14 for networking technologies that use your home's existing AC wiring and phone wiring. Chapter 14 also gives you the lowdown on wireless networks.

Tip

If you're planning to build your own house, you can add Ethernet wires and wall plates to the house while it's being built. Adding a networking infrastructure to your house during construction is far easier than rewiring the house later.

Find It Online

LinkSys (www.linksys.com) and NetGear (www.netgear.com) offer network starter kits for traditional Ethernet cabling. You can choose from several models; you may find one right away that fits your networking desires.

by the idea of laying bathroom tile or rewiring the kitchen yourself, but a little unsure of where to start wiring your house for a computer network. Not to worry. If you have just a little bit of handyman savvy, you can set up your very own Local Area Network the way the big kids do it: using dedicated networking cable to set up a traditional Ethernet network.

To get started on your home network, you either need to purchase the components for your network separately or purchase a networking starter kit. D-Link (www.dlink.com) offers a networking starter kit known as "Network in a Box," for about a $100. "Network in a Box," as seen in Figure 12-1, is a good place to start even for the not-so-handy. This kit is designed for the individual who has two desktop computers. If you have laptop to include in your network, see the special section in this chapter "For Laptops." The D-Link kit includes:

▶ Two NICs for your two desktop computers.

▶ A 4-port 10/100Mbs hub to pass information between the computers. The four ports allow you to add two new computers later; the hub can handle data at either 10 or 100 megabits per second.

▶ Two 20-foot cables to connect your computers to the hub.

▶ Instructions for setting up your new network.

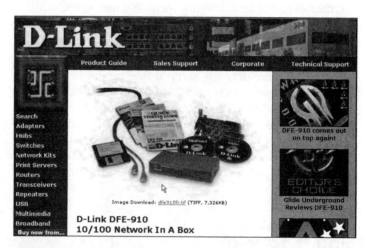

Figure 12-1. You can find Home Network Kits from D-Link.

The installation process is the same regardless of whether you get a kit; you still need all the same components for your network. You can purchase them separately from your local computer store or from online stores. If you decide to purchase components separately (rather than going with a kit), the following sections provide some pointers.

For Laptops

Including a laptop in the network means changing the standard kit. A laptop needs a PCMCIA Ethernet card, rather than a standard NIC. Slipping the card into the PCMCIA slot on the laptop is nearly all you have to do. The computer will recognize the new card and may ask for the drivers which will be provided with the card. I have found that the 3Com Megahertz 10/100 LAN Cardbus PC Card is a good product for laptops (as seen on the company Web page below). Kingston, Intel, and D-Link also have fine laptop products.

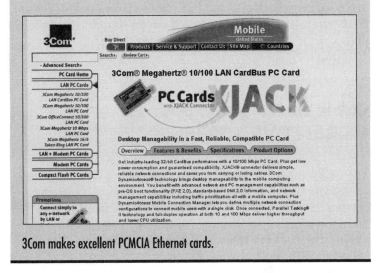

3Com makes excellent PCMCIA Ethernet cards.

Note

The Windows 98 Revision 2 operating system can not only connect to the Internet, but also share that connection with other computers on its local network. If your home network has two computers and you have Windows 98 Rev. 2 running on one of them, that computer can connect to the Internet with a modem and share its connection with the other computer — without needing any additional software.

Networks Cards

Network interface cards (NICs), sometimes called adapters, come in all flavors. A number of companies make good quality cards; picking one can be a draw from a hat. Reputable brands include 3Com, Intel, Kingston, LinkSys, and D-Link, to name a

Find It Online

When you have an idea of the computer hardware you want and cost *is* an important factor, look for the device on www.pricewatch.com, a Web site that allows hundreds of vendors to submit their lowest price for their particular products. Pricewatch then lists the vendors' price offerings for each product, with the lowest overall price at the top of the list. You can even use the site to price compare when shopping at your local computer store.

few. These companies provide excellent support for their adapters. Finding drivers for the cards on the company Web site becomes important should an install disk get lost. The following list gives the Web addresses for a number of NIC manufacturers as well as the names of their most popular product:

www.3com.com	Etherlink 10/100 (3c905)
www.intel.com	Fast Ethernet Controller (82559ER)
www.kingston.com	EtheRx PCI 10/100 Fast Ethernet Adapter (KNE120TX)
www.linksys.com	EtherFast 10/100 LAN Card (LNE 100TX)
www.dlink.com	D-Link 10/100 Network Adapter (DFE-530TX)

Although this list shows each company's Web site, one of the Ethernet cards the company offers, and the model number of the card, these models are only examples; I have worked with each of these brands and find them all to be reliable. First make sure any network card you choose is compatible with your system. Such information is usually prominently displayed somewhere on the packaging for the card.

Definition

PCMCIA stands for Personal Computer Memory Card International Association, the group who set the standard for making credit-card-size memory cards for laptop computers and mobile devices. The PCMCIA standard is no longer limited to memory cards; it includes many types of devices, such as modems, SCSI adapters, Ethernet cards, and more.

Cable at Network Speeds (10BaseT VS 100BaseT)

The two standard transfer speeds for network communication are 10 Mbs and 100 Mbs. Both standards require Twisted-Pair cabling for networks. (No, the wires aren't demented; they're wrapped together in a pair to reduce electromagnetic noise.) Cables that conform to these standards have names that correspond to their most obvious difference — speed: 10BaseT (10Mbs) and 100BaseT (100Mbs).

The *other* obvious difference between the two types of cable is price. One outperforms the other by a factor of 10, but speed costs money. You might not want the additional expense for the NICs and hubs. You can end up paying $50 more for each 100 Mbps NIC — and $100 more for a 100 Mbps hub. Two NICs and one hub — the minimum you'd need to go from 10 Mbps to 100 Mbps — add up to about $200.

NICs and hubs that use 100BaseT are still relatively new on the market; that means they still cost more to manufacture. 10BaseT has been around for a while, which means it's more common and easier to find — which is one big reason it costs less. Over time, the 100 Mbps NICs and hubs will also cost less, reducing the $200 gap — but until that happens, you may want to stick with 10BaseT. The operation of 10BaseT still allows you to play games, transfer files, and share devices.

When shopping for cable for your new network, you are sure to come across some new (and perhaps confusing) terminology. Salespeople will probably refer to some types of cable that sound more mysterious than they are:

▶ **CAT 5:** Short for Category 5, the industry standard for regular network use.

▶ **Plenum:** This term refers to the plastic coating on the cable.

▶ **Solid:** Used for Ethernet wiring in the walls of a house, this type of cable uses 8 solid strands, durable but too stiff to use in tight places.

▶ **Stranded:** Made of multiple thin strands, this type of cable is more flexible and better suited to the smaller spaces between the wall plate or hub and the NIC where they are moved often.

For a home network, you need only insist upon CAT 5 patch cabling to connect your computer NIC to the hub. CAT 5 cabling works for both 10BaseT and 100BaseT networks. You can find the cables you need at your local computer store or online at www.warehouse.com.

Hubs and Switches

Hubs also come in a rainbow of choices. The important thing to remember is the hub must have enough ports for the number of computers that will be connected to the hub. Obviously a four-port hub will not work with a five-computer network. You can always have more ports available than you have computers. Sometime later on, you may want to add a computer or two to the network and hub will be able to accommodate the additions.

Caution

Never run wiring across the floor. The wire becomes a trip hazard, could be damaged by being stepped on, and it makes the floor look cluttered. Use wire channels (which you can buy at a local office-supply store) that create a bridge, of sorts, that traffic can go over without crushing, nicking, or damaging the cables.

Caution

Never bend network cable in half; doing so can kink the wires and possibly damage them. This can cause the cable to break inside which will cause you hours of frustration.

Tip

If you have excess cable, wind it into a 6" loop then secure it with a twist-tie. This reduces the cable clutter while preventing the cables from getting snagged and damaged.

12

Wiring Your Home Network

Tip

If you find a *10/100 auto-sensing* on a hub, that means the hub can sense the speed of the NIC in the computer and adjust its port speed accordingly. This handy feature helps all the computers on a network communicate, regardless of whether their usual speed is 10 or 100 Mbps.

Another consideration is the speed of the hub. Be sure to choose a hub that matches the other components in your network. *The slowest component of your network determines the overall speed of the network.* If all the components can operate at 100Mbs, but the hub can only operate at 10Mbs, then your network speed will be 10Mbs at best. A 10Mbs hub cannot communicate with a 100Mbs hub unless a switch (or an auto-sensing hub) is working as a translator between the two speeds.

Figure 12-2. NetGear offers both switches and hubs.

Definition

In generic terms, a *packet* refers to a unit of data being transmitted on a network. On its way from one computer to another, the file gets broken down into smaller chunks (data packets) before being transmitted across the network to the destination computer and reassembled into the original file.

As you peruse stores and browse the Web looking for a hub, you will see the term "switch" (see Figure 12-2) used sometimes interchangeably with the word "hub." A switch cuts down the communication traffic on the network by sending little packets of information only to the port or connection of the recipient workstation. In other words, the information sent to a computer goes directly to the computer connected to the switch. The hubs broadcast an information packet to all the connections on the network. The autosensing hubs broadcast the 10Mbs packets to the port that operate at 10Mbs only and broadcast the 100Mbs packets to the ports that operate at 100Mbs only. Below are a couple of examples of available models.

Company Web Site	# of Ports	Model
www.Netgear.com	8	8 Port Switch (SW108)
www.Dlink.com	8	8 Port Hub with Auto-Switching (DSH-8)
www.LinkSys.com	5	EtherFast 5 Port Auto-Sensing Hub (EFAH05W)

Putting It All Together

Once you have all the devices picked out, you are ready to put your network together. The following three basic steps (each one devoted to a particular component) will help you assemble your network. (If you purchased a network kit, follow the instruction included with the kit instead of these instructions.)

1. **NIC installation:** The first step is to install an NIC into each computer on your network. Follow the instructions that came with the NIC packaging. (Each manufacturer may have a slightly different procedure.) The instructions should include installing the card itself as well as the software for the card.

2. **Setting up the hub:** Make sure the hub has enough ports to handle all the computers on the network. Hubs are usually the easiest pieces of hardware to set up and install for your network. As always, read the instructions carefully, but usually all you really have to do is take the hub out of the box, connect the power supply to the hub and plug the unit into a power outlet.

3. **Connecting the cable:** Cable is what ties the network together; it's a good thing that something so crucial is so easy to work with. For each computer, plug one end of an Ethernet cable into the NIC and the other end into a port on the hub. That's all.

In Figure 12-3 you can see an illustration of two computers connected by Ethernet. Notice the cabling and hub. Your new network should look similar to this picture, assuming that you only have two desktop computers.

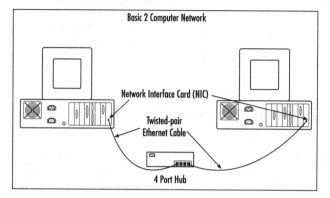

Figure 12-3. The basic network has three key components- NIC, Hub, and Cable.

Coming Up Next

After you have a physical network assembled, your computers have to be configured to talk to each other so they can share devices, information, and (let's talk priorities here) run multi-player games. Coming up in the next chapter are all the instructions you're likely to need to set up your software and make your network function.

Chapter 13

Bringing It All Together

IN THIS CHAPTER

Setting up Windows to work on a network

Sharing resources on a network

Using one printer among several computers

Diagnosing network problems

After you have a network physically set up, you still have to configure your software settings in order to get your network up and running. This chapter addresses those settings and gives step-by-step instructions so you can complete the network yourself.

Setting Up Windows 95/98 for Networking

Setting up the software is the final step in completing your network installation. As you might expect, the software is the key to allowing all the computers to communicate with each other. To get the software to do its job, however, you have to set up your network so the software can identify each computer on the network. This means giving each computer a unique name, one not shared by any other computer on the network. To complete the naming process, you also have to assign a Workgroup name to the network as a whole, so that the software knows which computers to recognize as part of the network. This next section covers computer names and workgroup names, followed by the step-by-step instructions on configuring the software.

Having Fun with Names

Giving a name to computers, files and printers can be fun. Your creativity can shine through when assigning names. The administrators of large networks often create themes to their networks (sometimes the nuttier the better). They choose names of characters, locations, or objects from cartoons, TV shows, or movies. Let your imagination roam when choosing names for your computer world.

You can use up to 15 characters (but no more) in each name you choose for your computers and workgroups.

For example, you could choose a name for your workgroup that comes from your favorite cartoon show, whether it be *The Simpsons, X-Men,* or (my own personal favorite) *Super Friends.* You can name your computers after characters on the show (for example, wonder woman, superman, and aquaman), and name the shared devices after super powers (such as golden lasso, xray vision, or sonar). There you have it — organization that's easy to remember because it's fun. Now to teach the computer those new names.

Setting Up the Software

Windows 95/98 makes configuring any settings you need to make the network operational easy. For this to work, however, you already had to have the NICs, hub and cable installed. I'm going to assume that the physical part of your network is complete and it's time to move on to the software.

To find the identification information for Windows NT and Windows 2000, right-click Network Neighborhood on the desktop and choose Properties.

1. Click the Start button from the taskbar and choose Settings⇨Control Panel.
2. Click the Network icon to access the Network Properties dialog box.
3. Click the Identification tab of the Networking Properties to reveal the fields that categorize the computer on the network, as shown in Figure 13-1.

Cross-Reference

This chapter refers to information and terms from previous chapters. Please look at Chapter 11 for definitions of terms.

Note

The right mouse button gives you access to special menus and commands when you click it.

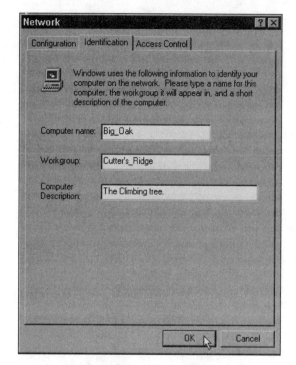

Figure 13-1. Creative names for your computers.

4. Enter a name for your computer in the Computer Name field. Each computer on the network must have a different name, just like every person in a family goes by a different first name.

5. Enter a workgroup name for your network in the Workgroup field. The Workgroup name must be the same for all the computers on the network, similar to the last name for a family.

6. Enter a description of your computer in the Description field. Use just a few words to remind you which computer this is on the network.

7. Next choose the Configuration tab by clicking it.

8. Confirm that the NetBEUI protocol is listed among the installed components. If not, check out the sidebar entitled Adding NetBEUI for installation details.

Adding the NetBEUI protocol

If you do not find the NetBEUI protocol in the list, follow these instructions to add it, otherwise, go on to Step 7 in the software-setup steps.

1. From the Network Properties dialog box, click the Add button.

2. Select Microsoft from the left column.

3. Select NetBEUI from the right column, as shown in the sidebar figure.

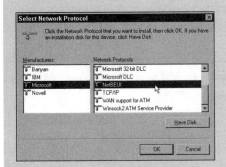

Adding NetBEUI to the list of protocols.

4. Click the OK button; then click the OK button again for the Network Properties dialog box. Watch the files install and restart the computer when asked.

This completes the core network settings for your computer. Repeat these steps for each computer on your network. When all the configuration steps are complete for all the computers, you should have a working network. The rest of this chapter offers pointers on how to start using your new network.

Sharing Drives

One advantage of having your computers on the network is that you can share their drives as resources on the network. The main (C:) drive is easiest to share; it can become a source

Note

Though you could share a CD writer (CDR-W drive) on a network, a more reliable approach is to create a folder on the drive's local machine to hold the data you want to put on a CD-ROM, and then copy the data to that folder from the remote computer. You can then burn the data onto the disc from the local computer.

of folders and files for the other machines on the network as needed; you can also share CD-ROM drives, CDR-W drives, and other file-storage devices. The following steps show you the process of sharing drives.

1. Open the Control Panel by clicking the Start button from the Windows taskbar, and then choosing Settings⇨Control Panel.

2. Locate and double-click the Network icon to access the Network Properties dialog box.

3. Click the File and Print Sharing button.

4. Check the I Want to be Able to Give Others Access to My Files box; then click OK (see Figure 13-2). Windows may install some of the needed files to enable the sharing.

5. Allow the files to install; then click OK twice to close the Networking Properties dialog box. When Windows asks whether you want to restart and put your changes into effect, restart your computer.

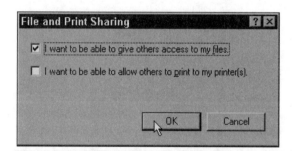

Figure 13-2. Preparing your computer to share files.

6. After Windows restarts, double-click the My Computer icon.

7. Locate the drive letter or folder that you would like to share on your network and click it with the right mouse button.

8. Select Sharing from the pop-up menu that appears.

9. The next dialog box shows properties for the drive or folder. Select the Shared As radio button. Figure 13-3 shows several fields you can fill in, depending on what kind of security your system needs.

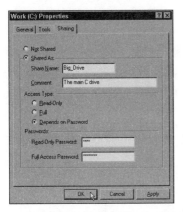

Figure 13-3. Several security options exist when sharing files and folders.

10. Assign a name to your new shared resource. This name shows up on your network, associated with the shared drive or folder. (You can use the optional Comment field to give a longer description of the shared resource.)

11. You will also need to choose the access permissions (Read-Only, Full, or Depends on Password) for the shared resource and enter a password associated with the permission level. If no password is given for the permission level, then none will be required to access the shared resource from the network. *Read-Only* permissions give the person accessing the shared files the right *only* to read, while *Full* gives the person the ability to read, write, modify, and delete. The last option, *Depends on Password*, enables both options to allow the person to perform the tasks for the password they were given.

12. Click OK and confirm the passwords if you used any. Your sharing is complete.

To share other drives and folders, simply follow Steps 6 through 12 for each additional shared resource. You may find that you like the ability to share files. For example, you can share the CD from one machine to install software on another machine that might not have a CD drive. The more you investigate possible ways to give your computers access to each others' resources, the more you can see of the power of networking and sharing.

Accessing shared devices over the network is as simple as sharing them. You can set them up so that as long as the shared computer is on, you will always have access to those devices. You will never need to do the floppy shuffle again to

Note

A hand under a drive, folder, or printer icon identifies it as shared on the hosting computer.

use a printer, move files, or back up data. The following steps will guide you to setting up a connection to a remote shared resource.

1. From a remote computer, you can assign a drive letter to a shared drive, device or folder by opening the Network Neighborhood.

2. Locate and open the computer name the shared resource exists on.

3. Right-click the name of the shared resource. This brings up a menu with Map Network Drive as one of the options. Select that option by clicking it.

4. You will see a dialog box similar to that in Figure 13-4. You can choose the drive letter that you want this shared resource recognized as locally.

Note

If you check the box labeled Reconnect at logon, the drive mapping will always try to reconnect each time you start your computer.

Figure 13-4. Creating a drive on a local machine for a remote shared resource.

Sharing Printers

Sharing one printer among several computers is a capability that leads many people to set up a computer network in the first place. Luckily for you, setting up printer shares is no harder than setting up drive shares; you follow many of the same steps. Here's how you get it done:

1. Open the Control Panel by clicking the Start button from the Windows taskbar and then choosing Settings⇨Control Panel.

2. Double-click the Network icon to access the Network Properties dialog box.

3. Click the File and Print Sharing button.

4. Check the I Want to be Able to Allow Others to Print to My Printer box; then click OK (see Figure 13-5). Windows installs any files needed to enable the sharing.

Figure 13-5. System option for sharing printers.

5. Allow the files to install; then click OK to close the Networking Properties dialog box. Windows will ask you if you want to restart to make those changes take effect. Click Yes.

6. After Windows restarts, double-click the My Computer icon.

7. Double-click the Printers folder.

8. Find the printer you want to share on your network, and right-click its name; a pop-up menu appears.

9. Select Sharing from the pop-up menu to access the specified printer's Properties dialog box.

10. Click the Shared As radio button in the dialog box to enable sharing (see Figure 13-6).

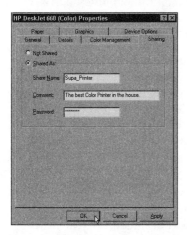

Figure 13-6. Sharing printers the simple way over a network.

11. Enter the share name and a description for the printer you want to share.

12. Click OK to complete the printer-sharing process.

Your network is now ready to access your printer on the network. When you are at a remote computer and you want to setup that computer to print to your printer, add a new printer, select network instead of local for the connection to the printer, and follow the rest of the Printer Install wizard.

Testing and Troubleshooting the Network

Testing your network is simply checking to see if the computers and their shared resources exist on the network. Assuming that you gave all the computers on your network the same workgroup name, you will be able to double-click the Network Neighborhood icon on your desktop and see listed all the computers on your network. If any of the computers are missing, double-check the settings and look again.

Definition

A *local* machine is a computer that makes one of its own folders, drives, or printers available to the other computers on the network as shared resources. Any other computer on your network is the *remote* computer.

Occasionally, a computer on the network may give you trouble (like not showing up anymore in the Network Neighborhood). You may be tempted to heave the offending machine overboard, but you shouldn't do anything hasty yet. Fortunately, you still have other options — in particular, two quick checks you can do that may identify the problem.

▶ **Check to see whether the indicator lights of the NICs and hubs are lit.** Generally, if a light is on for a port of the hub, there is a connection from the NIC to the hub. If not, check the NIC for lights and the cable connections. Refer to the NIC and hub manuals for color codes on the light. (In some cases, orange means ON but no connection and green means everything works.)

▶ You can also use the Windows Help guide. This guide will direct you by having you answer questions based on the symptoms that you experienced. Follow these instructions to start the troubleshooting for Windows 98:

1. Open the Windows Help dialog box by clicking the Start button on the taskbar and clicking Help.

2. In the left panel of the dialog box, click Troubleshooting to expose more options.

3. Click Windows 98 Troubleshooters to display all the different guides.

4. Click Networking to bring up the guide in the right panel for you to follow.

▶ Accompanying the NIC should be some diagnostic software. Follow the instructions for this software to validate that the NIC is functioning properly. This will tell you if there is a problem with the card itself.

▶ Sometimes, just rebooting all the computers on the network is enough to get them working and visible on the network again.

▶ Lastly, I must reiterate that all the computers on the network must have the same workgroup name. If not, they will not be able to see each other.

Coming Up Next

Such are the basics for building a home network. However, to learn more about new technologies that might guide you in your final decisions — from wireless innovations for your home network to new features that can help when you're on the road — check out the next chapter. The products available today only scratch the surface compared to what's on the drawing board.

Chapter 14

Look Ma, No Wires!

Traditional Ethernet cabling is the standard way to set up computers on a network, but recent technological developments give you a lot more choices. In this chapter, I introduce you to alternative devices, methods, and technologies that can help you create a far-beyond-standard home network. You may discover that one or more of these choices better suits your particular situation — and may even save you time, money, or both.

AC-Power-Line Networking

Power lines are everywhere you look — in homes, offices, and nearly every structure we build. Finally, someone developed a technology to use these lines for something more than moving power around. Intelogis (`www.intelogis.com`) has come up with a device known as the PassPort that enables you to transform your electrical wiring into a *data path* (in effect, a ready-made cable) for your home computer network. This little device, shown in Figure 14-1, is roughly the size of a portable tape player and goes between your computer and the wall outlet.

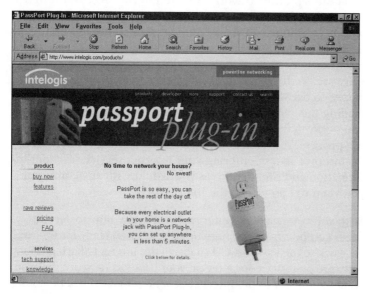

Figure 14-1. Network a home via the power lines with the PassPort.

Setting Up PassPort

The starter kit ($60) comes with three modules for two computers and one printer. You can add more modules individually (they're $40 apiece) as your home network grows. The PassPort modules include a cable that connects to the module and plugs into the printer port of your computer or printer (depending on the module). After you have physically set up the devices, just follow the directions to install the software on your computers from the PassPort CD, use the software to connect to shared printers, sit back, and enjoy. You now have a fully functioning home computer network, capable of sharing files, folders and other devices. Using power cables as a data path avoids the expense of installing dedicated network cable. If you consider the level of online noise and the 0.35-Mbps data-transfer speed you get with this setup, it's much better than a modem, but not even close to the speed of a conventional Ethernet network.

Sharing Internet Access with PassPort

The PassPort CD also comes with software that enables all computers on the network to share Internet access through one computer. Before you set up such shared access, decide which computer will act as your gateway to the Internet; make sure it has a modem or cable modem to make the necessary Internet connection. Install the Internet Sharing Server software on the computer you've chosen as the gateway (or *server,* to use the software's terminology). I strongly suggest reading the installation manual both before you install and as you perform the installation; to answer any questions during the process. You then configure the Sharing Server software for Internet access, entering your Internet service provider information and preferences as you would with any computer you want to connect to the Internet.

With your gateway computer set up, it's now time to get the other computers on the network (the *clients*) ready for Internet access. Use the PassPort CD to install the Internet Sharing Client software on every computer on your PassPort network that you want to connect to the Internet. Several programs will be configured automatically during the installation — such as the AOL Client, Netscape Navigator, and others. (This configuration information comes from the Internet Sharing Server software on your gateway computer; be sure to get that information right when you set up the gateway computer.) After all the machines are configured, you are ready to cruise the Internet from anywhere on your new AC-Power line network.

Be sure to plug your PassPort module directly into the wall outlet, rather than into a surge suppressor or line conditioner. Surge suppressors and line conditioners filter out the signals from the PassPort and diminish its effectiveness. All PassPort modules already have surge protection built in.

Make sure that the PassPort modules are installed before you load the software. Sometime during the installation, the software tries to detect the module; if the module is not in place, the installation fails.

The PassPort comes in two models; one is for a computer and the other is for a printer. They are not interchangeable.

Phone-Line Networking

Today, new homes are built with a phone jack in nearly every
room. Why not use them for home networks? This is precisely
what Intel thought when they developed the AnyPoint
Phoneline Home Network kit (shown in Figure 14-2). The
AnyPoint uses the existing, analog phone wires of your home
as data paths for your computer network. It enables you to
make phone calls at the same time you have your computers
running on the network, giving you the best of both worlds.
This technology allows computers to transfer either 1 Mbps
($89) or 10 Mbps ($99) of data from computer to computer,
depending on which model you purchase.

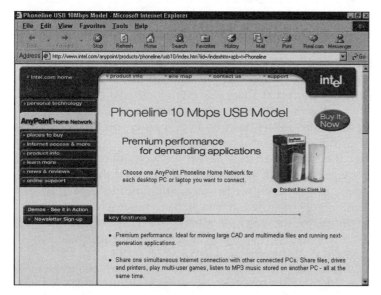

Figure 14-2. The AnyPoint Home Network operates over ordinary phone lines in the
home.

The simple instructions show you how to make the necessary
connections to the phone, wall jack, computer, and power
supply. After you make all the physical connections, insert the
AnyPoint CD into your computer to access the following options from the menu:

▶ **Install.** Start installing the AnyPoint software on your computer (be sure that you make all physical connections first).

▶ **Guided Tour.** Take a guided tour to learn more about what AnyPoint can do in your home. Learn more about Internet sharing, printer sharing, file and drive sharing, and multiplayer games.

▶ **Create Disks.** From here, you can create a set of disks with the setup software for any computers on your network that don't have CD drives.

▶ **Readme.** The readme file contains any last-minute details, changes, or notes that could not be included in the manuals.

▶ **Help.** Get help directly from the CD if you ever run into problems.

▶ **Exit.** Exit the setup menu program.

Note

You can connect the AnyPoint network hardware, a phone, and a modem into a single phone jack. Just follow the examples in the manual.

Setting up the software is easy; just click the Install option from the CD's main menu and follow the on-screen instructions. (The Internet Sharing Server software is optional and need not be installed if you do not intend to share one Internet account with the other computers on the network.) As with PassPort, only one computer on the network needs to have the Internet Sharing Server software. All other computers on the network act as clients and can use the Internet Sharing Server computer to access the Internet. The only requirement is that the Internet Sharing Server computer is turned on for the other computers to access the Internet. When you use AnyPoint with AOL, the following guidelines can help you ensure that AOL runs correctly:

▶ Only the Internet Sharing Server computer can use the AOL client software. All other computers sharing Internet access on the Network must use a non-AOL Web browser (such as Internet Explorer, Netscape Navigator, or others) to surf the Web.

▶ The AOL account password must be saved on the Internet Sharing Server computer in order to enable it to dial up AOL automatically. The clients then need only start a program (such as a browser) to get the Internet Sharing Server computer to initiate the connection process.

> ► Lastly, make sure the ad screen (which asks if you want to purchase the displayed product before you can continue) in AOL preferences is turned off. This enables the Internet Sharing Server computer to connect completely to AOL without requiring a person to intervene, so the clients can start browsing immediately.

Use the Sharing and Mapping Software to set up the drives and printers you want to share on the network. You see these options when you first install the mandatory program — but you can make changes later as your sharing preferences change over time. You can access this menu by clicking the Start button on the Windows task bar, then choosing Programs⇨Intel AnyPoint Network⇨Sharing and Mapping Software.

Wireless Connectivity

Every electronic device we own seems to sprout more wires to add to the tangle; computer systems are the worst offenders. Wouldn't it be nice to get rid of a few wires? One way to cut down on wiring clutter is to create your home computer network using wireless networking devices, now all the rage in computer-networking circles.

The wireless technologies work similar to cordless phones or TV remotes. Let us imagine that you have only two phones and no phone base. In the wireless networking world, these two phones can talk to each other. If you have two computers with wireless networking devices, then these can talk to each other also. No matter whether they are in the same room, separate rooms, or in the house and on the patio. When you add a base to the two remote units, you can add these two computers to an Ethernet network. In Figure 14-3, you can see an example of two remote units (floating) above a base, which then is physically connected to an Ethernet that happens to be connected to the Internet. Most wireless technologies use a radio signal like the cordless phones, but a few use infrared like most TV remotes.

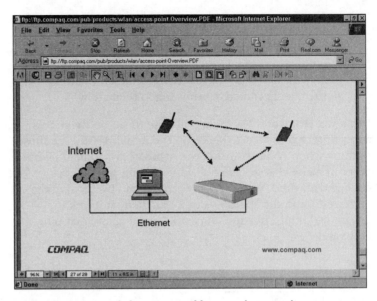

Figure 14-3. An example from Compaq of fitting wireless networking into an Ethernet network.

Note

Wireless networking products can range from $150 to nearly $1,000. Pick carefully and be sure to shop around for the best prices. New technology prices can drop quickly as products become more competitive.

Below you will find wireless networking sources for computers ranging from desktops to handheld devices. This area of the technology is growing rapidly. More companies every day are offering new products and services.

Desktop/ Laptop Computer	Intel's AnyPoint Wireless is similar to the phone-line models, but can communicate wirelessly at 1.6 Mbps with a range of 150 feet. www. intel.com/anypoint
	Compaq's Access Point gives wireless access to desktop, laptop, and other networking devices up to 300 feet away at 11 Mbps transfer rate. www.compaq.com/products/wlan
	WebGear's Aviator 2.4 provides wireless networking (with a 500-foot communication range among networked devices with 2 Mbps transfer rate) for home, small businesses, and large businesses alike. www.webgear.com

	Nortel's Baystack 600 is geared for the small-to-medium-size business, but its 2 Mbps transfer rate and 250-foot communication range is great for the home environment as well. `www.nortelnetworks.com/ products/wireless`
Windows CE	Wireless connectivity varies with Windows CE devices. Some can communicate with infrared; those with PCMCIA card slots can make use of wireless networking cards. (See Chapter 7 for details.)
Palm	The Palm III, V, and VII have a built-in infrared port enabling them to communicate with each other. The Palm VII connects the Palm.net Wireless communications service. (See Chapter 7 for details.)

Accessing the Internet from a Network

All the bells and whistles described in this chapter so far — the alternative wiring technologies, their features, and the clever ways to access the Internet through one connection — have a common limitation: They really don't help the people who have chosen to use traditional Ethernet for their home networks and still want to share Internet access. If you are one of those people, you may want to pay special attention to this section.

The function that enables you to use one connection to the Internet for an entire network is called a *proxy service* (what it does with information is called *routing*). Coming up is a look at some products that offer the kind of proxy services a home network owner needs to access the Internet through a one-account connection. This saves you money on extra Internet accounts, modems, and phone lines.

See Chapter 16 for more information about security and firewalls.

▶ The **UMAX Ugate 3000** (shown in Figure 14-4) is a high-end product designed for use with a high-speed broadband connection (such as a cable modem). It not only shares the connection to the whole network, but provides extreme protection from intrusion to your private network. This device comes with a 4-port 10/100MB auto-sense, dual-speed hub for immediate networking, works via a single IP address of a Cable/ADSL modem account, and offers Dynamic Domain Name Service to simplify configuring the other computers on your network. For more product information, check out the UMAX Web site at `maxgate.net`.

Some cable companies offering cable modem service may claim that sharing their service on a home network cannot be done — but it can, as the Ugate 3000 proves.

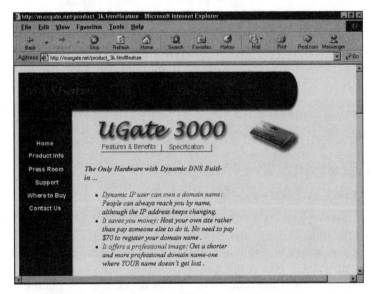

Figure 14-4. For cable-modem sharing, try the Ugate 3000.

▶ **Webramp 200i** does not require a high-speed connection, which enables a network to use a single, built-in 56K modem to access the Web for an entire network. The device includes an extra serial port to add another modem for increased access, software to share two modems at once, and a 4-port Ethernet hub. The software is easy to set up, enables you to add user accounts for each person on the network, and controls the services each account can access. Check out the Web site at `www.webramp.com`.

▶ The **Tiny Software WinRoute Pro** enables one computer connected to the Internet by modem, ISDN, or cable modem to share Internet access with a network of computers. The only requirement is an additional NIC in the connected computer; the software takes care of the rest. The program is small and easy to configure. Tiny Software is on the Web at www.tinysoftware.com.

The Future of Networking

What's in the future for wireless devices? Many say that the future, rather than being rosy, is actually blue. Bluetooth, that is. Bluetooth is a new wireless technology being developed and supported by a group of companies — including Ericsson, IBM, Intel, Nokia, and Toshiba, to name a few. The Bluetooth Special Interest Group (as this consortium is officially known) has over 1,400 members and the list grows longer every day.

What is so special about Bluetooth technology? Currently, electronic devices are designed for a unique purpose and communication between devices is limited by design and function. Bluetooth abandons this old way of designing products in isolation from each other. Rather than thinking of a cell phone as just a cell phone, for example, a designer using the Bluetooth model would imagine a cell phone enmeshed in a web of other Bluetooth-capable devices — including cars, phones, headphones, computers, and Personal Digital Assistants, to name a few.

Why would having a Bluetooth device be useful? Imagine for a moment that you are driving down the road and you remember you need to call Aunt Ruth to find out what time to be at her house for dinner next week. You happen to be wearing your Bluetooth-capable headset. You speak commands into the headset mic that makes the call to Aunt Ruth. Your mobile phone happens to be in your coat pocket, but your coat is in the back seat and the phone was turned off. Your Bluetooth-capable mobile phone turns on, searches for the Aunt Ruth's phone number, but doesn't find it. The phone then contacts your Bluetooth-capable electronic address book, which is

Note

Those of you who have Windows 98 Second Edition need not worry about finding special software to use one-connection access to the Internet. This particular version of Windows includes special options designed to share Internet access with all computers on your home network, through one computer. Look up Internet Connection Sharing in Windows Help for more information.

turned off in your suitcase in the trunk. The address book turns on, looks up the number, tells the phone the requested number, and shuts itself off. The phone then makes the call to your Aunt Ruth and you chat with her for a while over your headset. All this time, none of those devices were ever connected by wires — in fact, none had to be touched by human hands at all.

Coming Up Next

After you've set up a home network, shared devices such as printers and modems on the network, and accessed the Internet through the network, how do you protect yourself, your children, and your computers from the veritable nasties lurking in the Internet world? The next section of the book dispels some common (but incorrect) notions about the Internet, and shows how to protect yourself, your privacy, and your family.

IV

Protecting Your Privacy,
Your Kids, and
the Computer

CHAPTER

15

PRIVACY SETTINGS AND
PARENTAL CONTROLS
INSIDE AOL

Chapter 15

Privacy Settings and
Parental Controls Inside AOL

L yricists write songs about it. Governments pass laws to protect it. Everybody worries about it. Privacy issues loom large today, both in everyday life and on the Net — particularly when your kids are involved. Your online connection allows children to visit places they've never been (which might be good or bad, depending on the spot). A few well-placed clicks might reveal educational sites that enrich and enlighten or could dump little Harry and Harriet into the most "wretched hive of scum and villainy" you could imagine. As parents and adults, it's our job to keep those little eyes safe.

Of course, we adults use AOL as well — for work, play, research, communication, and more. AOL offers some great privacy settings to keep your productivity high and your interruptions to a minimum.

This chapter explores privacy and protection on AOL. It looks at privacy preferences inside the Buddy List system, takes a peek at AOL's Parental Controls, and offers a good look at keeping your kids safe.

Block Out the Interruptions

Using the Buddy List Privacy Preferences, you can block any and all AOL users, whether they drop in via AOL Instant Messenger or through the AOL service. To see the window for yourself, use AOL Keyword: **Buddy** and then click the Privacy Preferences button in the Buddy Lists window that appears.

Normally, the Privacy Preferences dialog box (shown in Figure 15-1), shows a mark next to Allow all AOL members and AOL Instant Messenger users. Depending on how much privacy you need, you can block AOL Instant Messenger users only, or block all AOL members *and* AOL Instant Messenger users. The dialog box also enables you to include or exclude particular members and if you've been plagued by one or two AOL members who found you in an open chat room one night, you can use the settings to block their screen names (and only those). For the screen names you specify, your screen name conveniently fails to appear in their Buddy Lists.

If you want your online world to be small (quite useful if you're working on a project with only a handful of people) set the preferences to let in only the people whose screen names you list in the Screen Names box. Then, to the rest of the world, you don't exist — at least as far as Buddy Lists go.

After you complete the settings in the Privacy Preferences dialog box, check either the Buddy Lists checkbox or Buddy Lists and Instant Messages (under the Apply Preferences to the Following Features option). Normally you find only the Buddy Lists option checked and which means someone can still send you an Instant Message (if taking the time to locate you online isn't deterrent enough). If you check both the Buddy Lists and Instant Messages check boxes, the system will tell anyone who tries to send you an Instant Message that you are not accepting Instant Messages right now.

Tip

If you spend a lot of time on-line, try the PowerTools add-on program from BPS Software (AOL Keyword: **BPS**). This application offers an incredible collection of tools for managing online privacy, chatting, e-mail, Instant Messages, and more.

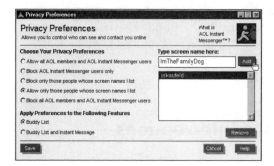

Figure 15-1. Set your privacy preferences and minimize intrusions, even from well-meaning friends.

Remember to click the Save button when you finish updating your preferences. Otherwise all that tweaking will be for naught. After you save your preferences, the dialog box disappears and your privacy selections go into effect immediately.

Chat Without the Noise

In an online chat room, *noise* can be audio tidbits from sound files on your computer and or random, repetitive comments offered on-screen by other members in the chat room. You can block out both kinds when you're in a chat room, and bask in the calm conversation that remains.

To block out sounds from an overactive chat room, click the Chat Preferences button in any chat window. Uncheck Enable chat room sounds, and then click OK. (Phew! Silence at last.)

It's a free country, and everyone has a right to their own opinions, but that doesn't mean you can annoy the living daylights out of your fellow chat members. For a look at what's okay and what isn't on America Online, check out the Terms of Service (AOL Keyword: **TOS**).

Sometimes you have to ignore a member who repeatedly types the same annoying drivel over and over, interjects meaningless comments, or continues to be offensive after you (or some other tactful member) asked him nicely to desist. To restore some peace and quiet, double-click the offender's screen name in the People Here list box. When a small dialog box titled with the person's screen name appears (as shown in Figure 15-2), click in the Ignore Member check box and close the dialog box. Presto! The newly ignored member's comments no longer reach your screen. Other people in the room still see what that person types — unless, of course, he or she managed to annoy the room so much that *everyone* used that handy Ignore Member feature.

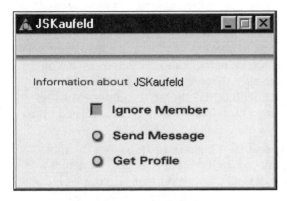

Figure 15-2. Check Ignore Member and restore some peace to your conversation.

When enough time has passed (or your curiosity gets the better of you), double-click the person's screen name again, uncheck Ignore Member, and close the box. You'll soon see whether the offender repented of the annoying behavior that made a roomful of other members "disappear."

AOL's Parental Controls

Some children need to stay in the front yard. Others can be trusted around the block at a friend's house. America Online provides customizable controls through its Parental Controls area (AOL Keyword: **Parental Controls**) so you can provide as little — or as much — freedom as you like.

To set up parental controls for your child, he first needs to have his own AOL screen name. Then you can attach as many, or as few, controls as you like to that screen name. The controls are divided into general age ranges:

▶ **Kids Only (12 and under):** Restricts children to the Kids Only Channel, created especially for children 12 and under. A Kids Only screen name can access age-appropriate content on AOL and the Web and interact with others online through e-mail and supervised Kids Only chat and message boards. Instant Messaging is turned off by default, but parents may turn Instant Messages on for their children by going to AOL Keyword: **Parental Controls** and clicking Set Parental Controls. (See Figure 15-3.)

Find It Online

SafeKids.com (www.safekids.com/kidsrules.htm) and GetNetWise (www.getnetwise.org) both list great safety guidelines for junior Net surfers. For a massive list of kid-safe resources, look at the American Library Association's 700 Great Sites for Kids at www.ala.org/parents/index.html.

▶ **Young Teens (13–15 years old):** Provides more freedom than a Kids Only screen name, but does not provide full access to content or interactive features. Young Teen screen names can access most AOL content, and Web sites that are age-appropriate. They may communicate with others online through e-mail, message boards and chat. Instant Messaging is turned off by default.

▶ **Mature Teens (16–17 years old):** Allows the most freedom of all controlled-access categories. Mature Teens can access all content on AOL and the Web except for Web sites that are known to contain explicitly mature content. Mature Teen screen names can locate others and communicate through all chat areas, e-mail, Instant Messaging, and AOL's Member Directory.

▶ **General Access (age 18 and over):** Gives wide-open access to the online world.

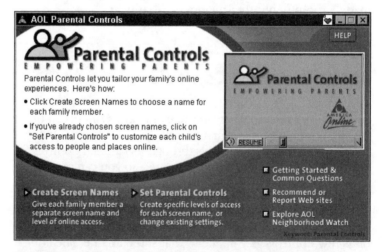

Figure 15-3. Use the Parental Controls window to set your child's boundaries.

Once you select a general age category for your youngster, you can then customize each of the following online features:

▶ **E-mail:** Allow or block messages from other America Online members and Internet mail users.

▶ **Chat:** Control where your child can chat within America Online's People Connection and other AOL-based chat rooms.

▶ **Instant Messages:** Allow or prevent receiving Instant Messages from other America Online or AOL Instant Messenger users.

▶ **Web:** Set age-based restrictions on what your child can see online.

▶ **Downloads:** Allow or prevent the child from downloading files and programs attached to e-mail messages, from the America Online file libraries, or through the Internet via FTP (AOL Keyword: **FTP**).

▶ **Newsgroups:** Block specific newsgroups, adult-oriented newsgroups, or newsgroups with certain words in their title. This control also lets you prevent the child from downloading files attached to newsgroup messages.

▶ **Premium Services (surcharged games):** Allow or prevent the child from getting into the pay-by-the-minute games and other online areas.

You'll find each of these features listed under the Set Parental Controls button in the main Parental Controls window. To place controls on a screen name, first select that screen name in the Edit controls for text box. Then either connect the box next to a specific control or select a general age range for the controls to find out what particular controls apply for each age range.

Shield Their Eyes

Although the Internet may wow you with its possibilities, you soon realize that like any huge entity, it has its dark side. Wherever large groups of people gather, you're bound to find a few that you wouldn't want to invite home for dinner. In much the same way, things lurk on the Net that you don't particularly want in your house. Anyone can put up a Web page, spouting whatever views they like. Because it's not illegal to talk or write, you can find lots of sites on the Web dedicated to immorality and violence — just the thing you don't want little eyes to see.

Tip

AOL introduced a new "on-line timer" feature that helps you control how much time your child spends online. For more about this new feature, visit AOL Keyword: **Parental Controls** and then click Discover the Online Timer.

15

Privacy Settings and Parental Controls Inside AOL

Innocence is one of those precious things that cannot be restored once destroyed. A chance browse through a Web site can make the little ones knowledgeable way before their time. Do your part by not allowing children online without some type of parental control in place.

Of course, the best control is the parent. No software, no matter how sophisticated, can match the watchful eyes of parents who know where their kids are going online — and who they're talking to. Sitting with them while they're online gives you the opportunity to share common interests — or develop a few new ones — while you watch out for their welfare.

Keeping Kids Safe in Cyberspace

Caution

Kids should never give out personal information online. Teach them to keep last names, addresses, and phone numbers to themselves.

A few simple rules go a long way toward protecting the kids' overall safety. Ensure that your child

▶ Never gives out her online password to friends.

▶ Keeps his full name, city, state, and phone number to himself.

▶ Creates an online profile that includes no personal information.

▶ Always tells a parent about any threatening or bad language online, and about strangers who send them e-mail, files, pictures, or Web site links.

▶ Knows how to use the Notify AOL button on the Instant Message window (if you allow your child to receive and send Instant Messages).

▶ Never agrees to meet in person anyone they met online.

AOL provides a place for kids to report harassment they encounter online. AOL Keyword: **Tell AOL** walks the kids through chat, e-mail, Instant Message, and message board problems, and shows them how to notify AOL.

Adding Extra Filtering Software

One option for guarding the kids is to purchase and install software that runs on top of your America Online connection. Rather than tweaking anything inside the AOL software itself, you set up the additional program to run with AOL and do the filtering or tracking. Depending on the package, this software can track Internet usage or block certain activities.

Several different vendors provide this type of software. Cyber Snoop, designed by Pearl software, www.pearlsw.com, provides reports detailing where each user went on the Internet without actually preventing anything. WinGuardian, a Webroot product (www.webroot.com, as shown in Figure 15-4), takes pictures of the screen in addition to logging each user's time on the computer.

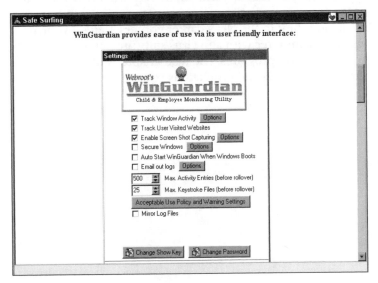

Figure 15-4. Customize a program like WinGuardian to follow — and report on — the kids' online romps.

A program like NetNanny, www.netnanny.com, is designed to block specific Web sites from view. NetNanny compares the sites you want to visit against a list of code words and denies the user access if the words match. For younger kids (or the children who have a few favorite Web sites they like to visit over and over), Internet Safe Kid Desk from Edmark, `www.edmark.com`, allows you to select the Web sites that the child *may* visit.

Breakability is one drawback to the software you install on your home computer. A determined teen with a fair amount of computer knowledge could probably figure out how to get around installed filtering software, given enough time. Because the software physically exists on your system, it's easier to jam, lock, or break than a filter set up at America Online.

Coming Up Next

It's a dangerous online world out there, particularly for an unprotected computer. Viruses, computer criminals, and snoops of all kinds lurk in the Net's darker corners. Defend yourself and your computer with anti-virus software, Internet firewalls, and encryption programs. The next chapter walks you through the perils and protections you need.

Chapter 16

Protecting Your Stuff

In the early days of home computers, *computer security* meant locking the house before going out to dinner, lest someone break in and steal the machine. Now that the Internet connects computers from Africa to Oceania directly to the one sitting on your desk, security means a whole different thing.

Issues that once only worried corporations and international spy agencies — hackers, crackers, viruses, Trojan horse programs, and other perils of the Information Age — now threaten the machine in your home office, kitchen, or bedroom. Protecting your computer and your information means entering a world of computer security applications. This chapter introduces some of these applications, including anti-virus programs, firewalls, and encryption software.

Computer Health Through Anti-Virus Programs

Although the media tend to lump computer viruses into a single seething mass, they come in several shapes, sizes, and attack types. Some viruses just annoy your machine, while others destroy everything they touch — some simply reproduce and multiply. What a particular virus does depends on how malicious the developer felt while creating the code (which makes you wonder about the people who write viruses).

With thousands of viruses cruising around the Internet, it's only a matter of time before one (or more) of them comes knocking at your digital doorstep. If you don't have a plan in place for dealing with the malicious little visitors, your machine could be in for a pretty bad time.

The best anti-virus plans include steps for prevention (keeping the critters out of your machine) and removal (showing them to the door if they sneak inside). Relying on one without the other leaves your computer uncomfortably vulnerable and exposed.

Virus prevention costs you only attentiveness and thought, yet it goes a long way toward keeping viruses at bay. (After all, the easiest virus to cure is the one that your computer never catches in the first place.) Luckily, preventing infections is a whole lot easier than it sounds. Following a couple of simple rules about downloading programs and files from the Internet stops the vast majority of computer viruses dead in their tracks.

First, download applications only from reputable public sources like www.tucows.com, www.cdrom.com, or information companies such as CNet (www.download.com) or ZDNet (www.zdnet.com). These sites exhaustively check their files for viruses, so you're reasonably safe getting programs from them. (Of course, it pays to virus-check the files yourself, just to make sure.)

Tip

What about viruses that infect without downloading — like the infamous Melissa e-mail virus? Luckily, America Online members are safe from those viruses because of the service's secure e-mail system. The Melissa code (and other viruses based on Melissa) relied on a flaw in Microsoft Outlook, Microsoft's e-mail program. America Online doesn't use Outlook in any form, so its members won't pick up Outlook-based viruses.

Find It Online

To learn more about viruses, virus hoaxes, and anti-virus programs, visit the Virus Information Center (AOL Keyword: **Virus**).

Note

For maximum protection, set your anti-virus program so that it continuously checks your machine and all newly-downloaded files. Check your anti-virus program's documentation for the details.

Most importantly, never download a file or program sent by someone that you don't know. No matter how interesting, useful, or intriguing the file looks, *leave it alone.* The virus can't hurt your machine if you never download it.

Anti-virus programs make up your machine's second line of defense. If you accidentally download an infected file or program, your anti-virus software takes care of the problem. Depending on how your software is configured, anti-virus scans may happen automatically (which is the best way to do things, because the computer needs no reminder from you) or work on a manual schedule which relies on you invoking the scan.

Either way, if the anti-virus program finds anything suspicious on your computer, it reports the problem. The program might suggest repairing the infected program or (if the virus can't be removed) recommend deleting the problematic file altogether. The options depend on the virus itself — some simply can't be repaired, so the only thing left is deletion.

If you don't already have an anti-virus application, check out the commercial programs from McAfee Anti-Virus (www.macafee.com) and Norton Anti-Virus from Symantec (www.symantec.com), or the various shareware and freeware programs at CNet (www.download.com). The AOL Store (Keyword: **AOL Store**) and Shop@AOL (AOL Keyword: **Shop**) offers its own anti-virus solutions as well.

After selecting and installing your anti-virus program, make a monthly visit to the manufacturer's Web site to check for new virus definitions. These definition files keep your anti-virus program armed against the latest threats. If your program doesn't know what a new virus looks like, then the virus gets a free pass straight into your machine. Most anti-virus applications include free updates for at least a year. After that, the companies frequently offer a paid subscription service that keeps the new definition files coming.

Some products — McAfee Clinic, for example — operate right over the Internet and don't require lengthy downloads to install. Best of all, McAfee Clinic automatically prompts you with any available software updates when you connect to the Internet so your anti-virus software is always up to date.

By contrast, with traditional anti-virus programs you must remember to download and install updates in order to keep your virus protection up to date.

Firewalls: Barbed Wire for Your Net Connection

A few years ago, only corporate computer departments worried about online security and Internet firewalls. Those things existed outside the realm of casual home users. The corporation's full-time, high speed Internet connection made its computers a juicy target for thrill-seeking hackers. Since the business computers were always online, they made easier hacking targets than modem-using home computers with temporary Net connections. For a while, at least, home computer users safely flew beneath the hacker radar.

Hackers started noticing home computers as high speed connections made their way into homes across the country. These always-on connections mirrored the capabilities of corporate systems, but with a huge advantage: home users lacked the security systems that guarded corporate America. Suddenly, home computers became very tantalizing for the hacking world.

This raises an interesting question: Why would a hacker care about your home computer? Apart from the basic hacker thrill of digital trespassing, why bother? The hacker doesn't particularly care about your computer — but if he breaks into your machine, he can enlist its help in attacking other computers on the Net.

Sound outlandish? Can't possibly happen? Think again. Several of the well-publicized "denial of service" attacks against Amazon.com, CNN, eBay, Yahoo!, and other sites relied on an army of so-called "zombie machines" — computers previously attacked and infected with remote-control software. When the hacker wants to strike, he activates the army of machines awaiting his call, and then watches them do his bidding. Without proper precautions, your computer might be among the foot soldiers.

Tip

Although computers con-
nected to the Net with cable
modems or DSL lines run the
greatest risk of hacker attack,
all online users experience a
certain degree of danger.
Thanks to advances in hacker
tools, even computers using
standard phone lines and
modems can fall prey. That's
why firewall applications are
so important regardless of
how your machine connects
to the Net.

Find It Online

For a quick and frightening
look at how vulnerable your
computer really is, visit Steve
Gibson's Shields Up testing
center (www.grc.com). If
you want a more in-depth
scan, try Hacker Whacker
(www.hackerwhacker.
com) or Secure-Me (www.
secure-me.net).

That's where a *firewall* comes into play. Like their real-world
namesakes, computer firewalls stop dangerous attacks from
reaching your machine. They do this by checking all your incoming and outbound Internet traffic for suspicious requests.
By watching the incoming requests, the firewall intercepts
hacker requests. The firewall also keeps an eye on the outbound messages to alert you in case a hacker application
somehow makes it onto the system.

For home environments, a simple software firewall handles all
your security needs. A quick search through any of the big
program libraries (www.download.com and www.tucows.
com, for instance) turns up a selection of firewall products, but
several programs stand above the rest:

▶ **ZoneAlarm** (from Zone Labs, www.zonelabs.com)
   tops my recommended list of personal firewall products. It monitors both incoming and outbound traffic,
   and pops up questions along the way that help you
   configure the protection (things like *Should Internet
   Explorer be allowed to access the Internet?*). Best of
   all, ZoneAlarm is free for individual use. Visit the Zone
   Labs Web site (shown in Figure 16-1) for more information or to download the program.

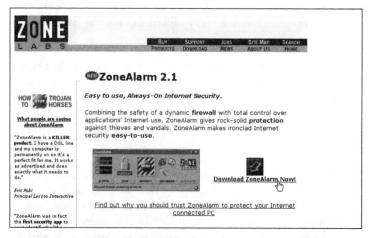

Figure 16-1. Zone Labs offers their incredible ZoneAlarm firewall to individuals for
free (businesses pay a small annual license fee).

▶ **BlackICE** (from Network ICE, www.networkice.com, shown in Figure 16-2) contains more bells and whistles than ZoneAlarm, but is a little too paranoid for my taste. In addition to a solid selection of standard firewall features, BlackICE includes a *backtracking* system which automatically chases down information about any computer that launches a hacking attempt against your machine. Although it offers strong security, its level of paranoia threatens to drive you nuts. Perhaps you can calm the program a bit through its esoteric setting systems, but I couldn't find a way.

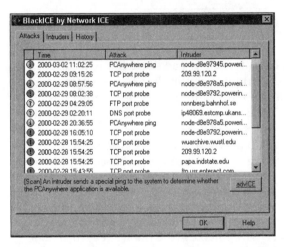

Figure 16-2. Thanks to an always-on Internet connection, hackers keep trying and trying to find vulnerabilities in unsuspecting computers. Firewalls like BlackICE keep the predators at bay.

▶ **Norton Internet Security 2000** (from Symantec, www.Symantec.com) builds on the successful AtGuard firewall system which Symantec purchased. The firewall uses a rules-based system, which looks somewhat overwhelming to an entry-level security user. The package includes a lot more than just a firewall (they throw in Norton AntiVirus plus a lot of other applications), which definitely pumps up the package's overall value.

For a slightly more powerful firewall solution, consider a simple line-sharing device like the UGate 3000 from UMAX (www.maxgate.net). Whether you want to split a DSL line or cable modem connection among several computers, these

Note

Looking for a password that's completely unique to you? Try a fingerprint scanner — it's just like a spy movie at home. The corporate market for *biometric* devices (fingerprint scanners, retinal scanners, and such) grows every year, and now it's bringing the home market along with it. Although it's a long time before your front door sports a retinal scan, companies like American Biometric (www.biomouse.com) already offer fingerprint scanners at less than $100. For more about these truly personal security devices, search your favorite news site on the term *biometric*.

16

Protecting Your Stuff

Find It Online

For more about line-sharing devices (including how they work, tips for installing them, and lots more), look at the extraordinarily helpful Tim Higgins site (www.timhiggins.com).

Cross-Reference

Chapter 14 contains lots of great information about sharing high-speed Internet connections among all of your home computers.

Cross-Reference

Encryption plays a big role in online shopping sites, where merchants are very much interested in ensuring their customers that any personal information sent over the Internet (such as credit card information) stays private. Check out Chapter 30 for more information on how online merchants are working to keep online buying safe and secure.

line-sharing devices do the trick. Better still, due to the way they organize the computers when splitting the online connection, line-sharing devices also act as very strong firewalls. Thanks to a technology called Network Address Translation (or NAT for short), each computer on your network uses a unique address when talking to the line-sharing device, but the Internet only sees the sharing device itself — all machines behind the device remain safely hidden from view and tampering.

Encrypting Your Messages

Keeping your computer safe is one thing, but what about the information you send through the Net? That's where encryption software fits into the picture. Encryption programs use a special mathematical key to turn a carefully crafted e-mail message, document, spreadsheet, or any other computer file, into a woeful conglomeration of garbage. The person who holds the decrypting key can turn the garbage back into its original pristine state. Only would-be spies in the middle of the process are left in the dark.

This style of encryption goes by the name *public key.* That's because you freely give one key (the public key) to anyone who wants to send protected information to you. When you receive an encrypted file, your software decrypts it with the *private key*, which you alone know.

Although encryption catches the fancy of many programmers, few encryption programs broke through the technical barriers into common use. The most popular of these is PGP, short for Pretty Good Privacy. Even with its advances, encryption software still takes a lot of effort to use correctly — and that's more effort than most people want to apply.

If you're a die-hard encryption person, take a look at PGP's latest Windows freeware, known by the clever name of *PGPfreeware.* Search your favorite software site (I recommend www.download.com) for the term *PGP,* then follow the links to the software. Note that *only* United States or Canadian citizens can legally download and use PGP.

Coming Up Next

Cookies here, cookies there — but what are cookies doing in your Web browser? They watch your every move, track your likes and dislikes, and generally personalize the whole Web experience for you, that's what! The next chapter looks into the mysterious browser cookie, and why you may or may not want to allow the little animals into your computer.

Chapter 17

The Question of Cookies

IN THIS CHAPTER

Magic cookie — the name may sound strange, but the words carry a lot of power. In the broad collection of online knowledge out there, cookie files remain one of the most maligned and misunderstood things in the technical universe. Some folks love them, others rant and rail against them, while most of us just wander onward through the Net, never suspecting that cookie files go with us on the journey.

But just what are these files? Where do they come from? For that matter, where are they staying? There's plenty to know, believe me.

Before delving into the world of cookies and personal privacy, you need to know a bit about cookie files themselves, so that's where the chapter begins. From there, it's time to expose some common cookie myths, take a look at software to tame the wild cookies on your system, and wander through the steps for tinkering with your Web browser's cookie settings.

Cookie Evolution: From Simple Entry to Simple Snooping

Cookies started with a noble, or at least useful, intent. After the overwhelming first rush of interest in the World Wide Web, Web site designers started looking for ways to make their sites more interesting and useful for the online public. Someone came up with the idea of adding personalization options — ways for an interested person to pick and choose what he wanted to see on a particular Web site (such as listing your favorite stocks on a financial news site).

For the personalization to work, though, the Web site needed a way to recognize you when you visited again. That's where the cookie idea began. Rather than make you remember some kind of user ID and password to see your personalized page, the Web site would recognize you automatically by leaving a little note on your computer that identifies you. In keeping with the computer industry tradition for giving things odd names, these note files were known as *magic cookies*. Because computer people also dislike long names (even when they invent them), the term quickly shortened to just *cookie*.

So just what *is* a cookie? It's a little file stored on your computer. That's it. The cookie file sits there quietly until the Web site that created it opens the cookie to see what's inside. Sometimes the Web site writes new information into the cookie file. Other than that, the file just sits around, taking up a tiny little corner of your computer's hard drive.

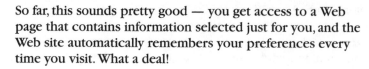

Tip

Cookie files are like a fortune cookie with a hinged back. A Web site opens the cookie, reads the fortune, puts in a new fortune if it wants, and then closes the cookie again. Believe it or not, that's exactly how Web sites use cookie files.

Note

In case you're wondering, AOL doesn't track its members as they click their way through AOL's own content.

So far, this sounds pretty good — you get access to a Web page that contains information selected just for you, and the Web site automatically remembers your preferences every time you visit. What a deal!

Well, at least it *was* quite a deal until the banner advertising and market research folks got into the act. At that point, someone (history doesn't remember precisely who) realized that if a site could track your movements from page to page, the site owners would know a lot more about what you did on the site, how you did it, and what interests you the most. This desire to track your every step grew during the last few years until it matured into the full-blown commercial advertising and tracking systems out there today.

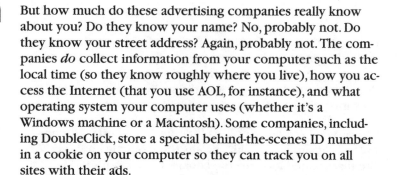

Thanks to some very clever cookie programmers, companies like DoubleClick (www.doubleclick.com) now keep tabs on the sites you visit, the pages you see, and sometimes the types of purchases you make — and they do the whole thing through cookies. The advertising companies then use this information to display custom-selected "targeted" ads relating to your interests (or at least related to the interests that the companies *think* you have). Through the clever use of cookies, they can also track your responses, noting which ads were more appealing to you.

But how much do these advertising companies really know about you? Do they know your name? No, probably not. Do they know your street address? Again, probably not. The companies *do* collect information from your computer such as the local time (so they know roughly where you live), how you access the Internet (that you use AOL, for instance), and what operating system your computer uses (whether it's a Windows machine or a Macintosh). Some companies, including DoubleClick, store a special behind-the-scenes ID number in a cookie on your computer so they can track you on all sites with their ads.

Common Cookie Myths

Although cookies wield a lot of power, they aren't some kind of all-seeing, all-knowing digital supervillain. Cookies live under specific technical limitations covering what they can and can't do. After all, a cookie is nothing more than a little data file on your computer that sits there quietly until its name is called. It can't do anything at all on its own. (It's not that bright.)

Unfortunately, the Internet is nothing if not a massive rumor mill, and dark whispers (the darker, the better) of secret Big Brother-like tracking programs make great mill fodder. Worst of all, the rumors get bigger and more outlandish every time they go around, so in no time at all they're completely out of control.

The following list exposes some of the most popular cookie rumors running around the Net. Like most rumors, they take a tiny tidbit of truth and stretch it unbelievably far. The following list takes on the Net's most popular cookie mistakes:

▶ **Cookies don't let people look at your computer's files.** Cookie files don't let *anyone* look at *anything* on your machine. Cookies are just little text files — a few lines of technical drivel and nothing more. Web sites can only look at cookies they created. Sites can't ask your computer for a catalog of all the cookies it contains, nor can one site open up cookies belonging to another site.

▶ **Cookies don't track your every move on the Internet.** Web sites can track where you go within that *site*. An Internet advertising company working with several sites that you visit regularly might track your activity across all the sites it serves, but nowhere else. Nobody can track you everywhere on the Internet (that's called *eavesdropping*, and there are laws against it).

▶ **Cookies don't fill up your hard drive.** Cookie files are very small, so unless you have a really tiny hard drive, you won't notice them, no matter how many you get. Just how *small* is small? Web browser standards say that cookie files can't be larger than 4,000 characters (what the computer folks call 4K). Compare that to an all-but-blank word processor document containing just one word, *test*. That file takes up 18,000 characters of space (18K) on the drive because of all the miscellaneous information the program stores along with your words. Comparatively speaking, cookies are tiny.

Find It Online

For more about online hoaxes (and there's a lot of hoaxes out there, believe me), go to AOL Keyword: **Virus**.

Want to check out a new cookie rumor? Visit www.cookiecentral. com (shown in Figure 17-1) for the latest scoop. It's truly a treasure trove of cookie knowledge (and completely cookie-free, I might add).

Figure 17-1. The Cookie Central Web site offers security information, histories, and all kinds of other great information about Web cookies.

Turning Off the Cookie Machine

Unlike most things in life, the America Online software and your Internet browser give you plenty of ways to control your world, even when it comes to cookies. If you don't want to bother (or be bothered) with cookie files, it only takes a few moments to block them from your online life.

Think carefully before completely shutting out cookies. Many online stores rely so much on cookies that you can't shop if they're turned off.

There are three ways to defend your computer against cookie files. The first two rely on settings built into your Web browser, while the other uses specialized anti-cookie software. The first two options don't cost anything, but they provide the least amount of flexibility. Using cookie control software puts you in full command over the cookies in your world, but you pay a little money for the privilege:

▶ **Warn when cookies arrive.** Internet Explorer and Netscape Navigator include an option to display a warning when a cookie arrives. You get to decide right then whether or not to accept the cookie. Although it's interesting (and very educational) at first, the newness wears off pretty quickly.

▶ **Block all cookies.** All major browsers have a security setting that automatically rejects each and every cookie that Web sites send. Usually it's an all-or-nothing thing — you either open your system to cookies or slam the door.

▶ **Use cookie control software.** Programs like CookiePal and Cookie Crusher do more than just block cookies from entering your computer. They include filtering options (accept some cookies while rejecting others), cookie management utilities, and much more. See the sidebar for more about these programs.

Taming Wild Cookies with Cool Software

Apart from automatically refusing every cookie that darkens your digital door or driving yourself insane with a near-constant stream of "should I accept this cookie" messages from your Web browser, what can you really do about controlling cookies? You can get some cookie control software, that's what!

Every interesting computer problem automatically draws software developers, and the on-going cookie crisis is no exception. The Net's various software libraries contain many interesting cookie control programs. For a good start, search any of the large libraries (www.cnet.com, www.tucows.com, www.download.com, and others) for the word *cookie*. Lots of prospects immediately respond to your call.

Two cookie control programs deserve special mention. CookiePal (www.kburra.com/cpal.html) and Cookie Crusher (www.thelimitsoft.com/cookie.html) go far beyond simply blocking cookies. Both of these applications allow you to set rules for accepting cookies (for instance, always accepting cookies that expire when you close the browser window). Both create lists of sites that may and may not leave cookies on your system, plus they help you list and manage the cookies already in place. In short, they're one-stop toolboxes for dealing with the whole cookie issue.

Changing your cookie preferences requires a quick trip into the Preferences dialog box of the America Online software. Here's what to do:

1. Choose My <u>A</u>OL ⇨ <u>P</u>references from the toolbar. The Preferences window appears, listing the myriad Preference settings available to you through America Online.

2. Click the WWW button to bring up the AOL Internet Properties window. This window controls all kinds of settings for Internet Explorer, which is America Online's default Web browser.

3. Click the Security tab along the top of the window. The Security settings hop into action in the dialog box.

4. Click the Internet button (the one with the picture of the world), then click the Custom Level button.

   Although the Internet button should already be highlighted, it never hurts to click again before going into the details. At this point, you come face-to-face with the Security Settings dialog box that governs how Internet Explorer works with your America Online software.

5. Scroll down the list in the Security Settings window until you find the two groups of Cookie settings.

6. The settings you choose depend on how well you like cookies.

   To turn off all cookies, click the round buttons marked Disable for both of the Cookie settings. *To continue accepting cookies normally,* click the round button marked Enable. *If you want the browser to annoy you every time a cookie arrives,* click the round button marked Prompt.

   Figure 17-2 shows a common selection of anti-cookie settings.

7. With all settings in place, click the OK button to save your changes.

8. Click OK again to close the AOL Internet Properties window. Finally, close the Preferences window.

   Whew — you did it!

You can come back at any time and change your cookie settings in case you change your mind — or if you suddenly go through online shopping withdrawal.

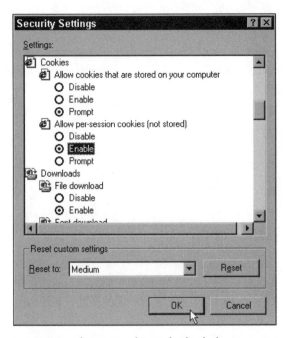

Figure 17-2. These settings let you decide whether to accept new permanent cookies, while letting your computer handle the temporary ones that your Web browser deletes automatically.

Coming Up Next

E-mail keeps you in touch with the world, but it does a lot more than that. Put your e-mail box to work with automated news, stock information, and more. The next chapter uncovers the mysteries of bringing a world of information to your online mailbox.

P A R T

Tools for Taming the
E-Mail Beast

INFORMATION
DELIVERED TO YOUR
DIGITAL DOORSTEP

Chapter 18

Information Delivered to Your Digital Doorstep

A t first glance, your online mailbox looks like a very passive piece of technology. It doesn't really do anything on its own — it just sits there and catches messages (which, of course, provides a lot of value by itself). But why let your e-mail get away with laziness? Turn your mailbox into a proactive information tool with America Online's personalized e-mail services. News, financial reports, America Online tips, and more await you.

This chapter explores several free *information-at-your-mailbox* services, giving you details on how each system works, what it does, and where to sign up for it. As an added bonus, the chapter closes with some cool tricks to control the newfound flood of messages arriving in your box.

Growing Information in Your Mailbox

America Online offers some great services that put your mailbox to work for you. Better still, they're free for the asking —

just go to the area and sign up! Whether you want to know more about America Online itself, keep a closer eye on the newswires, or watch your investments rise, America Online has an automated e-mail system that fills the bill.

The list below covers four of America Online's most popular e-mail services. If one of them tweaks your interest, give it a try — after all, they're free for the using:

▶ Learn more about America Online from the AOL Insider Tips (AOL Keyword: **AOL Tips**, as shown in Figure 18-1) newsletter. This biweekly e-mail newsletter offers up new and fascinating ways to use your America Online software. The information comes in quick, bite-sized pieces that focus on one particular aspect of America Online. One week it might point out a new online area; another week's tip could cover a new feature in the America Online software. The Insider Tips expand your online horizons, making America Online ever more valuable to your world.

Find It Online

Many forums in America Online offer newsletters (both snail mail an e-mail varieties) as well as announcements to keep you involved. Look in your favorite online areas for a Get our newsletter link or something along those lines. For a good example, visit AOL Live (AOL Keyword: **AOL Live**) and scroll through the list of chat events. At the bottom of the list sits a link you can use to get the official AOL Live newsletter.

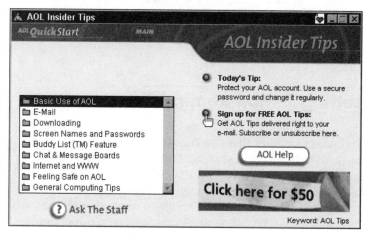

Figure 18-1. Uncover the secrets of using America Online with the AOL Insider Tips newsletter — delivered straight to your mailbox.

▶ Interest Profiles (AOL Keyword: **Interest Profiles**) delivers information about new AOL keyword areas that match your interests. To use the profiles, spend a few minutes in the Interest Profiles area describing the things that tweak your buttons. The lists go into a lot of detail, but it is worth the extra minute or two to make sure you paint a good picture of yourself. After filling out the interest surveys, expect a message from the Interest Profiles folks every week or so, describing a new or esoteric online area that matches your description.

▶ News Profiles (AOL Keyword: **News Profiles**) ships breaking stories straight to your mailbox. Tell the News Profiles system what you want more information about (such as a company, some stock market symbols, or even your own name), then pick the wire services you want to monitor for relevant stories. The News Profiles cover the various AP and Reuters newswires, plus business-oriented services like PR Newswire and Business Wire. To keep things flexible, the system lets you make multiple news profiles so you can monitor a variety of events.

▶ For the financial wizards out there, the Portfolio Direct (AOL Keyword: **Portfolio Direct**) system brings daily stock market news and company reports via e-mail. Plug in your favorite stock symbols, pick an index or two (or three), and tell Portfolio Direct when to deliver the goods. It's quick, easy, and free! The reports keep you *in the know* with ease.

Keep a close eye on your mailbox after you sign up for the News Profiles service — those stories tend to stack up quickly!

For a portable financial news solution, combine Portfolio Direct (AOL Keyword: **Portfolio Direct**) with AOL e-mail on your PalmPilot or Windows CE device. This pairing puts the latest news in the palm (so to speak) of your hand. For more about using e-mail on your handheld device, see Chapter 2.

Letting E-Mail Remind You

Did you remember that last Tuesday was your Uncle Rory's birthday? Or that next season's Little League signup happens next Saturday, even though the season won't start for two more months? It's tough enough just *living* in today's fast-paced environment, let alone trying to remember all the little details like birthdays, anniversaries, and random dinner engagements.

Technology creates lots of solutions for tracking your schedule, but few help as much as America Online's automatic e-mail reminder service (AOL Keyword: **Reminder**). This handy system remembers birthdays, anniversaries, and all the other dates you specify as important to your life; then it drops a reminder note into your mailbox two weeks before each event. It even includes some gift suggestions, which (of course) are available through America Online's various digital retailers.

To join the fun, go to AOL Keyword: **Reminder** and register for the service. Registration consists of entering your name, gender, and making a few choices about generic holiday reminders. After finishing your initial registration, the system drops you into the reminder tracking window. From here, you can add new reminder dates (one at a time, just like Figure 18-2) , as well as change or delete existing reminders.

Add a Reminder Here.   ⬛⬜✖

Add your reminder information and click "Save".

Gift Recipient's Name: | Madison |

Occasion: ○ Birthday   ○ Wedding/Anniversary

          ◉ Other | Every dog has a day |

Date: (mm/dd) | 5 | / | 41 | Does this event repeat annually?   ◉ Yes   ○ No

Optional recipient information to help us provide you with gift suggestions:

     Age: ○ Child   ◉ Teen   ○ Adult

     Sex: ○ Male   ◉ Female

[Help]   [Cancel]   [Save]

Figure 18-2. The Reminder system remembers everything you tell it about the important events in your world.

The reminder system works well for one-time-only events and annual reminders. If you need to remember an event that happens more than once a year, either enter the event multiple times or set up the event as a repeating entry in America Online's cool online Calendar feature (AOL Keyword: **My Calendar**).

Cross-Reference

For more about the America Online Calendar, see Chapter 4.

Other E-mail Tricks That Simplify Your Life

All of these new messages heading into your mailbox get overwhelming sometimes, but you aren't alone — those clever programmers at AOL built a lot of cool e-mail tools into the America Online software. These tools solve some of the

thorniest mail problems in your world, like forgetting an
e-mail address, accidentally deleting a message, or laboriously
typing your e-mail signature another time.

Some of these tools work regardless of whether you're signed
on to America Online, while others only function while you're
online with the service. Either way, these features simplify
e-mail handling, which makes your online life a little easier.

▶ Automatically save copies of all the e-mail messages
that you read and send with a handy feature in the Mail
Preferences (choose My AOL⇨Preferences from the
main menu; works without signing onto America
Online). To store a copy of everything that you read,
click the Retain All Mail That I Read in My Personal
Filing Cabinet check box, as shown in Figure 18-3.
Likewise, click the Retain All Mail That I Send in My
Personal Filing Cabinet check box if you want to
archive copies of your outgoing mail. Your America
Online software stores the messages in your Personal
Filing Cabinet, which is available whether or not you're
online. To open the Personal Filing Cabinet, choose My
Files⇨Personal Filing Cabinet from the toolbar.

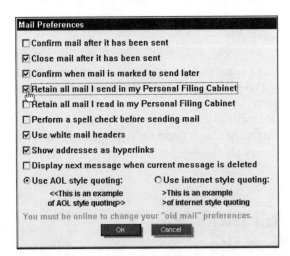

Figure 18-3. Save copies of your incoming or outgoing mail automatically with the
two Retain options in the Mail Preferences dialog box.

▶ If you hit the Delete key a bit too quickly while reading your mail last time and accidentally trashed a message you wanted to save, America Online has your solution. Recover deleted messages by choosing Mail Center⇨ Recently Deleted Mail from the toolbar. This command brings up a window listing all of the e-mail messages you deleted in the last 24 hours. To read a message on the list, just double-click the message title in the list. To restore a message to your mailbox, click the message title, and then click Keep As New. America Online puts the once-deleted message back into your mailbox. To totally delete a message, click the message title, then click the Permanently Delete button. Bye-bye, message!

▶ America Online's Address Book (AOL Keyword: **Address Book**) tracks individual e-mail addresses and helps manage whole groups of e-mail friends. Get into the Address Book by choosing Mail Center⇨Address Book from the toolbar, or by clicking the Address Book button in a new mail-message window. For a full overview of how the Address Book works, click the Help button on the Address Book window, or visit Member Services (AOL Keyword: **Help**), and look under E-mail for the Address Book section. It's great!

▶ Why type your name at the bottom of every e-mail message when you can tell America Online's software to do it for you? The e-mail signature feature (built into America Online's access software) automatically inserts whatever text you specify at the end of every e-mail message. To set up signatures, create a new e-mail message (you aren't going to send this one — you just need access to a button on the window); then click the Signatures button on the right-center side of the e-mail window (the button looks like a pencil writing). To make a new signature, select the Set Up Signatures option from the drop-down menu. There's a Help button handy to walk you through the whole process.

Find It Online

Creating your own mailing lists, discussion areas, or community groups (complete with group calendar, Web site, and such)? Several Internet sites offer the tools you need. For mailing lists, check CoolList (www. coollist.com), ListBot (www.listbot.com), and Topica (www.topica.com). To build a community, look to sites like eGroups (www. egroups.com) and Delphi (www.delphi.com).

Coming Up Next

America Online's e-mail system already offers lots of great options and capabilities, but with the right add-on software, the system enters a whole new dimension. Flip ahead to the next chapter for an introduction to PowerMail, one of the top add-on products for enhancing your America Online e-mail experience.

Chapter 19

Supercharging Your In Box with PowerMail

America Online's e-mail system gets better all the time. Features like text-formatting controls, multiple fonts, hyperlinks, and embedded pictures mean that your messages can look simply incredible. For some tasks, however, America Online's built-in tools handle only part of the job — or might not do what you need done.

Luckily, America Online planned for this situation by leaving a door open: a reserved place in their software for add-on programs. These extra applications hook into the America Online software, adding cool new capabilities and features.

When it comes to e-mail, BPS Software makes one of the best add-ons available: PowerMail. This chapter looks at what PowerMail does (and believe me, there's a lot to look at) and how to put the program to work for you.

How Software Saves Time, Keystrokes, and Your Sanity

With so many features already in the America Online e-mail system, what else could PowerMail possibly bring to the table? More than you might think — particularly if you spend a lot of time with e-mail. Here's a quick look at PowerMail's biggest and brightest capabilities:

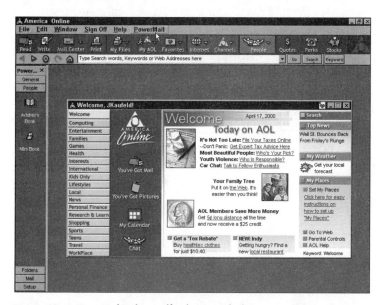

Tip

PowerMail attaches itself directly to your America Online software, changing the screen to look like Figure 19-1. To use PowerMail, double-click the PowerMail icon on the Desktop (or select the PowerMail item from your computer's Programs list). PowerMail first loads the America Online software; then it adds itself to the main menu, under the heading *PowerMail*.

Figure 19-1. PowerMail makes itself at home inside the America Online software, adding new buttons to the window and inserting an extra item on the menu bar.

▶ **Enhanced address book:** The Address Book feature built into the America Online software stores basic name and e-mail address information, but doesn't go much further. PowerMail's enhanced Address Book adds a full range of contact information — including address, phone number, and space for up to four e-mail addresses. For times when you need just an e-mail address, PowerMail offers its handy Mini Book, which displays only the basic information for each Address Book entry.

19

Supercharging Your In Box with PowerMail

▶ **Flexible message-folder system, plus special Archive and Recycle folders:** Tracking incoming mail takes some serious effort. America Online's software handles basic message organization through its Personal Filing Cabinet, but PowerMail goes the extra mile. Its customizable folder system does everything America Online's folders do, but it breaks new ground with the Archive and Recycle folders. PowerMail's Archive keeps messages handy without leaving them in your online mailbox. The Recycle folder catches messages deleted from your other PowerMail folders, so you don't lose messages killed by accident.

▶ **E-mail encryption:** Protect your messages with PowerMail's built-in encryption system. It works regardless of whether your intended recipients use PowerMail (if they don't, PowerMail can automatically send them a special message-decrypting program).

▶ **Address Book Import Manager:** PowerMail collects e-mail addresses from a wide number of sources. In addition to your America Online software's Address Book, PowerMail gathers e-mail addresses from Member Directory searches, incoming e-mail messages, and even chat-room member lists. For businesses or clubs, PowerMail also imports (and exports) address lists in plain-text files (just the data — no fancy formatting — which makes the file easier to compress and faster to send).

▶ **Style sheets and form letters:** Need to say the same thing to a lot of people? Want to give your messages a touch of pizzazz? PowerMail's style sheets and form letters give you all that and more. Style sheets are like digital letterhead — create a cool design, and then insert it into any mail message with just a click of your mouse. For a more automated reply, look at the form-letter options in PowerMail. Form letters combine your text with customizable additions, making them a powerful tool for business and group communication.

▶ **Custom Phrase Manager:** Save time and keystrokes in e-mail messages with the Custom Phrase Manager. The Manager inserts frequently-used phrases (even whole paragraphs) into your message with a quick click. It's great for announcing meetings, providing prepared definitions, and other moments when you need to say again what you've said before.

▶ **User-created keyboard macros:** Perform common functions at the touch of a button with PowerMail's customizable keyboard macros. Open a message and compose a reply in one step, or do any of the other programmable options. It's your tool to build!

Tips for Making the Most of PowerMail

A great application like PowerMail contains so many features that you might feel overwhelmed at first. Don't worry — that stage passes. Here are a few ideas to get you started on the way to PowerMail success:

▶ **Spend time exploring the program.** Set a goal of learning at least one new feature or function each week. Who knows what incredibly useful things you might find?

▶ **Create form letters to handle standard replies.** If you do business online, try making form letters that provide responses to product questions, or serve as a standard *we received your message* reply. It's a great timesaver!

▶ **Customize some digital stationery for your e-mail.** It puts a ton of pizzazz into normal correspondence, and puts a cool, creative look on messages from your home-based business.

▶ **Register the program! BPS Software runs their business with a shareware model.** They let you test and try their software free for 30 days, but after that it's time to buy! Do your part by registering the program. On the PowerMail main menu, choose PowerMail⇨ Registration Information for all the details.

BPS makes a whole collection of programs to simplify, enhance, and generally soup-up your America Online software. For more about PowerMail and their other products (including PowerTools, one of the most popular AOL add-ons on the market), visit AOL Keyword: **BPS.**

If PowerMail tweaks your interest in add-on programs, visit AOL Keyword: **BPS** and check out their other America Online add-on programs, or search America Online's download libraries for even more cool AOL-enhancing applications. Go to AOL Keyword: **Filesearch**; then click the Shareware button under Search for Software. Type **AOL ADD-ONS** in the search text area, click the Windows check box, and click Search. The system replies in just a moment with a whole list of add-ons for America Online (plus some add-ons for other programs, which the search system includes on its own).

Coming Up Next

Once you get the hang of it, the online world isn't much different from the real world. Unfortunately, the similarity extends from the good stuff (24-hour shopping and multiplayer games) all the way down to the stuff that you really wish wasn't there (junk mail and con artists).

The next chapter looks at two of the biggest online frustrations: junk e-mail and online scammers. It helps you identify the dangers out there, report them to the right people, and (most importantly) avoid getting swept up in their clutches.

Chapter 20

Stamping Out Spams and Scams

First, it was junk mail hand-carried to your door by representatives of the U.S. Postal Service. After that came the telemarketers who relentlessly invaded the dinner hours with their inane offers and infomercial-like "surveys." Then we turned to the Internet to escape all this unwanted commercial attention.

Unfortunately, the marketers followed us. Welcome to the world of unsolicited commercial e-mail, officially called UCE by those who make up such things, although most people know its unofficial name: *spam*. (For the record, Spam is a long-standing trademark of the Hormel company, which probably wishes that the pioneering Internet gurus honored some *other* canned meat product in this unique way.)

Even though junk e-mailers find new (and ever more clever) ways of pushing their messages into your mailbox, you aren't helpless in this battle. America Online created some great tools for ridding your world of junk e-mail. This chapter offers some background about the whole junk e-mail phenomenon, how the junk mailers find you, and what you can do about it. It wraps up with some important thoughts about online scams designed to steal your account password. Don't miss it!

How Bulk E-mailers Find You

The first time a junk e-mail message showed up in my America Online mailbox, I was stunned. How did the sender find my e-mail address? And why on Earth did that person think I was interested in mink farms as an investment vehicle? (Yes, despite the lewd nature of most junk e-mail today, my first junk message tempted me with furry animal pelts.)

You probably felt the same way the first time a weird, naughty, or downright stupid message landed in your e-mail box. The good news is that you didn't do anything wrong. Instead, you accidentally wandered into a bulk e-mailer's sights. But the question remains: *How did they find you?*

The folks who send junk e-mail get addresses from a variety of sources. Some do things the easy way by purchasing a list of e-mail addresses from some misguided company. (AOL, by the way, never sells the e-mail addresses of its members.) Others rent customer e-mail lists from Web sites. (Remember when your favorite Web site asked for your e-mail address when you registered there?) Others simply go looking for you (or someone like you).

Junk e-mailers frequently use special software that (in effect) hacks into America Online, searches the list of member profiles, or builds a list of people chatting. Even though it's against America Online's Terms of Service to do that, these scofflaws don't particularly care. Bulk e-mailers also scour postings to Internet newsgroups and mailing lists. If you're active on the Net or America Online, it's only a matter of time until they find you.

Stopping (or at Least Slowing) the Junk E-mail Flood

Once a spammer has your address, what can you do about it? Are you condemned to a life of hopelessly slogging through the repulsive junk e-mail that clogs your digital inbox? No, you aren't! America Online offers several ways to slow the flow of junk e-mail. By combining those tools with some other easy steps, you can reclaim your mailbox from the spammers' attacks.

Spam-stopping tasks fall into two categories: Slowing the current flow of mail and protecting yourself from future messages. The following sections go into detail on using America Online's e-mail tools to guard your inbox.

Setting the Mail Controls

America Online gives you your biggest gun in the battle against junk messages: the Mail Controls. Using these controls, you can tell America Online exactly which messages you do or don't want entering your online inbox. Properly set, the Mail Controls protect you from a broad spectrum of junk mail. Unfortunately, you can *over-set* the controls, which unintentionally blocks messages that you really wanted.

As you start using the Mail Controls, please *go slowly.* Picking the wrong settings usually blocks your inbox too thoroughly. If possible, ask a couple of e-mail-literate friends to check your settings along the way by sending test messages to your account. If the messages don't show up, then it's time to tweak your Mail Controls!

Tip

Use the Mail Controls to block all e-mail from your chat-only screen name.

Because the Mail Controls are part of America Online's Parental Controls system, only a Master Screen Name can adjust the settings. No matter which screen name's controls you plan to change, start the process by signing on to America Online with the Master Screen Name for your account.

After signing on to America Online, use AOL Keyword: **Mail Controls** to get into the right section of the Parental Controls system. Click the Set Up Mail Controls button at the bottom of the window to continue into the controls themselves. When the screen name list pops up, click the radio button for the name you want to work on. Finally, the Mail Controls window itself hops into action, as shown in Figure 20-1.

Note

A Master Screen Name is a screen name with Master privileges, whether it's the name you created when you first joined America Online or another screen name that you endowed with those privileges. See AOL Keyword: **Screen Names** for more about the Master Screen Names.

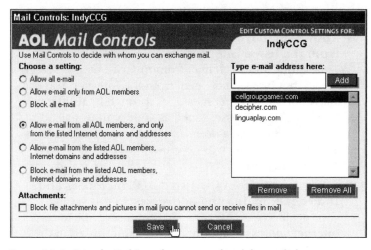

Figure 20-1. Using the Mail Controls, you can pick and choose which messages get into your mailbox.

As I mentioned earlier, the Mail Controls wield quite a lot of power over your inbox. To simplify using them, America Online's programmers created six primary ways to either allow or block mail. The first group of settings don't require any adjustment; they're *global*, affecting large categories of messages in a single stroke:

> ▶ **Allow all e-mail:** This is the normal setting for an adult's screen name. America Online passes along all messages addressed to your screen name.

> ▶ **Allow e-mail only from AOL members:** This setting rejects any message coming from outside America Online. If you choose this option, no e-mail from your non-America Online friends and coworkers can get through. This setting does, however, work pretty well for kids.

20

Stamping Out Spams and Scams

▶ **Block all e-mail:** Use this setting for your chat room screen name. This effectively closes your mailbox to all comers — it's like welding the mailbox door shut.

The remaining items are the surgeon's knives of mail controls. These settings deftly carve away unwanted messages while allowing others free and easy access to your mailbox. That degree of control requires a delicate touch, so think carefully as you apply these to your account:

▶ **Allow e-mail from all AOL members and only from the listed Internet domains and addresses:** This setting allows all mail from America Online screen names, but blocks most mail from the Internet. You can allow certain Internet messages through by listing either specific addresses (such as your work e-mail address) or domains (a *domain* is the part of the address after the @ sign, such as compuserve.com or linguaplay.com).

▶ **Allow e-mail from the listed AOL members and Internet domains and addresses:** In this setting, your mailbox accepts mail *only* from screen names, Internet addresses, and Internet domains listed in the box. Anyone you don't list cannot send messages to your America Online account. Use this setting carefully!

▶ **Block e-mail from the listed AOL members and Internet domains and addresses:** Want to keep out only a few particular people? This setting is just for you. Here, America Online allows all messages into your mailbox *except* mail from specific America Online screen names, Internet addresses, or Internet domains. This one works great if you don't *ever* want to hear from the folks at your old company again!

The setting at the bottom of the window, Block file attachments and pictures in mail, doesn't change *who* can send mail to your America Online account. Instead, it limits *what* people can send to you. When this is turned on, America Online automatically blocks any message containing a picture or attached file. (This works great for younger kids.)

Avoiding the Spammers

The second spam-stopping stage involves shielding yourself from future address-harvesters. After all, slowing the current flow won't make much difference if new spammers keep pummeling your account with messages. To shield your address from spammers, try these reliable techniques:

▶ **Make a chat-only screen name.** Online chat draws lots of people, so it only makes sense that more than a few spammers show up for the party as well. Luckily, it's easy to foil a spammer's harvesting techniques by adding a chat-only screen name to your America Online account. Many people use a variation of their existing screen name as their chatting name (such as using JKaufeldChats as a chat-room replacement for JKaufeld, which is my primary America Online screen name). Before taking the new name into a chat room, go into the Mail Controls area (described in Setting Your Mail Controls) and block all e-mail to your new screen name. After that, sign on with your new name, and then create a nice profile that includes a note giving your real screen name in case someone wants to e-mail you a real message. At that point, take your new name into the People Connection, then sit back and enjoy the fact that the scammers can harvest your new name all they want, but they can't send mail to it!

▶ **Spam-proof your e-mail address in the newsgroups.** Your e-mail address goes into every newsgroup posting you make. Stymie the spammers by obscuring your address with this simple trick. In America Online's Newsgroup area (AOL Keyword: **Newsgroups**), click the Set Preferences button. In the Posting Preferences area, put some text such as *nojunk* or *spam.begone* into the Junk Block area of the newsgroup preferences window. From that point on, America Online's software automatically tacks that text onto the end of your e-mail address in Internet newsgroup postings. When spammers pull your address out of newsgroup postings, they get a useless bunch of text like *jkaufeld@aol.com.spam.begone* instead of a working address.

Tip

You can always go to AOL Keyword: **Screen Name** to create a new screen name.

20

Stamping Out Spams and Scams

Reporting Junk E-mail

Unfortunately, some junk e-mail messages might still sneak into your mailbox. When that happens, take a moment to report the messages to America Online's e-mail-abuse group. Because spam comes in various types, America Online uses several screen names for spam reports. Here's a quick rundown of the spam-reporting addresses:

▶ If the e-mail came from an America Online screen name and contains an unsolicited commercial advertisement (or violates AOL's Terms of Service in some other way), forward the message to screen name TOSEMAIL1 (that's the word TOSEMAIL with the numeral 1 appended to the end).

▶ If the unsolicited e-mail contains commercial advertising but *didn't* come from an America Online screen name, forward the message to screen name TOSSpam.

▶ If you get an e-mail with a file attachment or an inappropriate graphic file attached, forward it to screen name TOS Files. In this case, it doesn't matter where the message originated (whether inside or outside America Online), it's outta here.

Be sure to *forward* the original e-mail by clicking the Forward button when your e-mail message is displayed. *Don't* copy and paste your e-mail message into a new e-mail form, because you lose lots of technical drivel that's important to America Online's spam-hunters.

Beware the Password Scammers

I'm convinced that some people just need more activities in their lives. Maybe if everybody were a bit busier, the online world wouldn't have so many misguided folks trying to steal other people's account passwords. (Unfortunately, nobody ever asks *me* for advice on running the world, so don't expect significant changes soon.)

Password scammers love trying, as their name implies, to separate you from your America Online account password. They come up with lots of interesting tricks and lies to accomplish this, including some traps that look frighteningly close to real America Online screens. The good news is that you won't fall prey to the scammers — because you found this chapter!

The simplest password scams use a tried-and-true method: The scammer contacts you through an Instant Message or in an e-mail and asks for your password. Granted, the request often comes dressed up the request in a fanciful way ("Due to an incredibly technical computer malfunction, we lost all record of your account password."), but the refrain — *tell us your password* — stays the same no matter what.

If you receive a scam message in an Instant Message, click the Notify AOL button at the bottom of the message window, then follow the instructions that appear. If the window doesn't include a Notify AOL button, then the person sending it used AIM (AOL Instant Messenger). In that case, just close the window and go on with your life.

Some scammers work overtime creating incredibly elaborate hoaxes that look almost good enough to fool the practiced eye. Glance at Figure 20-2 for a moment. It looks like an official America Online Web page, doesn't it? Now look more closely at the address in the navigation bar. (Hmm ... America Online doesn't *normally* store its pages on the Angelfire Web service, now does it?)

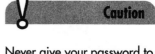

Caution

Never give your password to anyone, no matter who they claim to be or why they say they need it. Period.

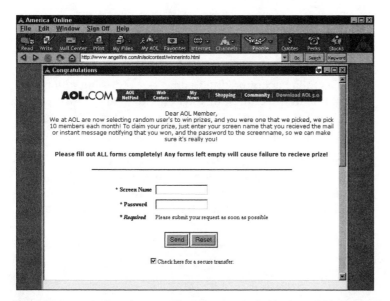

Figure 20-2. Apart from the misspellings, the screen looks like the real thing — but it's a scam!

No, it doesn't; this is a scam site. I received the link to this particular site in an e-mail. The message went into marvelous detail about how my name was picked in an America Online membership contest, and that I could collect my prize by clicking the enclosed link. The link led to the official-looking site in Figure 20-2.

This elaborate scam borrowed the artwork from America Online's Web site to enhance the scam's believability. If you face something like this, remember the first rule of avoiding scams: America Online only asks for your password when you sign on to the system. *After that, they don't ask again.*

If you're still unsure of a particular site, look at the address in the navigation bar on the America Online software. If the address doesn't include `www.aol.com`, then it's possible you're facing a scam site. When in doubt, get an opinion from a friend who knows more about the online world.

To report a "Grand Scam" like this, forward a copy of the e-mail that advertised the Web site to screen name TOSSpam. If the message was from an America Online screen name, send a copy to TOSEMAIL1 (that's T-O-S-E-M-A-I-L with a number 1 behind it) as well.

What to Do if You Get Scammed

If a scammer somehow latches onto the password for your America Online account, don't panic — everything *will* turn out just fine in the end. Unfortunately, the road to closure contains a few rocks along the way, so get ready for a bumpy (and sometimes frustrating) ride toward fixing the problem.

Disconnecting a scammer from your America Online account involves immediately shutting off his or her access by changing your password, and then removing any password-stealing programs from your computer. Here's the step-by-step solution:

1. Change your account password *immediately*. Go to AOL Keyword: **Password** and follow the instructions from there.

2. Go to AOL Keyword: **Virus Info** to download America Online's free copy of VirusScan.

   If you lost your password to a viral program (often known as a *Trojan Horse*), VirusScan should find and remove the offending software. The free version works for only 60 days, but that's long enough to fix your current problem.

3. Reinstall your AOL software.

   Many Trojan Horse programs irreparably mess up your America Online software, so this step makes sure that your America Online software works just fine in the future.

4. Go back to AOL Keyword: **Password** and change your password one more time.

   Although it looks like a bit of overkill, don't skip this final step. If your system had a hacker program running secretly during Step 1 (when you changed your password the first time), then the hacker already knows your new password. Changing your password again completely shuts the door on the scammer.

It's worth repeating: Never, never, *never* give your password to anyone who asks, no matter what they say or who they claim to be. Also, *never* download files from people you don't know. Those files almost always contain hacker programs designed to break into your account and steal your password.

Coming Up Next

The next chapter explores the wild world of photography in the computer age. Dive into the file formats, terminology, and other details of this incredible new hobby. It's all there for you!

For now, pick an easy-to-remember word or two as your password. You're going to change the password *again* after cleaning up your computer, so save any cool password ideas for that step.

If you download lots of things from the Internet or America Online, spend the money on a good antivirus program. They usually cost between $30 and $50, which makes them a inexpensive form of protection for your computer.

Chapter 21

Picturing Life in Digital Images

P hotography steadily advanced through years and years of new technology, film types, and image quality. What started with gigantic contraptions and glass plate negatives eventually worked its way to hand-held cameras and high-resolution film. But nothing in history prepared photography for the changes wrought by the explosion of computer technology in the last 10 years. In a relatively sudden burst of technological activity, digital photography arrived on the scene.

Unlike many changes wrought by technology, you needn't spend a ton of money to join the digital photography revolution. In fact, you can start with nothing more than your beloved film camera, your America Online account, and the information in this chapter. The chapter lays a foundation for you by explaining some key digital imaging terms; then it turns to information about creating digital images by scanning or by shooting with a digital camera.

The Language of Digital Images

Just like everything else in the world of computers, digital images come in a variety of types. Although the end goal remains the same, different companies and technical groups developed a collection of formats for storing and displaying digital images. Here's a quick look at the most common formats awaiting your jaunt into the world of computerized imagery:

▶ JPEG images draw their name from the Joint Photographic Experts Group, which developed this standard. JPEG images are compressed, so they take up a lot less space than some of the other image formats (particularly TIFF files). Compressing the image dulls its quality a little, but not enough for most people to worry about. JPEG files usually end with a *.jpg* extension.

▶ TIFF files (Tagged Image File Format) started as an industry-based specification created by Aldus Corporation (now a division of Adobe), with help from several other firms including Hewlett Packard and Microsoft. Some upper-end digital cameras use TIFF to store images at the camera's highest quality setting. In their natural form, TIFF files take a lot of space, although some cameras and image editing software offer TIFF compression options. In any event, the image quality of TIFF files makes up for their size — at least in the eyes of graphics and photography professionals. TIFF files traditionally carry a *.tif* extension.

▶ GIF (Graphics Interchange Format) is the most common image format for the Web. Like JPEG, GIF uses image compression to save space and downloading time. Thanks to its compression system, GIF files don't sacrifice quality when compressed — the compressed image still looks great. GIF files usually end with a *.gif* extension.

▶ PNG (Portable Network Graphics) came into being as a patent-free alternative to GIF. (The compression scheme used in GIF files is covered by a couple of patents owned by major corporations.) Members of the Internet community created PNG specifically to support the needs of online systems, so it's a natural match for the Web. GIF had a huge head start in the market, so it's still the graphics standard, but PNG slowly expands each year. Time will tell whether this format ultimately wins or not. PNG files typically end with a *.png* extension.

Tip

If you plan to put images on the Web, use your favorite image editing program (Adobe Photoshop, Microsoft PhotoDraw, Ulead PhotoImpact, or other application) to convert the images into GIF or JPEG formats. For a cutting-edge approach, try the still-emerging PNG format.

Find It Online

Take a quick lesson in digital photography or swap tips with other camera buffs in America Online's Digital Photography area (AOL Keyword: **Digital Photography**).

Note

If you already invested lots of money in a good 35mm or APS camera, it makes a lot of sense to use your current equipment and then scan the negatives or prints to create digital images.

Note

Film cameras capture colors better than digital cameras when a scene includes both very bright and very dark areas. Thanks to their size and capacity, digital cameras work well for snapshots and vacation pictures.

Turning Normal Photos into Digital Images

Starting your digital photography experience with a regular film-based camera adds some steps to making digital pictures, but everything works fine in the end. In fact, the results of starting with regular film often look better than images from mid-range digital cameras (a fact that depresses many digital camera owners, including me).

Turning regular film images into digital photos involves *scanning* the image. For the do-it-yourselfers out there, many companies make scanners that turn both color prints and documents into digital form. Hewlett-Packard makes some great scanners in a broad price range, but units from PaperPort, UMAX, and other companies perform very well, too. All of the scanners include some kind of photo editing software that also handles the scanning process. For a great start to your scanner shopping, check the Scanners section of the AOL Store (AOL Keyword: **AOL Store**) for the latest offerings.

The only drawbacks to scanning photos at home are the cost of the scanner (most cost about $100 by the time you get the scanner and cables), the time to do the work, and the fact that you can scan only prints, not the original negatives (scanned photos have a lower quality than scanned negs). But if you want to digitize a lot of existing photos, the scanner makes a lot of sense and pays for itself over time.

If you prefer a hands-off approach, most photofinishing companies now offer scanning services as part of their suite of products. For an extra fee (usually charged per roll), the film processor makes a high-resolution scan of your photos directly from the negatives, which ensures the best possible reproduction. Some companies put the pictures on disk or deliver them to you online, while others burn them onto a CD-ROM. Either way, your pictures look great.

Although photofinishing companies scan existing negatives and prints as well as newly-developed film, they charge significantly less per picture when they develop a roll of film and scan it at the same time. If you send them existing negatives or prints, expect to pay about 50 percent more per image for the scans. Prints and existing negatives cost the company more to scan because they require special handling. Scanning the images during the developing process takes less time and effort because automation handles everything, so the photofinishers charge less.

Figure 21-1. Develop film and get digital copies of your pictures in one easy step with America Online's You've Got Pictures service (AOL Keyword: **Pictures**).

Find It Online

For an incredibly easy way to get digital images from your newly-developed film, check out America Online's "You've Got Pictures" service (AOL Keyword: **Pictures,** shown in Figure 21-1). This service, offered through Kodak's film processing labs, scans your pictures and delivers them directly to your AOL account where you can email pictures, organize them into virtual albums, and then share the albums with friends and family. (Of course, you can download the pictures to your computer as well!)

Diving into Digital with a New Camera

If digital photography really clicks your shutter, consider turning your back on film and going all digital with a digital camera. The manufacturers offer plenty of cameras at almost any price point — even kiddie digital cameras for the kids. It's definitely a buyer's market, so this makes a great time to take the plunge.

Things always end better when you start with a clear goal in mind, so start your shopping excursion by answering one easy question: How will you use the camera? This one question covers a lot of ground. For example, if you want the camera for travel pictures, then size and weight mean a lot. Serious amateurs want a broad range of creative control like they enjoy with traditional film cameras. Happy parents who plan lots of toddler snapshots need something that's quick and easy to

Looking for a cool way to experience digital photography and video while keeping the kids involved? Look for kid-friendly products like the X3 Video Microscope and the Me2Cam, both from a partnership between toy giant Mattel and technology wizard Intel. For more about these products, visit www. intelplay.com.

Combination still image/ movie cameras typically record moving images in either MPEG or QuickTime format. Both are industry-standard formats, and work with PC and Macintosh computers. Although you find proponents and detractors of both formats, either one works well for simple movie clips.

use. Knowing your goal gives a clear direction on which camera features mean the most to you — and that ensures you purchase the best camera for your money.

When comparing digital cameras, start with the basic features to identify your best prospects, then dig further into some behind-the-scenes details to pick your winner. Here's what to look for:

▶ **Resolution:** Any discussion of digital cameras starts with resolution, the most basic measure of camera performance. A camera's resolution tells you how sharp its pictures are. Low-end cameras start around 640x480 pixels (the dots that make up your digital images). Most mid-range cameras use at least a million pixels, which earns them the moniker *megapixel cameras.* The latest round of cameras moves the bar even higher, as resolution moves into the two megapixel range.

▶ **Still images and movies:** Digital cameras started by imitating existing equipment — in this case, still image cameras. As technology advances, the limitations of old devices fall away, and whole new types of products emerge, such as the combination still/movie digital cameras. These cameras not only shoot great regular pictures, but they also record short (usually 15 seconds to 60 seconds) video clips in digital format. Dual-purpose cameras sit toward the upper side of the price scale, but look for them to drop as more devices come onto the market.

▶ **Capacity:** Welcome to the most bedeviling aspect of digital photography. Everybody wants a camera that turns out beautiful pictures, but high quality images take more space, which means that your camera holds fewer of them. The digital camera manufacturers compound this problem by advertising the camera's highest resolution while simultaneously saying that it holds "up to" an incredible quantity of images. A look at the fine print reveals that an average megapixel camera with factory-installed memory holds only 1 to 5 images at the highest possible resolution, but stores 80 or more images at lower resolution.

▶ **Memory Expansion:** All cameras except the ones at the very bottom of the scale store images in some kind of removable memory. (It's the digital camera's version of film.) Most cameras use one of two "industry standard" memory types: Compact Flash or SmartMedia. Of the two, it looks like Compact Flash is winning — lots of cameras and other small computing devices use Compact Flash, while SmartMedia is usually limited to digital cameras. Some cameras (notably the Sony Mavica line) store pictures on full-size 3.5-inch floppy disks, which are handy but make the camera itself quite large.

▶ **Physical size and weight:** Of all the issues surrounding a camera purchase, this is the most personal. Some people cherish lightweight gear, while others gleefully lug heavy camera bags everywhere. Whatever your leaning, check this specification as you shop for a camera.

▶ **Battery type:** Believe it or not, this is my second question (I look at resolution first) when shopping for a camera. Many digital cameras rely on esoteric, expensive "photo batteries" for their power supply. A growing number of cameras shun these odd batteries in favor of standard AA-size rechargeables. If you travel a lot, remember your camera's batteries. If your device uses one of the special "photo batteries", go to a local discount store and get a spare for your trip. If it uses rechargeable batteries, remember to pack the charger and power cord.

Coming Up Next

With your pictures converted to digital format, it's time for some fun. How about removing the red-eye from your son's birthday party pictures, or darkening the sky a bit in those gorgeous landscape photos? Heck, you might even have some fun by adding glasses to Uncle Louie's face or dropping an ocean liner into those Times Square pictures from your last vacation. With digital photography, anything is possible. The next chapter explores the options with image editing software.

Note

If your digital camera *doesn't* use floppy disks for storing images, then how do you get the pictures out of the camera and into your computer? With a digital film *reader*, that's how! Many companies produce readers that attach to your desktop or laptop computer. Some devices handle both Compact Flash and SmartMedia memory, although most only work with one type or the other. Lexar Media produces a very good reader that covers both memory types, and connects to your computer's USB port. Laptop users can also try a PC Card-sized reader that slides into the PC Card slot of the computer.

Tip

Cameras that use AA batteries work very well for travel. Even if the camera includes rechargeable batteries, they still run on standard alkaline batteries in a pinch.

Chapter 22

Image Tweaking 101

Creating, capturing, and scanning images aren't all there is to it. When you've put those images into your computer, you can custom-tailor them now that they're in digital format; this chapter takes you through that process. You also find out how to "get the red out" of photos that show people with red eyes, apply special effects to your photos, and polish them with a professional attention to detail.

Shutterbugs of all types have a use for photo enhancements — even skilled professional photographers who take multiple shots of single subjects. Mistakes will happen — why else take the multiple shots? Of course, the professional is also trying to capture *one* breathtaking image during the shoot — but sometimes even that shot has a flaw. Maybe it's too dark, or overexposed, or has an object in the background that detracts from the overall appearance of the photo. What to do?

Removing Flaws with the AOL Picture Gallery

With the help of your computer, you can remove these blemishes from your photos after you've made them into digital images. AOL client software has its own photo-manipulation functions, which enable you to make simple changes to an image. The following steps show you how to access the AOL Picture Gallery tools:

1. Make sure your AOL software is running. To open the Picture Gallery, select File⇨Open Picture Gallery from the Main menu.

   The Picture Gallery opens.

2. Select the (local) folder that contains the image(s) you want to modify.

   The images appear on-screen, six at a time.

3. Scroll through the list; click the image you want to modify.

After loading the image file you want to modify into the Picture Gallery, you can begin to change it (or even work on several images at the same time — each one opens in its own window). When you're satisfied with the changes you've made, you can save the image or send it to someone by e-mail.

Editing Images with AOL

Getting a photo to open in the editor is just the start; getting handy with the tools is the next step. Fortunately, practice makes perfect — the best way to learn how to use the editing tools effectively is to *use* them. Open an image and use the tools one at a time (as shown in Figure 22-1). If your experiments turn the image into a mishmash, no problem: Click the Revert button (between tools) to restore the image to the way it looked before you made any changes.

Cross-Reference

To find out how to get your picture into your computer, read Chapter 21 for details.

Caution

If you want to save the original image as well as the new one, save the new one under a new name. Clicking the Save button in the lower-left corner of the Editing window saves the image with its current (unchanged) name, which replaces the original; you can then never go back to it.

Tip

The Revert button always restores the most recently saved version of an image. Save the image now and then while you're working on it. Many a sadder-but-wiser user has adjusted a photo to near perfection, tried *one* last change, and made a last-minute goof that couldn't be undone. That means clicking the Revert button — and starting all over.

22

Image Tweaking 101

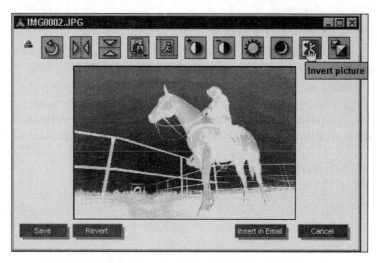

Figure 22-1. An inverted image converted to grayscale.

The editing tools themselves are pretty straightforward. Here's a list of available tools (from left to right on the toolbar) and what they can do for you:

▶ **Rotate Picture:** Clicking this button rotates the picture counterclockwise by a quarter of a turn. You can use it to orient your image in 90-degree increments.

▶ **Flip Picture Horizontally:** This button flips your image sideways, putting its right side on the left (and vice versa) so it becomes a mirror image of itself.

▶ **Flip Picture Vertically:** Use this button to flip the image upside-down. The top ends up on the bottom and the bottom on top.

▶ **Zoom In/Out:** Use this feature to focus in on a specific part of your picture or back out to see everything at once.

▶ **Select and Crop Picture:** This tool works in two stages. You use it to select an area of the picture that has only the parts you want to keep. When you're satisfied with the selection, you click the scissors button to crop away the rest of the image, leaving only the selected area.

▶ **Increase Picture Contrast:** Use this button to make dark portions of the image darker and light portions lighter.

- ▶ **Decrease Picture Contrast:** This button brings all the colors together to the same tone by darkening the light colors and lightening the darker colors.
- ▶ **Brighten Picture:** If you want to lighten a dark picture, this button does it for you.
- ▶ **Dim Picture:** Use this button to darken an overexposed, bright image.
- ▶ **Invert Picture:** Click this button to create a photo-negative version of the image you are editing.
- ▶ **Convert Picture to Grayscale:** Use this button to replace the colors in your image with shades of gray.

With all the tools available to you from the Picture Gallery, you can make simple changes to your digitized photographs. As you use these tools, you may discover that simple changes are just not good enough; sometimes you want to perform some radical surgery on your images. The rest of this chapter covers other applications that have some advanced features for making those major changes.

Other Software

A number of other software packages can modify, enhance, and adjust images; one of them may have just what you need. Each program offers different features for enhancing photographs — some of the possible changes are fundamental, others incredible.

Paint Shop Pro

Paint Shop Pro, by JASC Software (www.jasc.com), is a great way into creating and modifying images. Using it, you can either create images from your own imagination or touch up photos stored on your computer. As Figure 22-2 suggests, you can get your photos to retain (or regain) their sharpness and color. Editing tools are readily available, and floating control panels are a snap to move out of the way. All these features make this application friendly and fun.

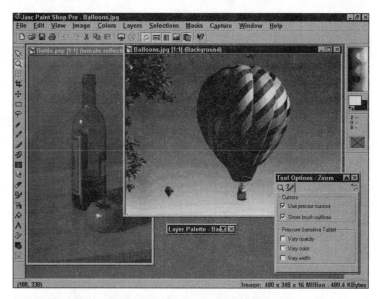

Figure 22-2. Paint Shop Pro, showing a couple of images awaiting touch-up.

You can download a 30-day evaluation copy of Paint Shop Pro from www.jasc. com/psp6dl.html.

Paint Shop Pro handles several types of graphic files — and you can convert one to another. Open a graphic file with (for example) a .bmp filename extension and you can save it as a .jpeg or .jpg file. Editing tools include the familiar set you can find in the AOL Picture Gallery (zoom, crop, contrast), plus many more special effects, such as resizing the image, creating shadow effects, and others. You can even create images with multiple layers. Usually, anything you add to an image gets blended into everything else of the image. But, when you add shapes and colors to the image in different layers, each layer remains a separate part of the whole image so you can make changes and add effects to the different components of the image.

PhotoSuite III

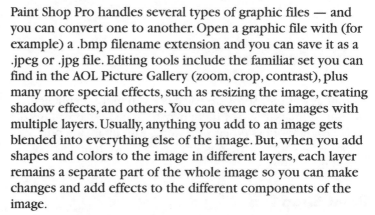

AOL users can find out more about Paint Shop Pro at AOL Keyword: **PSP**.

PhotoSuite III (www.photosuite.com), developed by MGI Software, keeps the beginner in mind when making adjustments to photos. The interface to this software is easy to adjust to fit your way of working; you click easy-to-read buttons and the program obligingly lays out step-by-step instructions for each modification task.

Figure 22-3 offers an example of this program's power, flexibility, and features: You can transform a normal photograph of a lighthouse into an image that looks like a cartoon. PhotoSuite III walks you through the process.

Figure 22-3. Getting artsy with PhotoSuite III, turning a photo into a cartoon.

Of course, you can do more with PhotoSuite III than change photos; it also helps you organize, share, and print your images. It even has templates you can use to create business cards, greeting cards, bookmarks, and other creative products. For the money, PhotoSuite III gives you the richest set of options for working with photos.

PhotoDraw

PhotoDraw, a Microsoft product (www.microsoft.com/office/photodraw), adds greatly to the collection of picture-manipulation tools in your software toolbelt. By automatically adjusting your graphics, PhotoDraw makes photos easier to edit (and graphic files easier to format). You can remove red-eye from photos, change tint, modify brightness and contrast, and that's just for openers.

Note

PhotoDraw 2000 Version 2 comes as part of the Microsoft Office 2000 package or can be purchased separately.

To give you an idea on how to use PhotoDraw, take a look at the steps needed to remove that creepy-looking red-eye effect from photos:

1. With PhotoDraw running, open the image; then select it so it shows in the workspace.

2. Use the Zoom function to magnify the part of the photo that shows the red eyes.

3. Click the Touch Up button on the toolbar and select Fix Red Eye from the drop-down menu that appears.

4. Click the red area of one or both eyes. PhotoDraw should automatically select the area you want to fix.

5. Select Fix from the Red Eye toolbar.

6. Adjust the Correction slider to shrink or expand the adjustment area.

7. You can continue the make changes to the image by repeating Steps 4, 5, and 6. Click Finish from the Red Eye toolbar when you are done making your adjustments.

Easy-to-follow wizards guide you through routine editing tasks. Hundreds of professionally designed templates offer starting points for creating your own graphics.

Photoshop

Adobe Photoshop (www.adobe.com/products/photoshop/main.html) is fundamental software for the serious photo artist. A powerful application to create your own graphic works of art, modify digitized photos, and much more. Figure 22-4 gives you a peek at the tools and options available by showing a photo ready for cropping.

Photoshop features include animation creation, image-slicing, and Web optimization (same picture, but smaller files size for faster downloads). These features enable you to open, modify, and prepare pictures for your Web page.

Figure 22-4. Easy-to-use tools make touch-ups effortless in Photoshop.

PhotoDeluxe

This Adobe product (www.adobe.com/products/
photodeluxe/main.html) offers guided instruction to help
you get photos into the computer as digital images. It then
steps you through the process of touching up the image. You
can even apply special effects such as removing red-eye from
photos, fading the edges of images, and adding other
attention-getting effects. This product is as readily usable as
PhotoSuite III. A beginner can work comfortably with this
product to create calendars, cards, and similar projects.

Coming Up Next

Capturing images, fine-tuning those images, and publishing
them on the Web is fun. What about sending those images to
the Web in real time? The next chapter covers just that topic.
You get to know webcams, how they work, and the software
that helps you put webcams to good use. Learn how to chat
visually and hold meetings face-to-face on the Internet.

CHAPTER

23

BROADCASTING YOUR
WORLD WITH WEBCAMS

Chapter 23

Broadcasting Your World with Webcams

As digital photography and Web video gain popularity, a variety of devices can help you put pictures in your computer. This chapter shows you another such device that connects to the computer to capture pictures, video, and provide live video feed on the Internet. This device is especially fun for chatting with others; using such programs as CU-SeeMe or NetMeeting, you can see who you are chatting with. Read on to find out more.

Webcam Basics

The Web camera, or *Webcam* for short, is a small digital camera that fits on your computer; typically sitting on top of the monitor to look at you. It's capable of taking only one picture at a time, or a series of photos in sequence (to approximate video) to send over the Internet. People use Web cameras to see each other while they chat online, put a face with a name, or to enhance a conference meeting. This works great for video conferences, where people are scattered around the world. You can also use these cameras to take snapshots to send through e-mail, make greeting cards, or post an image on your Web page for viewing.

Picking a Camera

When you're ready to pick a camera for the Web, you have several available choices. Most of them are major name brands like Logitech, Intel, and IBM. Still, of these recognized name brands, one stands out — the Logitech *QuickCam* (seen in Figure 23-1). So firm is Logitech's foothold in the Webcam business that you may hear the QuickCam brand name used interchangeably with the generic term *Webcam*.

Figure 23-1. The Logitech QuickCam, for sale at the AOL Shop.

Use the AOL Keyword: **AOL Shop** to check out products made by Logitech (as well as products made by the competition). After the AOL Shop Direct window opens, showing all the possible areas to shop in, click the Hardware tab to display all the computer hardware offerings. Click the Digital Cameras link to access a listing of digital Web cameras to be mounted on your computer as well as handheld, take-it-with-you digital cameras. The following table gives you an idea of what's available (in alphabetical order by manufacturer), as well as current prices:

Manufacturer	Product Name	Price
IBM	PC Camera	$49.95
IBM	PC Camera (2 Pack)	$99.95
Intel	Camera	$79.95
Intel	Camera (2 Pack)	$99.95
Logitech	Pro Video Camera	$129.95
Logitech	Quick Camera (2 Pack)	$99.95
Logitech	QuickCam Express	$49.95
Logitech	QuickCam Express (2 pack)	$89.95
Logitech	Video Camera	$49.95
USR	Bigpicture Video Camera and Card	$159.95

With so many digital cameras to choose from, picking the right one for you may seem like a daunting task. To help you keep the decision-making process as painless as possible, follow these simple rules:

▶ **Buy as much camera as you need:** Web cameras offer different features depending upon their intended use (chatting on the Web, videoconferencing, digital stills, instant photos). If all you really want is a simple way to send digital images via e-mail, don't buy a digital camera loaded with other features — but if you intend to take advantage of all that Webcams can offer, don't plunk your money down for a camera that may prove too limiting farther down the road.

▶ **Check the hardware requirements:** Be sure to buy a digital camera that works on your system. For example, you can't use a USB camera if you don't have a USB port on your computer (USB stands for Universal Serial Bus; see Chapter 6 for details). Before you purchase a particular camera, compare its specifications with those of your computer.

▶ **Compare prices:** If you're forced to choose between two major-brand products with similar features, go for the less expensive one. Note, however, that I said major brand. Be wary of no-name products offered at a rock-bottom price. You may end up getting less camera than you bargained for.

What kind of added bang do you get for the extra bucks you put down for a higher-end digital camera? The more expensive cameras often include additional features that you may find useful — including (for example) higher resolutions to make the pictures larger, more vivid and realistic colors, and clearer photos. The higher end cameras are good for people who videoconference often and want to show detailed presentations (like the latest sketch of a dress design or a prototype electronic mousetrap) through the camera with the best possible visual impact.

Making It Work

The installation process can vary from one brand of Webcam to the next. Generally, digital cameras are very simple to install and set up. The Logitech QuickCam Express, for example, has an installation procedure that's typical for most USB cameras.

If your computer is running Windows 98, installing the QuickCam Express is pretty straightforward. First you put the accompanying disc in your computer's CD-ROM drive and use the program's handy Installation Wizard to load the software that runs the camera. Then you make the physical connections between the camera and your computer, using the USB port in the back of your computer. After you make the connection, Windows 98 discovers the new camera hardware, installs the necessary drivers, and completes the setup.

Note

The software that comes with the Logitech's QuickCam Express camera lets you capture stills, make movies, post images to the Internet, and send snapshots in e-mail.

23

Broadcasting Your World with Webcams

CU-SeeMe

You, too, can join the CU-SeeMe (www.cuseeme.com) world, which is a community-based environment whose members can communicate by video chats. To share your images with this community, you must have a working Web camera connected to your computer (though it's not required if you simply want to chat without pictures), working sound system with microphone, and an Internet connection.

The CU-SeeMe software, produced by White Pine Software, is available for purchase from their Web page — or you can join one of the free Web communities such as the Family, Pets, Relationships, Sports, Teens, Travel, or Women communities. Membership to the Web version is free (and is required to join).

The interface only allows you to see three of the others in the community discussion, and has an overall limit of around 10 people. Once the maximum allowed have entered the session, the session becomes full, locking out anyone else. The default CU-SeeMe Web interface, shown in Figure 23-2, includes three view boxes, a text chat area, and a send/receive voice feature for complete group chat coverage. The sessions are monitored 24-7 against nudity, hatred, or anything else deemed offensive to keep the chat rooms safe for families, friends, and even children.

Figure 23-2. Using the CU-SeeMe Web client to chat visually with others. (Oops, no one has shown up to chat yet.)

Note

Web cameras are not required for using CU-SeeMe. You can use the software or Web site to chat, but no one will see you and you could miss out on some of the fun.

To gain entry to CU-SeeMe world, visit their Web site at www.cuseeme.com and click the Join/Login button on the left side of the page. Enter a nickname (so others have something friendly and appropriate to call you), as well as your first name, last name, and e-mail address. Then click the Submit button; you get a password that gives you a free login to the CU-SeeMe system. When you have logged in, join one of the existing groups or create your own.

If you decide you want to venture beyond what you can do on the Web site, the available CU-SeeMe Pro software opens the video Web world even more. You can include several people in a session and still see each one on your screen. Of course, you must purchase the client software to get these capabilities; fortunately, it's just under $70 — not too pricey, considering it offers the capability to talk to, look at, and collaborate with others.

NetMeeting

For fans of the Office suite of programs, Microsoft offers a product called NetMeeting — which connects two or more people to share information by means of video, voice, and viewing applications for demonstrations. This works really well for online meetings whose participants are calling from far-flung locations. Just launch NetMeeting and connect to a session. It's that easy.

The following steps show how it works:

1. At a predetermined time, launch NetMeeting from the icon on your desktop, which displays the Net Meeting - Connection dialog box.

2. One person hosts the meeting by clicking Call and selecting Host Meeting from the menu options.

   Everyone else scheduled for the meeting uses the host's IP address to join the meeting. (The meeting's host can find the IP address by pressing the Start button on the taskbar and clicking Run.)

3. Type **winipcfg** in the space provided on the dialog box; then click OK.

   The IP Configuration dialog box appears, showing the IP information for each adapter.

4. Select AOL Dial-up Adapter from the drop-down list near the top of the dialog box to see the needed IP address.

   The number should not be made up of all zeros (0.0.0.0); if it is, select another adapter, such as the PPP Adapter.

5. With the host's IP address determined, the participants enter this number in the top bar (black) of the NetMeeting - Connection dialog box and press the Call button, as shown in Figure 23-3.

Find It Online

You can get a free copy of NetMeeting for yourself at www.microsoft.com/ windows/netmeeting/ download/nm301x86. asp. Next stop, a videoconference with your Webcam.

Note

After the installation of NetMeeting, launch the application to complete the configuration of sound input and output. You also set the connection speed for the type of online connection you have — modem, broadband, or LAN.

23

Broadcasting Your World with Webcams

The host gets a connection request, which you can then accept by pressing the Accept button to establish the session.

Pressing the first button in the middle row of buttons (below the picture) starts displaying the video from your Webcam. The second button below the picture shows picture-in-picture, where yours is the small image and the other person's is the large one.

Figure 23-3. NetMeeting session in progress, with full audio and video features.

The row of buttons at the bottom of the NetMeeting - Connection dialog box gives you even more flexibility for using NetMeeting. These buttons (reading from left to right) access the following features:

- ▶ **Program Share:** Sharing programs lets everyone in your session see the program you're running on your desktop by projecting that image onto the NetMeeting viewing screen. This feature is good for demonstrations of software, helping a friend learn to work with a program, or training groups to use an application.

- ▶ **Chat:** Chatting gives you the option of communicating with someone through a text conversation, rather than through a voice application.

- ▶ **Whiteboard:** You can create on-screen sketches with the whiteboard portion of NetMeeting, just as you would using markers on a board in a conference room.

- ▶ **File Transfer:** The button at the far right is for transferring files. You can send one or more files to one or all the people in the NetMeeting session. This is useful if you need to send everyone a copy of the minutes from the last meeting and don't want to go to the bother of opening another program to do so.

Caution

Using NetMeeting can benefit you, but be careful. Collaborating with others via videoconferencing does mean giving someone else control of a program running on your computer, even if only for a limited time; offer that control only to people you trust. Accidents do happen; the effects on your machine can be worse when someone else has caused them.

Coming Up Next

By any of the methods presented here, you can capture, modify, and display pictures with your computer. But why stop with still pictures? The next chapter ventures into making movies with your computer. Nothing beats a good movie — especially when you made it yourself — and sharing it with the AOL community can be great fun.

Chapter 24

Making Better Movies with Digital Video

Taking pictures with a digital camera, scanning images, and creating your own graphics can be wonderful ways to beautify a Web site or any other presentation. But all these graphical forms still just lie there on the page, with none of the added visual interest that comes when images hop, skip, and jump across the screen. There is a way, however, to put some motion into your pictures. This chapter takes a look at the technology and shows you some tools to help you create your own movie productions.

Digital Video Technology

Movies have come a long way from the early silent movies. The newest New Thing to come to movies (as well as to home entertainment centers and computer screens across the country) is the Digital Video Disk (or DVD), a truly remarkable bit of technology that provides the clearest, best reproductions of cinematic movies for home viewing. Remember how the dependability and crystal-clear clarity of audio CDs made the old vinyl LPs obsolete? DVDs, because they can provide clear, clean pictures and sound, are set to make traditional VHS tape join vinyl LPs on the scrap heap of history.

As with most things, newer technology that promises bigger and better results also comes at a bigger cost. In the case of digital video, better video requires better hardware to take full advantage of what the new technology can offer. A case in point is your system's memory requirements. Depending on the quality of captured digital video, the resolution (screen size), and sound quality of the video, you need *approximately 10MB for every minute of the video.* An hour-length movie, then, takes up around 600MB of disk space. That's a lot of disk space — over half a gigabyte! Then you have speed to consider. The best hard drives for video applications spin at 7200 revolutions per minute (RPM) *or faster* to keep up with the stream of video. Slower drives and systems will work, but sometimes display jerky movies. I would recommend a *minimum* of a 300-MHz computer system with a 3D accelerated video card for working with video production.

Cameras and Other Video Capturing Devices

You can easily find digital video cameras on the market for making home movies. The trouble is, such cameras are still relatively expensive (although prices may drop as demand grows). The Ultura, made by Canon, is "cheap" at $1,000, with other models costing much more. The table shown here compares some cameras available on the market today, and includes the manufacturers' Web sites if you want to get more information about a particular camera.

Cross-Reference

Digital video can take up quite a bit of space on a computer hard drive. If you need to make room, you can find out more about expansion options for hard drives in Chapter 36.

Definition

Digital means that the information, be it movie, picture, or sound, is represented in the binary language common to computers — as a series of ones (1) and zeros (0); every aspect of the information corresponds to either a 1 or a 0, with no in-between states. The *analog* form of the same information is represented as a continuous stream of changing frequencies and amplitudes (like the wavy lines on an oscilloscope).

24

Making Better Movies with Digital Video

Note

Other cameras, such as those mentioned in Chapter 24, can capture movies in digital form.

Digital Video Camera	Web Site	Price
Canon Ultura	www.canondv.com	$1,000
Canon Elura	www.canondv.com	$1,400
Sony DCR-TRV310	www.sel.sony.com	$1,099
Panasonic PV-DV950	www.prodcat.panasonic.com	$2,700
JVC DVL9500	www.jvc.com	$2,000

Digital video cameras work similarly to the regular ones; they each take movies, storing them on tape to save the memories for later. They differ, however, in how they do their work. Digital video records the pictures as — you guessed it — digital information, which means the camera has to work more like a computer than an old-fashioned tape recorder.

Although the tapes used for digital video resemble VHS tapes, the tape medium itself is of higher quality so it can store digital information accurately; it's also smaller, though generally it holds more video recording time. The most popular mini-DV cassette used with compatible Canon recorders contains a quarter-inch tape (compared to half-inch VHS tape) and records up to 4.5 hours of home movies. Tape requirements may vary for different manufacturers and models of video camera.

When you have created your digital video, you still need some means of transferring it to your computer. Pinnacle Systems (www.pinnaclesys.com) StudioDV provides the hardware and software for your computer to capture any movie you create for around $150. The hardware is an add-on board that goes in a slot in the computer and uses the FireWire standard (IEEE 1394 — see Chapter 6 for more details) to transfer video information at high rates of speed from your camcorder to the computer. The software can take one hour of digital recording and save it in 150MB of hard drive space as .MPEG files, .AVI clips, or RealVideo files.

Although digital video cameras are certainly the current rage, most people still have handheld video cameras that are not digital. How, then, do you get analog home movies and other video onto your computer (a digital medium) for viewing? As you might expect, you need a specific product that converts analog signals into digital information. Several products do exactly that; the more popular ones include the Dazzle Video Creator, manufactured by Dazzle, Incorporated. The next section fills you in on some of its main features.

Dazzle

Dazzle (www.dazzle.com) bridges the gap between an analog video camera and the computer — for about $100 for the Digital Photo (& Video) Maker and around $200 for the Digital Video Maker. Both products include all necessary hardware and software; you can use either one to capture images as stills or as a movie. To make this happen, first you need the little Dazzle converter (seen in Figure 24-1) to physically connect the video camera, VCR, or other source of composite video signals to your computer. Dazzle uses a USB cable to connect to the computer and an S-Video or RCA cable to connect to the video device.

Find It Online

Find Dazzle Video Creator in the AOL Shop by using AOL Keyword: **Aol Shop**. Just click the Hardware tab, choose Digital Cameras, and scroll down the listing until you find Dazzle Video Creator.

Cross-Reference

Many of the new cameras can download what they have captured to a computer that uses the FireWire standard. To find out more about FireWire, check out Chapter 6.

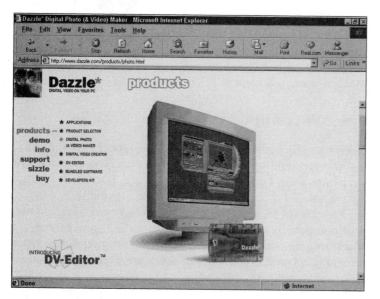

Figure 24-1. Information on Dazzle is available at www.dazzle.com.

The second part is the software, which can capture a single frame from a movie or a whole clip of the movie. When Dazzle Photo Maker opens, it shows three buttons on the right side of the screen — Record Mpeg Video, Capture

Note

This program uses a data-base to store all the thumb-nails. The program may have an error when it opens if Microsoft Access is not in-stalled on your computer. To get some help with this prob-lem, contact the Dazzle sup-port team by filling out their form at `www.dazzle.com/support/supform.html`.

Screen Shots, and Record Audio. Clicking any of these buttons enables you to capture information in one of the three media. At the bottom of the main viewing window are the play/record controls. The left side opens to show a *thumbnail* (small picture of original) archive of all the snapshots and movies you have recorded. As a special bonus, you can select from this archive list any pictures or clips that you want to use as a screen saver.

Video Mixing Software

After you have some video clips in digital format on your computer, your next step is to edit out any unnecessary footage and then put the clips in the order you want. Professional editing equipment to do the job costs thousands of dollars (not very practical if you're editing a family wedding), but there's no need for you to take that path. Video editing software designed for home computer use can do the job almost as well and much cheaper. The Dazzle Video Creator outlined in the previous section, for example, does a very good job of editing, but it's not the only product out there. VideoWave III, made by MGI Software, is a great alternative.

VideoWave III

VideoWave III, made by MGI Software, is a very economical ($100) video-editing software program that gives you many of the professional controls you would find in packages selling for a whole lot more. Most of all, it offers flexibility. You can use VideoWave III with video clips that have been copied to your computer, animations created on the computer by an-other program, or (in conjunction with your own digital video camera) captured live. Using this software, you can cut and paste video, pictures, and audio.

Creating your own movie is easy with the help of VideoWave III's snazzy-looking user interface (see Figure 24-2). Running down the left side of the window is the program's toolbar, where you can click the buttons to open, save, produce, and

Find It Online

You can find out more about VideoWave III online at `www.videowave.com`.

edit a project. The mini-screens at the top of the window contain the video clips you're working on at the moment. Think of it as a storyboard, where you can arrange (and rearrange) the order in which you want your video clips to appear. Finally, near the center of the window, you can see the main screen for showing each individual video clip.

VideoWave III comes with some sample video files to play around with. The following steps use these sample files to illustrate some of the basic features of VideoWave III:

Note

When you work with multimedia files, you encounter several different extensions to the files. Files that end in .wav refer to audio (such as voice or music). Files that end in .avi or .mpg refer to movie/video clips.

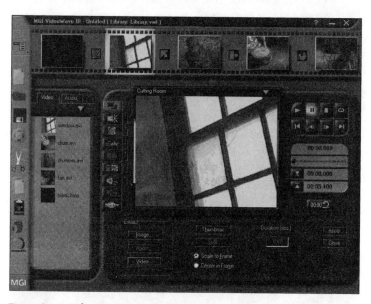

Figure 24-2. VideoWave III's interface graphically looks like a piece of studio-equipment.

1. Start out by finding the video clips you want to work with. To do this, right-click in the video library area; then select Add Files from the menu to begin choosing video clips. Then, using your mouse, drag-and-drop one of the files into an empty frame at the top of the storyboard.

2. Keep placing video clips on the storyboard in the order you want the movie to play them.

3. You can smooth out the breaks between video clips by inserting any of various transition effects (such as Dissolve or Wipe Up or Wipe Left) between the clips. To add a transition, click the Transition Effects button located between the two clips you want joined together (as displayed in the storyboard at the top of the window). A Transition Effects menu appears to the left of the window; the two clips then appear in two mini-screens at the bottom of the window (see Figure 24-3). Select the transition effect you want by double-clicking its icon in the Transition Effects menu.

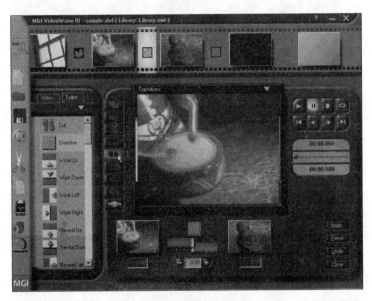

Figure 24-3. You have a variety of transitions available for creating amazing effects for a final product.

4. Repeat Step 3 for each transition in the storyboard.

5. When the story board is complete, click the frame where you want sound to start and then click the Audio tab in the menu on the left side of the window. An empty box appears underneath the main viewing screen. Drag-and-drop the desired audio file from the menu to that box. Figure 24-4 shows the result when you use the sample Excite.wav file.

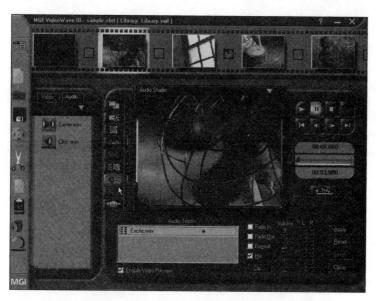

Figure 24-4. Add sound to a production, simply by dragging and dropping.

6. Lastly, click the Produce Video button (the one that looks like a movie reel) on the toolbar to have the program mix down the audio and video files to create a single .MPEG file.

Keep in mind the these are just the basic steps for creating a simple movie. When you are comfortable with the basics, you can move on to working with more advanced controls, such as setting the duration of the effects, adding text as titles and credits, and blending images as they transition. With those under your belt, you'll have all you need to give your creativity free reign.

Coming Up Next

Graphical content is only the visual part of multimedia. Online music, covered in the next chapter, opens up a whole new audio world delivered over the Internet right to your desktop. Time to put on your dancing shoes!

24

Making Better Movies
with Digital Video

Chapter 25

Listening to Online Music

For most people, listening to recorded music means putting a CD into a stereo's CD player and cranking up the volume. More recently, the technologically proficient have noticed a new and magical possibility: With a CD drive in the computer, a good sound card, and a pair of killer speakers, you can transform that computer of yours into a $2,000 CD player (in addition to all those other tasks it does for you). Folks who are *really* on the cutting edge, however, know that (with the help of the Web) you don't even need a CD anymore to hear great music.

Music from the Internet

Listening to music over the Internet happens in a variety of ways. You can listen to files that you download, go to a Web site that has audio built in, or use an application that turns your computer into a pretty expensive radio. Whichever method you use to hear the music, a program on your computer has to be associated with that method, interpret the signals, and re-create the musical sounds you hear.

If you use the Internet as a music source, you need software as an interpreter. Like radio, Internet music has a transmitter (the server) and a receiver (the client). The client programs are what the listeners see on their computers. Both the client and the server programs see the music as a stream of data — called an *audio stream* because it's used to create musical sound.

RealAudio

RealAudio (`www.real.com`) pioneered audio streaming technology, introducing both RealPlayer and RealJukebox, the trendsetting applications in the field. RealPlayer, as seen in Figure 25-1, plays both audio and video over the Internet, transforming your computer into a true entertainment center.

Figure 25-1. RealPlayer features audio and video streaming over the Internet.

Many Web sites have integrated RealAudio technologies into their broadcasts, several of which can be found on Real.com's site. Radio stations, music sites, and such keep the Internet community entertained with their transmissions.

Audio streaming is a continuous flow of information from the server to the client, used to create physical sound — a process that resembles the continuous flow of radio waves transmitted from a radio station to your car radio. *Video streaming* is the same concept applied to video signals; *media streaming* combines the two.

To find out more about RealJukebox, go to Chapter 26 for the details.

Find your favorite popular performers online with music and videos at `www.launch.com`. Watch top music videos, download featured songs, or chat with other music fans — all from the Launch Web site.

 **Note**

Both RealPlayer and Media Player are available free on the Internet — RealPlayer at www.real.com and Media Player at www.microsoft. com/windows/ mediaplayer.

Using RealPlayer and Windows Media Player with IE5

Microsoft's answer to Internet media-streaming is Windows Media Player (see Figure 25-2), available at the company Web site (www.microsoft.com/windows/mediaplayer/en/ default.asp). Although both RealPlayer and Windows Media Player perform the same basic function, the technology behind them is different. Windows Media Player is based firmly on Microsoft technology: Internet Explorer 5.

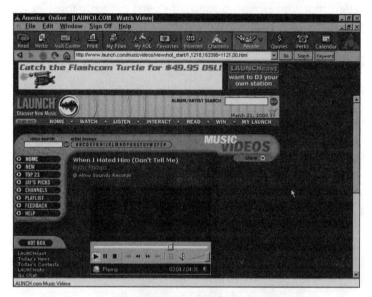

Figure 25-2. Microsoft Windows Media Player plug-ins work for Web pages.

The RealPlayer Option

If you install RealPlayer, the setup program offers you the option of adding RealPlayer to Internet Explorer 5 (IE5). This puts a button icon on the browser; when you click that button, you get immediate access to the Real listings of radio stations. You can search for music and video or check out *Take Five*, which gives you a quick look at news, sports, movies and music.

The Media Player Option

If you want to go the all-Microsoft route to music on the Internet (and you have IE5 with the Media Player plug-in installed), the following steps get you started in that direction, while also giving you a typical picture of the procedure involved in using online radio:

1. On your desktop, double-click the Internet Explorer 5 icon.

2. With Internet Explorer open, choose View⇨Toolbars⇨ Radio. The Radio toolbar appears below the Address bar.

3. Click the Radio Stations button. A drop-down menu appears.

4. Click Radio Station Guide. The WindowsMedia.com Web site opens.

5. Click the Radio tab if it's not already open.

6. On the Radio tab, click the Launch Radio Tuner button. The Radio Tuner opens in its own window.

7. In the Radio Tuner under STATION FINDER, click the down arrow next to <Find By>. A list of ways to search appears.

8. For now, choose Format⇨Select Format. A list of radio-program formats appears (Rock, Jazz, Classical, and so on).

9. Click a format; a list of radio stations appears.

10. Pick a station to play and then click it; a round Play button appears to the left of your selection.

11. To play your selected station, click the Play button. Details about the station appear in the oblong blue window at the top of the Radio Tuner screen.

12. To stop listening, click the Stop button on the Radio toolbar.

Spinner Plus

Spinner Plus (www.spinner.com), the first multichannel Internet broadcast application, offers 120 plus different channels with 21 presets, from which you can choose your favorite type of music — such as New Jazz, Swing Dance, Pop, Rock, Top Country, or Classical 101. After you make your choice, your selections on that channel come to your computer via the Internet, one at a time.

Note

Because your computer must take in and save up the first batch of streamed audio (a process called *buffering*), you may have to wait a few seconds before you hear the music.

Caution

Remember that you are still online as long as the globe icon in the upper-right corner of Internet Explorer is rotating. If you aren't planning to listen to online radio again for some time, close Internet Explorer after you click Stop.

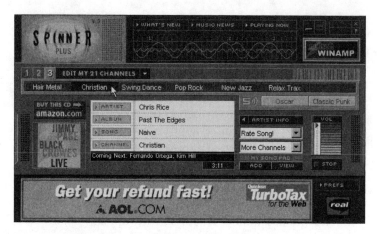

Figure 25-3. The Spinner Plus control panel packs features everywhere.

You can download the software for Spinner Plus for free from www.spinner.com. After you install the software, an audio tutorial gives you a guided tour of the available features.

You can switch from channel to channel with the click of a button, access one of two featured (preselected) channels, and even buy the CD containing the selection you're listening to (with the help of Spinner.com's quick link to amazon.com, as shown in Figure 25-3). If you really like the selection currently playing, say so to the folks at Spinner.com by giving it a high rating (using the Rate Song feature). Songs with higher ratings are played more frequently.

QSound

QSound technology, developed by QSound Labs, Inc. (www.qsound.com), can significantly improve the quality of the sound coming from your computer speakers, whether the sound source is audio-streaming, the sounds of your computer system, gaming sound effects, or even pre-recorded CDs. QSound Labs developed plug-ins to enhance audio-streaming players (such as Windows Media Player); with their help, your standard two-speaker computer can sound like a true surround-sound system with truly amazing virtual-3D effects.

The higher your Internet download speed, the smoother and clearer the music will be when it comes out of your speakers.

How significant is the actual improvement in sound? QSound lets you hear the difference for yourself on the demo page of its Web site (www.qsound.com/soundstg/demos.asp). There you can find a program that shows you, visually and audibly, what QSound technology does to improve — and place — the signal. You can use the demo (shown in Figure 25-4) to place sound effects (helicopters, jackhammers, dogs, bells) at different locations around you; then you can choose to hear the results in standard stereo and QSound stereo. For example, if you set up the on-screen indicators to place the helicopter sound above the head of the human figure, the sound of a helicopter will seem to come from overhead.

Find It Online

You can get more information on QSound's plug-ins for various audio-streaming players at www.qsound.com/ products/conpc.asp on the Web. Visiting their Web site, you will also discover some of their other applications like AudioPix which lets you create your own audio-visual presentations. AudioPix allows you to incorporate JPEG/GIF/BMP images with MP3 song files into a outstanding multimedia display created by you.

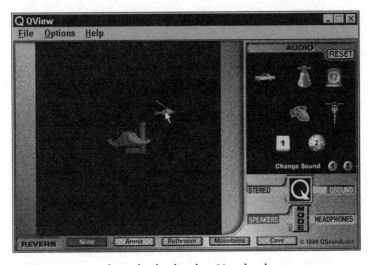

Figure 25-4. Mess with your head and see how QSound works on your computer.

To check out the QSound demo (known affectionately as QView) for yourself, first download the installation file to your local drive. Here's how:

1. Go to the www.qsound.com/soundstg/demos.asp Web page and click the word *QView* to begin the download process.

2. After the file qviewinst.exe is on your local computer, execute that program by double-clicking the filename.

   The Welcome dialog box appears, welcoming you to the setup application and recommending that you close all other windows before continuing to install this application. When you are ready to continue, click the Next button.

3. The next dialog box asks you where you want to install this demo. Unless you have objections to the default location, click the Next button to proceed to the Program Folder dialog box.

   The setup program creates a new program group called QSound.

4. Click the Next button to continue.

   After the files are installed in the appropriate locations, a dialog box opens to let you know the setup is complete.

5. Click the Finished button to close this program.

Now you can run the demo for yourself and see (that is, hear) the difference QSound makes to your computer sound system. To run the program, click the Start button on your Windows taskbar and choose Programs⇨QSound⇨QView. When the application opens, play around with its options and compare the differences between QSound and stereo sound. You can even experiment with the sound quality of your own .WAV files.

WOWThing

Other companies out there are also working hard to improve the sound coming out of your computer speakers. SRS Labs (www.srslabs.com) has come up with WOWThing (www.wowthing.com), a stiff competitor to the range of products offered by QSound. In a nutshell, SRS Lab's WOWThing can make the audio coming through a normal two-speaker system sound like audio coming through a multi-speaker surround-sound system.

The WOWThing is available in two forms: (1) a software plug-in that works only with WinAmp and (2) the WOWThing Box, a piece of hardware that installs into your speaker system. The control panel for the WOWThing plug-in (shown in Figure 25-5) gives you control of WOW (the surround-sound feature) and TruBass (for enhancing bass sound).

Cross-Reference

Look to Chapter 26 for details about WinAmp Media Player.

Figure 25-5. Add enhanced surround-sound quality to your two-speaker system with the WOWThing plug-in.

The WOWThing Box has the same purpose as the software plug-in. This is the device you use to connect the computer sound card to your VCR (or portable player) and your speaker system. An external power supply provides energy to the device. You have on/off, volume, and bypass controls. You even have controls for WOW and TruBass, which are what makes this little apparatus special. You can see from the SRS Labs Web site, the WOWThing box looks as modern as the technology used in it (see Figure 25-6).

Figure 25-6. The WOWThing Box as it looks from the Web site.

Coming Up Next

Listening to music over the Internet is a step into a new world: Various kinds of audio-streaming players are available to you, as well as enhancements to sound quality that you can make with the help of plug-ins and extra hardware. To complete the online music picture, all you need is an intro to a new technology that makes CD-quality sound easily accessible and easily portable. Next stop on the audio train — MP3s.

Chapter 26

Jamming with MP3

Online music delivered directly to your computer over the Internet is a great addition to anyone's listening options, but streaming audio only *begins* to expose the wealth of music available to computer users. Recently, a new wave of musical madness has begun to wash over the music industry: MP3. This chapter gives you all you need to know to ride this new wave of music technology.

The Makeup of MP3

Motion Picture Experts Group (MPEG) Audio Layer 3, better known as *MP3,* started in the movie business as a way to store audio efficiently. It uses a high-tech compression technology to shrink audio, music, or other digital sounds to a tenth their original file size — and yet still retain the near-CD-quality sound as perceived by the human ear. The average audio track on a CD contains around 45MB of digital sound. When you compress that to an MP3 file, you end up with a file closer to 5MB in size.

With MP3 file sizes as small as they are, storage becomes less of a problem. One major advantage of such smaller files sizes is that they're relatively easy and fast to transfer over the Internet. Music fans knew a good thing when they saw one, and adopted MP3 as the technology of choice for storing audio files. This led to the first stirrings of an MP3 craze a few years back — and enthusiasm for the new technology has grown ever since. As sound cards, computer speakers, and computer storage have improved, so has the abundance of these MP3 files, players, Web sites devoted to free MP3 music, and other MP3-related items.

Because of its file size and the quality of its music, the MP3 audio format is a hit with the computer-using public. However, simply having the capability to create these compressed files does not mean it's legally or ethically right to simply create and distribute copies of someone else's creative work any way one sees fit. Lawsuits threaten to pop up all over the place as record companies worry over the growing popularity of MP3. The record companies are concerned that they are not being compensated for songs distributed over the Internet.

MP3 Programs

Check out for yourself what MP3 can offer. To do so, you first have to familiarize yourself with the different software programs currently available that can play MP3 files. The following programs are the most popular; generally they can play other audio formats as well.

WinAmp

WinAmp (www.winamp.com) was one of the first MP3 players on the market; it remains a popular choice among enthusiasts. When first introduced a few years ago, WinAmp was a bare-bones player with no added features. Now it comes equipped with an equalizer for fine-tuning your sound, a playlist editor

Caution

Despite what many music fans may think, copyright laws still definitely apply to music. CD covers will have a warning stating that "unauthorized reproduction is a violation of applicable laws." The degree to which replication is allowed for personal use varies from one record publisher to the next, but all the variations agree on one principle: By law, you can copy music *that you have purchased* for your own use, for as long as you possess the original, but you are not allowed to sell, trade, or give the copy away.

26

Jamming with MP3

for selecting the songs you want to hear, and much more. WinAmp has even included a minibrowser for (limited) cruising of the Web into the WinAmp site's collection of features (see Figure 26-1) or any other sites of interest.

Figure 26-1. WinAmp, shown here in all its glory, displays all the wonderful features of this interface.

You can download the program from www.winamp.com to install it on your own system. When you've installed it, playing MP3 files is a snap. The application is organized according to function; Main control, Equalizer, minibrowser, and playlist editor occupy separate windows. Each of these four windows floats on its own; you can place it wherever you want it. If you double-click the title bar (top) of a typical WinAmp control, its panel shrinks to one line but still gives you easy access to the control. The main control shows the current song, volume and balance controls, continuous-play and random-play buttons, and all the normal buttons for controlling a player. Also on the main control panel is a sine-wave symbol in the upper-left corner that opens a menu for its options when clicked. This is the equalizer; it gives you control over treble, bass, and midrange sound frequencies (for finicky audiophiles who are particular about their sound). The third panel shows the songs lined up to play in the playlist.

WinAmp will play MP3 songs downloaded from the Internet, saved on your computer, or created from CD (which must be performed by another program). As long as WinAmp is the default MP3 player, any MP3 song will play through WinAmp when double-clicked.

If you want to play a song right away, use the mouse to drag-and-drop the song icon onto the WinAmp player from the song's stored location. The song will start playing immediately.

A WinAmp bonus is its *skin*, an option that changes the appearance of the WinAmp interface. Pick one that fits your mood or just looks cool. The basic function of the player remains the same; only the look of the player changes (see Figure 26-2). A wide variety of skins is available from the WinAmp Web site for free downloads. Check out some of the five-star skins available for free at the following Web address:

```
www.winamp.com/customize/browse.jhtml?component
Flag=S&categoryNum=0
```

Figure 26-2. Changing WinAmp's skin converts the player into an electronic circuit board (one of hundreds of available skins).

Lastly, WinAmp accommodates a variety of plug-ins designed to enhance the player in some way. Some of the plug-ins do nothing more than display a psychedelic visual representation of the music being played, while other plug-ins serve to provide a function, like enabling WinAmp to play additional audio formats (such as RealAudio files) outside of the already large default list of compatable audio formats.

MusicMatch

If you want a simple MP3 player that lets you easily create playlists, listen to audio CDs, and record audio tracks from the CD to the computer, then you can find it in MusicMatch Jukebox (www.musicmatch.com). MusicMatch will help you organize your MP3 files on the computer, make playlists of your favorite MP3 songs, and offers some customization such as changing the skin of the player.

Cross-Reference

One of the plug-ins, covered in Chapter 25, called WowThing enhances the sound output for a more three-dimensional sound.

MusicMatch also lets you change the appearance of the interface. (They call such customized interfaces *themes* rather than *skins,* but the principle is the same.) Figure 26-3 shows how the Digital Age theme gives the interface a cool techno look. You can change your own interface by clicking the Options button at the top, selecting View and clicking Download Themes to get more themes or Change Theme to select a different theme.

If you don't want MusicMatch crowding your desktop, you can switch between full view and a view just of the player by clicking the little arrow button next to the "X" in the upper-right corner.

Figure 26-3. MusicMatch combines flashy visuals with functional audio listening.

As this young MP3 technology grows, so do its improvements. New methods of creating MP3-like files produce smaller files with higher sound quality. Some of these new methods of creating MP3-like files even use a *secure* format to help prevent piracy. (True MP3 formats are not secure.)

If you get tired of the visual themes stored in the default library, you can access even more themes by selecting Add New Features from the Options menu. This opens your Web browser to a Web page where you can download any of the new plug-ins. When you have added a new feature, click the Options button again and choose View⇨Visualization⇨Select Visualization from the menu that appears. You can then pick a visual theme from the list (there was only one at the time of this writing, but I expect more will follow).

Additional features include a minibrowser called Net Music, which you can use to look up other songs (basing the search on the songs you have listened to), preview 30-second album samples, or purchase CDs online.

RealJukebox

RealJukebox (`www.real.com`) covers the bases for playing
MP3s and includes its own audio file format. The player can be
used in either Full View (where you can see all the songs,
check the ones you want to hear, and load other songs) or in
Reduced View (where you see the minimal player controls
and the current song). When using Full View, you have access
to the Record/Play CD, Music Library, and Get Music buttons
on the left side. Use the Record/Play CD button to play your
CDs on RealJukebox; the Music Library button lets you manage your song library to keep it organized; and the Get Music
button connects you to a special RealJukebox Web site where
you can access, download, and play new songs.

The small version of the player can take on different looks
with skins available from the Real Web site. As you can see in
Figure 26-4, the basic format of RealJukebox is much like that
of the other players on the market.

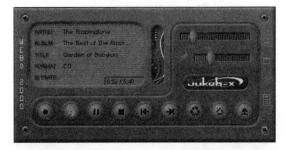

Figure 26-4. RealJukebox with the Webo 2000 skin applied.

This player also comes ready to download songs to some models of MP3 personal players (such as Nomad, Rio, and Lyra). In
fact, the Lyra uses RealJukebox as the default method of transferring songs to the device. It also offers an upgrade to the
free verson of RealJukebox (to a Plus version for just under
$30) that adds more program features.

RioPort

The RioPort (`www.rioport.com`) software was designed to
manage the songs for your Diamond Rio portable player, but
makes a great MP3 player when used all by itself. After you install the program, it searches your hard drive and finds all the
MP3 files stored there. You can then add and remove songs

from the list, as you desire, creating your own virtual MP3 albums. You can add more songs to the RioPort list by manually searching for the song files, extracting them from a CD, or downloading them from the Internet.

You can add files manually by choosing File⇨Add tracks and then browsing for the music file(s) you want to add. To add multiple songs at once, you simply hold down the Ctrl key while selecting songs. Also, using the RioPort program, you can insert your favorite CD in the computer and click the Read a CD button to read (and extract) any of the songs you want to add to your MP3 collection on the computer. Lastly, the RioPort program includes a Web browser that you can use to download MP3 songs directly from the RioPort Web site.

Skins and themes are all the rage among the MP3 crowd, so it should come as no surprise that RioPort comes with its own set of skins. Figure 26-5 shows how a skin can even change the look of RioPort's small player. (More skins are available from the RioPort Web site at www.rioport.com. Figure 26-5 also shows the G-Force plug-in, an extra bit of software you can install to add visual effects that dance with the music. Some plug-ins can be found at the RioPort Web site, while others, like those used with WinAmp, can be found at the WinAmp Web site (www.winamp.com).

Tip

Use the keyboard key F8 to switch between the small RioPort player and the larger one.

Find It Online

The RioPort Web site (www.rioport.com) offers many MP3 songs plus spoken-word MP3 files on topics ranging from business to comedy.

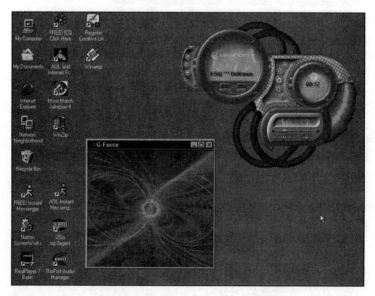

Figure 26-5. Get cool player looks by applying skins to the RioPort.

LAVA

If you are looking for an MP3 player with a twist, you can find it in LAVA (www.lava.com) from Creative Technology. This little player includes a customizable graphic display to watch while you listen. The player offers the basic functions you'd expect from a player — volume controls, play/pause buttons, and an on-screen bar that shows you how much of the song has played. Nothing very exciting there, but that quickly changes as you go to the playlist — which functions like any other playlist, with a major exception: It associates each MP3 song with a live-motion interactive 3D music video, as shown in Figure 26-6.

Figure 26-6. 3D visual effects from LAVA dance with the music.

LAVA comes with some ready-made music videos that you can associate with the music you listen to. You can also modify the videos — or create new ones that may fit better with the music. Use the Settings button on the player controls to reveal the control panel for the 3D graphics. After you have the graphics modified the way you want, simply save and associate the new music video with the MP3 song by clicking the File button on the video control panel and selecting the last option (Save and Associate with MP3).

Creative Technology doesn't recommend using sound cards based on the Voodoo, Voodoo3, and Banshee chipsets. You may experience performance or stability problems with these cards.

The program works smoothest on a fairly high-performance system. The minimum system requirements are as follows:

▶ Intel Pentium II 300 processor (or higher)

▶ 64MB RAM or more

▶ Any OpenGL 3D graphics card (Creative Technology recommends Graphics Blaster Riva TNT or better). OpenGL is a 3D graphics language that improves performance. Usually used in 3D games for maximum performance.

▶ Any PC-based sound card

▶ Windows 95/98 (Sorry, Mac owners.)

▶ DirectX 6.1 and above (to enable the graphical shows, which can be found at www.microsoft.com/directx)

Making Your Own MP3s

Listening to MP3 files created by others is definitely cool, but that's only half the fun. MP3 technology also makes it easy to create your own MP3 music files — either by taking the music directly from an audio CD or by translating another music format into an MP3 file. Because an MP3 file is a digital audio file, using the computer to create the files becomes effortless — provided you have the proper software.

Some programs don't have all their controls labeled clearly; putting the cursor over the control usually produces a label with a description.

To create MP3 files using audio CDs as your source, first you have to download a program capable of extracting songs from CDs. This isn't as complicated as it sounds, because a number of the players mentioned earlier in this chapter have such a feature. MusicMatch, RealJukebox, and RioPort, for example, all can extract audio tracks from a CD, convert them to MP3 files, and save the files on your computer. Each program accomplishes this in a slightly different manner:

▶ Using MusicMatch to turn CD music into MP3 files is a three-step process: Insert the CD in the drive, select the songs you want from the Recorder window, and click the Play button to start recording the songs as MP3 files to your computer hard drive.

▶ RealJukebox is just as easy to use as MusicMatch. Just put the CD into the computer's CD drive, select the songs you want, and click the Record button.

▶ The RioPort lets you extract songs while listening to other MP3 files you already have on your computer. Simply insert the CD that you want songs from, open RioPort, and click the Read a CD button. The program may go out to the Internet to retrieve the album title and song names. When the list of songs appears, check the boxes of the songs you want to extract. Then click the Start Ripping button to copy the songs to your computer.

MP3s You Carry Around

Listening to MP3 files on your computer is fine, but what if you want to listen to the songs while away from the computer? Portable MP3 players are the answer — and (unlike the portable CD player) you no longer have to worry about bumping, jarring, or shaking the personal music device. MP3 players have no moving parts to interrupt your listening pleasure while doing aerobics. You can actually shake the player as hard as you can (making sure not to lose your grip), without disrupting the song. Listed below are a few of the available MP3 personal players:

Manufacturer	Product	Price
Diamond	Rio Player 500	$267
Creative Technology	Nomad II	$240
I-JAM Multimedia	IJam	$99.95
RCA	Lyra	$250
i2Go	eGo	$220

Not all MP3 players are made alike, so it makes sense to take a look at each player individually. Some of the players have added features that may sway you toward them or away from them. Many of these players come in various styles and colors.

Note

Even though the downloadable versions of these programs are fully functional, they may be subject to some limits or restrictions until they are purchased or registered. The RioPort, for example, will only allow 50 songs to be extracted before the user has to register the program. To extract more, you have to unlock the player with a certificate code obtained (after registration) from its Web site for free.

26

Jamming with MP3

Find It Online

AOL offers the Rio Player 500, IJam, and Lyra players for sale at the AOL Store. Use AOL Keyword: **AOL Store** and click Hardware; then click the red dot next to *MP3 Player*.

▶ **Rio Player 500** (www.rioport.com): One of the first MP3 players on the market, it comes with 64MB of memory and is upgradable to 96MB. The Rio 500 lets you download MP3s from the Internet as well as create your own from CDs. You can mix the songs together that you want to listen to and play them back instantly. If you change your mind about the current list of songs, then just download some new ones to the player and take off listening again.

▶ **Nomad II** (www.nomadworld.com): The new generation of the Nomad player, the Nomad II, is upgradable so you can listen to other, newer audio-compression formats such as Windows Media Audio (WMA). In addition, Nomad II includes an FM radio, a USB connection for faster downloads, and voice-recording capabilities. They seem to have thought about everything when making this powerful player.

▶ **IJam** (www.ijamworld.com): The IJam player also includes an FM radio; if you're out and about and get tired of the songs you have with you, just change over to the FM radio and keep going. This is a true MP3 player, so you don't need any special program to convert or load the songs for the player's memory. The only needed software that comes with the player controls the memory card station (MusicMatch is also included for your convenience). Loading songs for the player is as simple as copying any MP3 songs to the memory card (which shows up, looking like a drive, under My Computer). It comes with 32MB (two 16MB cards) of memory and uses a MultiMediaCard by SanDisk, making the memory card the smallest part of the device. For the price, it's hard to beat this player.

▶ **Lyra** (www.lyra.com): One of RCA's smallest entertainment devices, the Lyra has amazing sound. It comes with preset equalizer settings, or you can customize the bass, midrange, and treble yourself. Repeat, random, and continuous-play settings provide playback versatility. The Lyra, however, isn't a true MP3 player. MP3 files change slightly as RealJukebox loads them into the player's memory. Simply copying a MP3 file to the memory card will not work; you must use RealJukebox to load the songs. Lyra does, however, offer as much as 64MB of memory for hours of listening pleasure.

▶ **eGo** (www.i2go.com): The i2go.com company has
   room to boast: They've come up with a product that's
   not only an MP3 player for music, but is also a mobile
   audio office. eGo is a design for the busy person who
   travels. You can connect it directly to your computer
   with a USB cable — and then let the iGo MP3 Agent
   software (see Figure 26-7) send songs, audio versions of
   news reports, and even your e-mail in audio format to
   your eGo. When you have set your preferences, the
   downloads can take place automatically. Because the
   eGo only works with MP3 files, the Agent software converts your e-mail from text to voice. How does one little device do all this? Not by itself; the i2Go.com Web
   site handles the fancier conversions and downloads. I
   give the eGo two thumbs-up for innovation. It's an excellent device for the busy traveler.

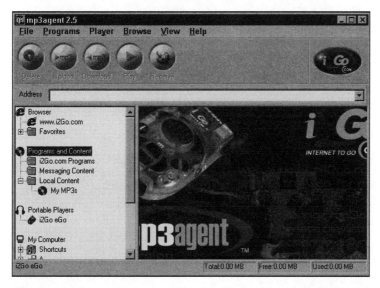

Figure 26-7. The i2Go MP3 Agent includes a minibrowser to connect to the i2Go Web
site for your information downloads.

Coming Up Next

Looking for something to do with your computer other than work? How about some fun games to play? The next chapter introduces you to the exciting world of games within AOL. You don't need to know anything about the games to start playing, buy any additional software, or know anyone to play with. Just show up. Learn the what, how, and where of AOL games in the next chapter.

PART

VIII

Playing the Night Away

PLAYING IN
AMERICA ONLINE'S
AMUSEMENT PARK

Chapter 27

Playing in America Online's Amusement Park

When friends come over for the evening, few things make a better activity than games. Whether it's a few friends in your living room or a big group at the company party, games break the ice and bring people together like nothing else.

About 22 million people wander the digital rooms of America Online — it only makes sense that games play a big part of the online service. When you feel like taking a break from the stress of daily life, head into AOL Games (AOL Keyword: **AOL Games**) to relax and unwind. This chapter looks at the channel's main areas — EA Lounge, EA Clubroom, EA Worlds, and EA Sports Arena. It also points out cool games lurking elsewhere on America Online.

AOL Games

To give you an easy starting point for finding online games, the America Online programmers created AOL Games, shown in Figure 27-1. You get here by either clicking the Games button on the left side of the Welcome window or by using AOL Keyword: **AOL Games.**

Note

Games change quickly, so don't be surprised if the whole AOL Games window looks a little bit different by the time you read this chapter. It's part of the ever-new world of online games!

Figure 27-1. America Online's Games window, home to some great online stress relievers.

AOL Games contains these main areas: EA Lounge, EA Clubroom, EA Sports Arena, and EA Worlds. Your America Online monthly membership includes unlimited access to everything in EA Lounge, plus lots of other games scattered elsewhere throughout the Service (see "Other Games Lurking around the Service," later in this chapter for more about the free games).

Click on the GameStorm logo from the EA Clubroom window or the EA Worlds window (or type in the AOL Keyword: **GameStorm**) for *premium games,* which, as you guessed it, cost extra to play. Currently, diversions in GameStorm cost 99 cents or $1.99 per hour, depending on the game you play.

The following sections go into detail about the games in each of the main areas. If you're new to online games, start with the EA Lounge area (particularly Strike A Match and Out of Order, two of my favorites) to get the hang of the whole online game thing. When you feel more adventurous, take a spin in the EA Clubroom or EA Worlds. Most of all, enjoy yourself!

Tip

27

Playing in America Online's Amusement Park

By default, new screen names *cannot* play premium games. (This protects you from unexpected credit card bills once the kids discover the EA Worlds area.) To allow a screen name in your account into the premium games, sign on with a master screen name, then visit the Parental Controls area (AOL Keyword: **Parental Controls**). Change the *Premium Services* setting for that screen name so premium services aren't blocked.

Note

By the way, most online games require you to download a helper program that makes the game work. These programs don't require much space, which means they come down to your computer pretty quickly. The first time you try a game, don't be surprised when America Online puts a window on the screen telling you it wants to send you a program before you can play. Just follow the on-screen instructions and you'll be playing in no time at all.

Note

Your monthly America Online membership covers everything in the EA Lounge area, so play as much and as long as you want!

EA Lounge

For the best free games in the online world, visit the EA Lounge area. Go there by either clicking the EA Lounge link on AOL Games window or by using AOL Keyword: **EA Lounge**. Either way, the EA Lounge window in Figure 27-2 hops into view, ready to meet your gaming needs.

Figure 27-2. The EA Lounge area features free, quick-playing games to fill those gotta play something moments.

Online game shows build on the success of TV game shows, combining the fun and challenge of their TV cousins with the interactivity of the online world. If you haven't tried them yet, here's a quick look at what's available:

▶ The best online game shows imaginable come from the folks at BoxerJam Games (AOL Keyword: **BoxerJam**). They specialize in highly interactive word games like Out of Order, Take 5, and the ever-popular Strike A Match. If you like fast-paced thinking games, you'll love BoxerJam's great creations.

▶ Games Paradise (AOL Keyword: **Games Paradise**) features chat room, e-mail, and discussion board games for all ages. Whether you love trivia, word games, music, or imponderable conundrums, Games Paradise has your games. These games rely more on mind power than reflexes, so if you want a game with a slower pace, look here.

▶ For fast-paced trivia with a head-to-head twist, try choosing Know It All from the drop-down list in the EA Lounge window. In the resulting window, you can see how many players are currently online and the top scores of players from all over the country. Just click the Play Now link to join the game.

▶ Feel like teasing your brain a bit? Dive into the Puzzle Zone (AOL Keyword: **Puzzle Zone**). The goodies here include Flexicon (a five minute crossword puzzle with a flexible twist), Elvis Lives (an anagram challenger), Clink (a stream of consciousness word game), and more.

▶ Feel like a game of chance? The EA Lounge area delivers casino-style games in Slingo (AOL Keyword: **Slingo**).

EA Clubroom

The EA Clubroom (appearing in Figure 27-3) contains a selection of America Online's free games and links to premium games. Join the fun by either clicking the EA Clubroom link in AOL Games window or by using AOL Keyword: **EA Clubroom**.

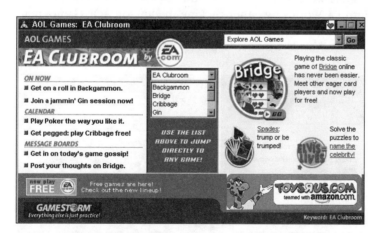

Figure 27-3. The EA Clubroom delivers the best in premium board and card games.

These titles focus on classic card and board games. Here's a look at what's available:

▶ Bingo, Backgammon, Bridge, Spades, and more await you in EA Clubroom (AOL Keyword: **EA Clubroom**), the home of classic multiplayer games. The games require a small downloaded program (don't worry — it's free) which takes a few minutes to get the first time that you play. The program installs automatically, then whisks you away to the games.

▶ You can find premium games at AOL Keyword: **GameStorm** or by clicking the GameStorm logo in the EA Clubroom window. Bowl online, yell out Bingo, and win at poker at GameStorm. Premium games currently cost 99 cents or $1.99 per hour, depending on the game you play.

EA Worlds

When nothing but the biggest, boldest, and most engaging games could possibly meet your entertainment needs, turn to the EA Worlds area. Like the other AOL Games sections, tune into EA Worlds by either clicking the link on AOL Games main window or by using AOL Keyword: **EA Worlds**. Either way, the EA Worlds window hops into action, as with Figure 27-4.

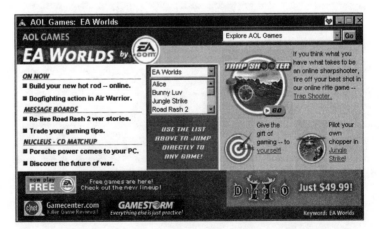

Figure 27-4. Whether you enjoy strategy, action, or role-playing, the EA Worlds deliver plenty of entertainment for your money.

If you're interested in high-end action or other premium games (costing 99 cents or $1.99 per hour), you can find them by following links from the EA Worlds window. Click on the GameStorm logo or use AOL Keyword: **GameStorm.** In the resulting GameStorm window, you can choose games from the drop-down list or select one of the featured games. Here's a look at what's available:

▶ Take to the skies in Air Warrior III (AOL Keyword: **Air Warrior**). Whether you fly a single-person fighter or take part as a crew member in a bomber, it's non-stop 3D excitement. Air Warrior III not only offers great action, but also an incredible community of gamers.

▶ Multiplayer BattleTech (AOL Keyword: **BattleTech**) puts you in command of a gigantic battle robot. Join a team or go head-to-head against all comers in this thrilling game of high-tech combat.

EA Sports Arena

You sports fans won't be disappointed with the online game selection available from the EA Sports Arena window (see Figure 27-5). Click the EA Sports Arena link from the AOL Games window (or use AOL Keyword: **EA Sports Arena**) to find out what's available. As with the other game area windows, you can choose from a drop-down list or click on links to find online games for major team sports, as follows:

▶ **Football:** Test your skills at rushing, passing, tackling, and even building a team with games like Running Back Challenge and Front Office Football 2001.

▶ **Baseball:** Choose Triple Play 96 to relive the excitement of the classic video game or It's Outta Here to find out how well you hit those homers under pressure.

▶ **Basketball:** Try out your speed, accuracy, and timing while shooting baskets on the Pro 3-Point game.

▶ **Soccer:** Check out FIFA 97 Gold Edition to help your squad on its drive for the World Cup.

If you're new to online sports games, check out the rookie tips under the Message Boards section of the EA Sports Arena window.

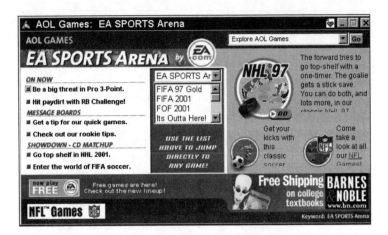

Online gamers enjoy more than just playing games — they also join together in great online communities. For more online fun, take part in the online community of your favorite game. To find these groups, check the game company web sites for fan pages and community links.

Figure 27-5. Go to AOL Keyword: **EA Sports Arena** to play your favorite sport online.

Other Games Lurking around the Service

Although AOL Games sits like a jewel at the center of America Online's game playing world, a lot of great games are scattered here and there throughout the service. The trick, of course, is finding them.

The following bullets list several of the lesser-known game areas, complete with brief descriptions of the games and keywords for going there. Grab your calendar, cancel some appointments, and get ready to play the day away:

▶ Whether you enjoy online games, board games, card games, or role-playing, there's something for you in the Gamers Forum (AOL Keyword: **Gaming**). The forum, shown in Figure 27-6, offers customizable card game discussions, strategy game forums, plus links to the popular Red Dragon Inn and Spaceport free-form role playing games.

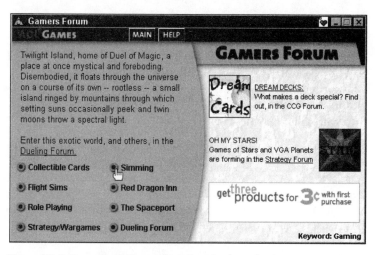

Figure 27-6. Love games? Meet and mingle with others who share your passion in the Gamers Forum (AOL Keyword: **Gaming**).

▶ Some people love the wide-open world of free-form role playing games, but others like a bit more structure in their simulations. That's where the Simming Forum (AOL Keyword: **Gaming**, then click the Simming button) comes into play. Simulations are role playing games taken to another level. Plot lines run deep, characters are better developed, and the games are more fun. The Simming Forum sponsors a broad variety of games, including Victorian Mystery, FBI Paranormal, Space Wars, Space Fleet, Dark Gothic, and others.

▶ AOL Games' Cool Links page (AOL Keyword: **Games Cool Links**) provides one-stop access to an incredible collection of games and game-related areas all over America Online and the Net. When you just don't know what to do next, spend some time exploring here. Goodness only knows what you might find!

▶ Interested in politics? Frustrated over deadlocks in Washington? Try your hand at the wheels of government in the Senate Simulation Game, one of the hidden jewels of America Online. To get there, go to AOL Keyword: **Members Speak Out**, then scroll through the Members Speak Out index until you see an entry for the News Message Boards. Keep scrolling a bit further until you see a link for the Senate Simulation Game.

Coming Up Next

Still more games await you on the Internet itself. The next chapter looks at the world of free online games on the Net, including where they are, what you can find out there, and tips for making it all work.

Chapter 28

Playing for Free on the Net

The Internet changed just about every facet of computing, but it *really* shifted the world of games. Computers boasted cool single-player games for years, but multiplayer games just didn't catch on well. The problem wasn't the games, but rather the computer — after all, it's not that easy for several people to crowd around a single computer.

Once the Internet connected multitudes of computers into a gigantic network, the world of multiplayer games exploded with possibilities. When the Net solved the communication problem (how to make the computers talk with each other), programmers started answering the *what shall we play* question. Their work resulted in a torrent of wonderful multiplayer games that await you right now. Best of all, the games don't cost a dime to play — what a deal!

This chapter takes you on a wild entertainment ride through free games all over the Net. Whether you love classic board or card games, game show-style competitions, sports, or role-playing, there's something in here for you.

Classic Board and Card Games

The magazines may jabber about complex, high-powered games like Half-Life, Quake, and StarCraft, but when it comes down to which games the *most* people play online, classic card and board games win hands-down. For a relaxing evening of online entertainment, few things beat a spirited round of Spades, Hearts, Bridge, or Euchre, complete with the conversational table talk that makes the games such fun in real life.

Classic games thrive all over the Net. Different sites offer different implementations of the games, so if you don't like the Spades game on Yahoo!, don't give up — try playing it somewhere else! Most of the games listed require a small downloaded program that lives on your computer's hard drive to play. The good news is that the Web sites help you get and install the game software by automating everything they can. And now, on to the list:

- ▶ Yahoo! games (games.yahoo.com) offers a wide variety of classic games. All the games work through your browser, but each one requires a small Java program that downloads automatically the first time you go into a game. To play, you must register with Yahoo!, which costs nothing (and gives you yet another e-mail address in the process).

- ▶ For younger kids (the 6-to-10 range), Yahoo! created a special game system devoted exclusively to them. Just go to the Yahooligans games page (games.yahoo.com/games/yahooligans.html), pick one of the preset names from the drop-down list, then dive into a game. To maintain the child's privacy, Yahoo! *does not* ask the child to register (which makes me feel better as a parent).

- ▶ Won.net (the World Opponent Network, shown in Figure 28-1) creates an incredible playing experience in its Web-based games. Brought to you by Sierra, one of the industry's premier computer game developers,

Note

Some of these games play directly through your Web browser, but others require a downloaded program. Don't worry — regardless of how they play, the games still don't cost anything!

Tip

Games that rely on downloaded software generally offer better graphics and sound than Web-browser games. On the other hand, downloaded games take up hard disk space, which might cause problems on older computers with small hard disks.

Won.net offers online versions of their Hoyle card and classic board games at www.won.net/channels/ hoyle. The games are free for online playing. Most Won.net games require a brief download (it takes about five minutes on a 56K modem) to play.

Figure 28-1. Won.net's extensive online game offerings include classic card games, game shows, strategy games, and more.

▶ Game site Pogo (www.pogo.com) definitely shows its roots as one of the first major online game sites (it used to be the Total Entertainment Network, or TEN). Pogo provides one of the easiest-to-use game systems out there, plus a good variety of classic games (and a bunch of single-player ones, too). The games play exclusively through the Web browser, so there's nothing to download. Pogo *does* go a bit overboard with advertising (particularly when you're entering a game room), but at least you get plenty of time to refill your drink or grab some snackies.

▶ Everybody knew the folks at Microsoft loved computers, but one look at the MSN Gaming Zone (www.zone.com) tells you that they adore games, too. Although their list of free, classic card and board games impresses even the most jaded Internet user, the games themselves can truly blow you away. All require small software downloads, but the site handles the down-load-and-install process for you.

▶ For a round of checkers, backgammon, or a wild six-person chess variant called Duchess, point your Web browser to PhatGames (`www.phatgames.net`). Their games rely on Java applets, so they play straight through the browser (no downloading required).

Sports and Game Shows

Apart from talk shows and afternoon soap operas, sports broadcasts and game shows form the backbone of television entertainment. These paragons of TV time make a natural match with the Internet, thanks to the Net's interactivity and broad audience. Whatever your pleasure, grab a bowl of popcorn and get ready for some Web-browser quarterbacking with these great sites:

▶ Bezerk delivers laughs (and occasional winces) in their wild and wacky online game shows. Part of the Won.Net family (`www.won.net/channels/bezerk`), Bezerk's games include their hilarious flagship game show, You Don't Know Jack, plus several other titles in the same genre. Each of the games requires a download, but they take less than five minutes to arrive on your 56K modem.

▶ The same BoxerJam game shows that you know and love from America Online's Game Shows area also live on the Net at `www.boxerjam.com`. In addition to favorites Strike a Match, Take 5, and Out of Order, the BoxerJam Web site adds Napoleon (draw poker with a French twist), two Take 5 variants focused on sports and entertainment, plus a whole bunch of single-player puzzles. The puzzles play directly through your Web browser, but the games require a three- to five-minute download.

▶ Drawing from an incredible stable of TV properties and technical expertise, the Sony Station (`station.sony. com`) lives up to its promise with a great selection of brand-name games and game shows. Jeopardy and Wheel of Fortune (along with several variants like

Note

The Java computer language revolutionized online games by giving developers a relatively easy way to write their programs for more than one kind of computer. Most Web browsers understand Java; almost any device with a Web browser can play Java games.

Sports Jeopardy) lead the way, with an online version of the classic board game Trivial Pursuit following close behind. The Station also offers some of BoxerJam's on-line game shows, plus plenty of single-player puzzle games. Because of the in-game graphics, all the Sony Station games require downloaded software.

▶ As the reigning king of TV sports, ESPN offers some incredible fantasy sport leagues in the ESPN Fantasy Sports Games site (games.espn.go.com). The good news is that their fantasy leagues cover baseball, basketball, football, and more. The bad news is that few of their leagues are free. Most cost $30 for the first team in a particular sport, with discounts (thank goodness!) if you spring for multiple teams. Their games run exclusively in your browser, so at least you don't need to download any programs to play.

▶ First they cover the Web itself, now they run the gamut of fantasy sports games! Yahoo! Fantasy Sports (fantasysports.yahoo.com) includes all the major United States "ball" sports, plus auto racing, soccer, golf, and hockey. All the games run in your browser, so there's nothing to download at all. What a deal!

Role-Playing and Strategy Games

Find It Online

If you love the TV gameshows, check out their online offerings for still more fun. The major network Web sites include www.abc.com, www.cbs.com, www.fox.com, www.nbc.com, and www.wb.com.

The thrill of the great unknown draws people into amazingly precarious situations on the sides of mountains, in fast-moving cars, and deep in the briny seas. If the desire for adventure reaches out and grabs you, hike over to your computer and take an inexpensive trip into the fantastic world of online role-playing and strategy games.

These games pull, push, and generally exercise your mind as you play. They cover the range of time and space as well, with settings in deep space, the Old West, and lands of mystical enchantment. Because of their complex graphics and immersive atmosphere, most of these games require downloaded programs.

▶ Build your real estate development savvy in Netropolis (`netropolis.lineone.net`), a fun and challenging game from LineOne in England (see Figure 28-2). The money may be Pounds Sterling, but business works the same! Start with a nest egg scraped together from your savings, then buy and sell your way to corporate success. Watch the dirty tricks, too, or you might end up in jail! This game plays entirely in your browser.

Note

If you discover a fondness for online strategy and role-playing games, flip ahead to the next chapter for a peek at playing store-bought games like StarCraft, Half-Life, Alpha Centauri — and many others — against opponents on the Internet.

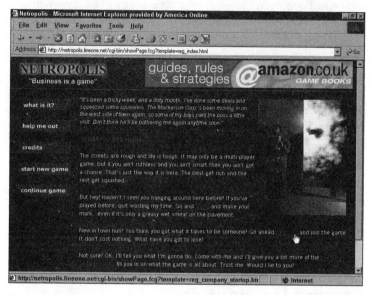

Figure 28-2. Test your real estate development skills in Netropolis, a free online game originating in Great Britain.

▶ SharePlay (`www.shareplay.com`) develops massively multiplayer online games that run entirely through your browser — you don't need any downloaded programs. Their games include Panumbra (role-playing), Space Merchant (intergalactic business), and Monarchy (turn-based strategy), with more on the way. SharePlay's high-quality games cost nothing to play.

▶ Although their popularity started soaring in the last year or two, multiplayer online games aren't really a new idea. For instance, Stellar Crisis (`stellar. gamestats.com/SC.main.html`) started life back in 1993, before the Internet caught the world's attention. This game of deep-space empire-building and conquest plays through your Web browser, without any downloaded components.

28

Playing for Free on the Net

Find It Online

Feel like exploring a little? Take a peek at the Multiplayer Online Games Directory (www.mpogd. com) or Starting Page's list of online games (www. startingpage.com/ html/games.html). These directories cover major game manufacturers, various game types (chess, board games, and such), and games in different stages of development. Starting Page even includes different platforms (PC, game console, and such) as well.

▶ Building on the mythos of the popular StarCraft strategy game, NetNexus (www.netnexus.com) created Terran Legacy, a role-playing game where you take the part of a Terran marine in a hostile world. Their other game, World at Ruins 2, takes you into a fantasy world of sword and skullduggery. Both games play through the browser alone.

▶ For a journey deep into the realms of fantasy fiction, visit Forgotten World (forgotten.acs-isp.com). In this browser-based game, you command a civilization of elves, dwarves, ogres, humans, or another of the 18 available races of creatures. Through clever strategy, military prowess, and timely alliances, your civilization claws its way to the top.

▶ U-Planet (u-planet.tourma.com) rounds out the strategy-game line-up. Instead of focusing on the *blow things up* model of gaming, U-Planet requires thought and diplomacy rather than a quick trigger finger. Starting as the newly-appointed governor of an unexplored planet, you build, develop, and explore your world while interacting with your alliance-mates for mutual growth and protection. This browser-based game doesn't use any downloaded components.

Coming Up Next

Individual games offer lots of fun, but there's more to playing on the Internet. The next chapter looks at the Net's leading online game services, where you sometimes pay to play, but find lots of new opponents and incredible game experiences.

Chapter 29

Online Homes for Serious Gamers

You rushed home from the store with the newest game on the shelf. The game looks *so* cool. And you already figured out some incredible multiplayer strategies. It loads on your computer like a dream, and blows you away with its potential. But where do you go now? How do you find an opponent? What perils await as you attempt to play the game online? Fear not, good gamer, for that's why the Internet contains so many game services.

This chapter introduces you to the Net's havens and help for multiplayer games, the online game services. These sites feature the hottest games and the best-quality support, a combination that means you get to spend more time playing than fiddling with arcane software settings. The chapter opens with a look at the commercial game services (both free and fee-based ones), and then dives into the game company-sponsored sites that support various retail-purchased games.

Online Game Services

Amusement parks make great destinations for family fun because they offer something for everyone. Fast rides, slow rides, kiddie areas — the parks wrap everything into a package of family fun. If you translate that "everything under one roof" model into the online game world, you get the *online game services*, the Net's answer to the large-scale group fun.

Most game services offer a variety of in-house games (titles that the service developed or exclusively distributes), plus some online versions of classic board and card games. Some services also provide the behind-the-scenes technology to play multiplayer-capable retail games (that you purchased at your local software boutique) against other people through the Net. Message boards and chat rooms round out the list of popular game service features. Sometimes it seems that the only thing gamers love more than playing is *talking* about playing.

All of this cool stuff costs money to produce; many online game services charge a fee to offset their costs (advertising and product sales cover the other expenses). Some use a monthly fee (usually between $4.95 and $9.95) for unlimited access to everything on the site, while others institute a per-hour for playing specific games. All the sites do a good job explaining their various fees and charges, so you needn't worry about accidentally running up a huge bill.

Here's an overview of the Net's most popular games services. Each list item includes the site's address, notes about their current games, and any fees the site charges. Enjoy yourself (but not too much — the best is yet to come)!

▶ 2am (www.2am.com) moved to an all-for-free format after experimenting with monthly membership fees for their exclusive collection of multiplayer games. 2am's games lean heavily on multiplayer strategy games, with some interesting forays into political strategy.

▶ Echelon Games (games.eesite.com) provides two multiplayer strategy games, Earth 2025 and Utopia, plus trivia and bingo. All the games are free to play.

 **Find It Online**

Things change so quickly on the Internet (particularly fees and product lists), that it pays to visit the various game-service Web sites for up-to-the-moment details about their offerings.

▶ If cost is no object and the game itself truly *is* the thing in your world, visit Fantasy Sports (`www.fantasysports.com`) for some of the fanciest and most expensive play on the Net. Build your fantasy baseball, basketball, football, or hockey team, then manage it through a full season of games. Brace yourself for the price — a single sport season (that's one sport, not all of them) costs between $80 and $90.

▶ First-person action gamers, your ship just came in. GameSpy3D (`www.gamespy3d.com`, shown in Figure 29-1) might be the most important application in your world. GameSpy3D collects and organizes information about available game servers, new software patches, and game modifications, presenting everything to you in an easy-to-use program designed to keep you *playing* your favorite games instead of *wishing* you could play as you track down the right add-ons. Because GameSpy3D is shareware, you can download a full-featured copy for free directly from the GameSpy Web site. Register the software for access to the latest features and updates.

Figure 29-1. GameSpy3D makes first-person gaming on the Net easier than ever before.

▶ Gamestorm (www.gamestorm.com) mixes a good selection of free classic games with several proprietary premium games. Classic games are free by registering on the site, while the premium games cost $9.95 per month for unlimited access.

▶ The Ientertainment Network (www.iencentral.com) houses the wildly popular multiplayer flight simulation WarBirds, plus a host of other free and premium games. Premium games use a prepaid-time model; you pay a monthly fee ($9.95, $19.95, or $29.95) that pays the premium games' per-hour charges. If you play more hours than your prepaid time allows, the extra time gets charged to your credit card.

▶ Kali (www.kali.net) and Kahn (kahn.descent4. org) fit in a special multiplayer gaming niche. These services provide Internet support and player match-up for games originally designed to run over a Local Area Network (LAN). The Kali and Kahn Web sites list the games each product supports. Kali costs $20 for a lifetime registration (including all future updates); Kahn recently started giving its product away for free.

▶ Microsoft Gaming Zone (www.zone.com) stands as one of the largest game services out there, with a very strong collection of classic games, multiplayer match-up services for retail games (including both Microsoft games and popular titles from other companies), plus several unique premium games. Most games, including both classic and retail match-up) cost nothing, while the premium games use an unlimited-play model: You buy a subscription. Most of these premium games give you the first 30 days free; you have plenty of time before you buy.

▶ Mplayer (www.mplayer.com) primarily offers free games, but with a twist. In addition to free classic card and board games, the site offers free multiplayer matching services for lots of retail games like Alien vs. Predator, Rogue Spear, MechWarrior, and such. Mplayer also hosts a few subscription-only games, which cost $9.95 per month for unlimited play.

Tip

To find out if one of your retail-purchased games works online, check the game's documentation. Look for things like "TCP/IP support" (which means that the game probably works on the Net) and "IPX support" (which should work with Kali and Kahn).

▶ Sandbox (www.sandbox.net) put together a unique combination of fantasy sports and fantasy stock games. The best thing about their games (apart from the broad selection of topics and titles) is the price: Everything is free!

▶ Sony PowerStation (www.station.sony.com/powerstation) includes Sony's hot multiplayer titles *Everquest, Everquest: The Ruins of Kunark,* and *Tanarus,* plus a small group of other potentially high-end games. Cost to play varies depending on the game. Some games cost a flat monthly fee for unlimited play, while others use a pay-per-play model.

▶ Uproar (www.uproar.com) started with some simple trivia and bingo games, but recently expanded into a much broader variety of game shows, arcade hits, and more. Game play is free with sign-up.

Company-Sponsored Mayhem

As the multiplayer gaming hobby grows on the Internet, more companies get into the business. Some game-makers jumped into action early; others started their online focus only recently. Either way, a wealth of online-capable games roll out of the industry development centers each year.

To make the online experience as easy as possible, many companies built dedicated multiplayer game systems for their products. These company-sponsored sites offer the latest game updates and patches, and often include add-ons like extra units, maps, and player discussion areas. Best of all, they're free for your use — after all, you *already* bought the game, so it only makes sense to give away the playing time.

The following table lists online offerings from the top computer-game companies. Look through their sites for details about multiplayer options, procedures, and such. If the table doesn't include the maker of your favorite game, visit that company's Web site and look into multiplayer options directly.

Company/Service	Web address	Supported games
Blizzard	www.battle.net	WarCraft, WarCraft II, StarCraft
Boneyards	www.boneyards.com	Total Annihilation, TA: Kingdoms, AMEN
Bungie	www.bungie.net	Myth, Myth II
Electronic Arts	www.ea.com/ multiplayer_matchup/ main.cfm	Support for more than 50 games including Populous: The Beginning, Sid Meier's Alpha Centauri, the Jane's combat titles, and Tiger Woods Golf
NovaWorld	www.novaworld.com	Delta Force 2, Armored Fist 3, F-22 Lightning 3, Commanche Gold, and others
Sierra	www.won.net	More than 50 top games including Star Trek: Armada, Homeworld, Half-Life, Starsiege Tribes, NASCAR Racing 3, Trophy Bass 2, and 3D Mini Golf Deluxe
Westwood Online	www.westwood.com	Command and Conquer series, Nox, and Dune 2000

 **Find It Online**

Hungry for more games? Search the Online Game Library (www.oglibrary.com), Multiplayer Online Games Directory (www.mpogd.com), Multiplayer Dot Com (www.multiplayer.com, see Figure 29-2), and the Internet Gaming Guilds (www.igg.net).

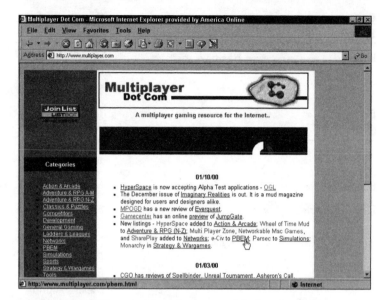

Figure 29-2: For information about the universe of Net-based multiplayer games, go straight to the source — Multiplayer Dot Com.

Coming Up Next

The Internet single-handedly put a whole new face on shopping. With malls, boutiques, chain stores, and specialty shops all just a mouse click away, it's easier than ever to find exactly the product you wanted. Of course, all those options do mean some lurking pitfalls as well, so the next chapter guides you through the perils and payoffs of the online shopping experience.

Chapter 30

Shopping from Your Favorite Chair

Shop till the stars appear while never leaving home with a little help from your Web browser. Whether you want toys, music, or a brand new car, your Net connection is the key to stress-free, leisure shopping. At the end of a spree, your credit card may be exhausted, but your feet won't hurt a bit. Thanks to highly competitive pricing on the Web, online shopping usually saves money while conserving gasoline.

In the Dark Ages of the Net, shoppers were lucky to find more than one or two merchants who braved the unknown and placed their products online for all to see. Today's web-based shopping, however, gives power to the credit card holder. You can purchase practically anything online if you know where to find it.

Because knowing where to look is more than half the battle, the chapter begins there. Then it discusses buying those big-ticket items online and comparison shopping that gets the most for your money. It ends up talking about the ins and outs of credit card transactions. Once you've placed the order, you can relax and wait for the shipping service to drop the package at your door.

All the Web's a Mall

Lands' End. eToys. Barnes & Noble. Where do you begin to find the Web vendor who sells what you want to buy? Or, if you've had an Internet connection for a while, how do you select from the huge number of available shops?

Just as in every other area of your life, you vote with your on-line spending dollars. Purchasing an item from one online store says that you prefer that store's selection or price to any other you might have available to you. From the shopper's standpoint, that's a good thing — it keeps the vendors on their toes and induces them to provide good products, fair prices, and reasonable service.

While you venture into Web waters to get your toes wet, sticking with the stores you already know gives you a feeling of security. It eliminates a few of the jitters that come with jumping into the unknown. If you've purchased your clothes from Eddie Bauer (or J.C. Penney) for the past ten years, you can be pretty sure that using their online stores (at the duly named www.eddiebauer.com and www.jcpenney.com Web sites) will present few surprises. You already know the store's price range and you're comfortable with the products they provide, so the only "unknown" here is the online shopping experience itself.

A quick Web search shows whether your favorite stores offer online shopping, and it's probably faster than digging out that last bag you brought home from the store. Depending on the store, the product selection offered on screen may be identical or somewhat different than what you'd find if you visited their location. Many stores add a closeout section online that they don't offer in their physical shops or catalogs — bagging a bargain definitely adds to the online shopping experience.

Once you move beyond the stores you frequent, you can add new favorites to your online repertoire. Even our local grocery store is online these days, so we can place an entire order

Find It Online

Great places to search for online merchants include AOL's online shopping search (Keyword: **Shopping Search**), plus Web sites like www.google.com, www.yahoo.com, aolsearch.aol.com, and www.altavista.com.

online and someone brings the groceries to the house. You might not immediately think of ordering groceries online, but that convenience could mean the difference between being able to entertain at home and having to meet at a restaurant on some evenings.

Also use a Web search to find that esoteric item you've been looking for. For example, if the local toy store doesn't have that coveted item, you might find it at www.etoys.com, www.toysrus.com, www.fao.com, or www.redrocket.com. From fishing lures to automobiles, you can find — and order it — online.

Help with the Big Decisions

If you're in the market for electronics or a new car (or a perfect pet, for that matter) you might want to take a look at the Personalogic Decision Guides, at www.personalogic.com. (see Figure 30-1). They guide you through decision making by asking your preferences on price, color, model, features, and a host of other options. They then crunch your answers and present a whole list of possible selections.

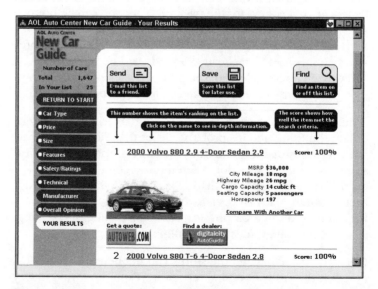

Figure 30-1. Decision Guides help identify the best possible choice for that new purchase.

Once the guide shows what it recommends, you can select any item in the results list that interests you, and the guide then provides comprehensive information on that product. Its suggested price, features, and options all appear in an organized column. When you like what you see, click the dealer or manufacturer button to open a Web site that allows you to purchase — or request a dealer for — the item.

If you find yourself torn between two or three options, use the Personalogic guides to compare your choices side by side. All the product information appears in column format so it's an easy process to select two or more and compare them. Any large discrepancies among the choices (such as comparing totally different products, huge price differences, or important variations in feature or function) appear highlighted in yellow so that you can easily spot them.

Start the Spree

Beginning your shopping experience in the AOL Shopping channel (AOL Keyword: **Shopping,** shown in Figure 30-2) effortlessly leads you to some of the biggest names in retail. Whether you want an executive gift from The Sharper Image, clothes from Gap, or housewares from Tupperware, the AOL Shopping channel provides it all without making you memorize dozens of individual Web addresses.

Figure 30-2. The AOL Shopping Channel.

If you're looking for a particular store, try the A-Z list on the shopping main screen or perhaps browse by category: apparel consumer electronics, and so on.

Once you master the hundreds of stores in AOL Shopping — or determine that none of the vendors carries that particular shade of green you really want to finish that outfit or decorating scheme — you can use one of the big search engines to locate a particular Internet shopping category or even a specific store on the Web. After browsing for a while, you'll locate some true gems. Save these sites in your Favorite Places list so you can find them again (click the little *heart-on-the-paper* icon in the upper corner of the site's window inside America Online). It saves brain cells — nobody wants to spend time memorizing fifty or so favorite shopping sites, and who can find that pile of scribbled sticky notes when they need them?

Alibris, at www.alibris.com, acts as a clearinghouse for out of print and rare books. It's a treasure trove for bibliophiles.

So you troll the Net and locate an item that makes your heart flutter. Next, you get to claim it as yours with a credit card. Click the Buy Now or Add to Cart button (or look for something similar) and the site drops the purchase into a virtual shopping cart. Think of it as pulling an item off the shelf so you can carry it around the store for a while. Selecting an item with the Buy This button does *not* obligate you to purchase it. Instead, it holds the item for you in an online bin so that you can find it again when you're ready to check out. If you change your mind, you can reset the total to 0 (or uncheck the Buy this box, depending on how the site is designed) and the site forgets you ever selected the item (see Figure 30-3).

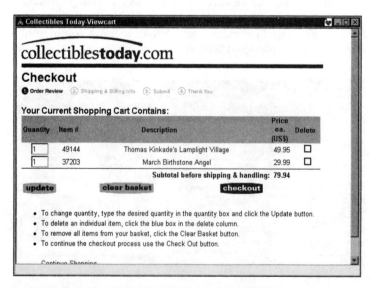

Figure 30-3. Set the quantities back to zero if you decide against an item.

Visit the checkout area of the site to complete your order. Here the site asks for your credit card number, your name and address, and your e-mail address. Fill in the required information and click the Finish or Complete Checkout button (or something similar). The site then processes your order and presents you with an order confirmation number. Most of the time, the confirmation screen also recaps the items and your mailing information. If you shop online quite a bit, printing the confirmation list helps you remember what you bought, and from whom.

It's a good idea to print your shopping confirmation number and final selection list in case problems should arise later.

Compare Those Prices

Nobody wants to feel like they've been taken. Realizing that you've paid more for an item than you needed tends to feed buyer's remorse. On the other hand, spending hours trying to shave fifty cents from an item here or three dollars from an item there gives you a tension headache.

Comparing prices on big ticket items is wise. Some sites, like the computer information wonderland known as CNET (www.cnet.com), include price comparisons as a feature. You can visit CNET's site and compare computer hardware and electronics prices from many different vendors and still stay within one site. If price is important to you, a site like CNET could prove to be a valuable addition to your favorite places list.

When you compare prices, keep in mind a few factors that might affect your decision one way or the other:

- ▶ **Watch out for unusually high handling fees.** Shipping costs can vary widely, and some companies try to make up for low prices by jacking up their shipping and handling.
- ▶ **Compare apples to apples.** Especially with computer components, you get what you pay for. If a vendor advertises a rock-bottom price on electronics, there's a reason: the model is outdated, it uses nonstandard components (which means it's not guaranteed to work with anything you might already have, such as software), or it's a refurbished item.

America Online's Shopping Search (Keyword: Shopping Search) prowls through the online catalogs of AOL's Merchant Partner Sites, looking for the products you specify. It's a great tool for easy price comparisons on popular products.

30

Shopping from Your Favorite Chair

▶ **Refurbished electronics can save you money and provide you with a good product.** Refurbished means that a store or customer has returned an item for repair. The manufacturer repairs the item and then sells it at a lower cost. Usually, these components carry a standard "bought it like new" warranty, so you aren't out anything if you get it and it doesn't work — you can always send it back for service!

▶ **Look at the extras.** What perks might come with a higher price tag? If a vendor will wrap a gift at no cost and ship it to the recipient, that item might be worth a few dollars more. Especially with computers, technical support is important. Check to ensure that a lower price tag doesn't mean you're purchasing a product that includes no after-sale support.

That said, once you make the best decision you can with the information you have, purchase the item and forget about it. Worrying whether you shopped enough, compared enough, or spent too much causes stress you're better off without, and it takes some of the joy away from the ease of online shopping.

Tip

Your time is worth money. Beware of spending hours comparison shopping only to save a dollar or two — you lose money in the long run. After all, wouldn't you really rather watch a movie, fly a kite, or spend time with your family instead of shaving another 36 cents off your video camera's purchase price?

Note

Almost every shopping site uses an "account number" or "member ID" of some kind to identify you. To keep your personal information safe and secure, they also require a password to use the account. Don't use your America Online password for these other accounts — come up with something different instead. Be sure to write down your account number and password somewhere safe!

Scammers in the Shadows

Unfortunately, you're going to find a few unscrupulous agents anywhere a huge number of people gather. The Internet is no different — in fact, it seems to foster attempted cons and scams because the Net seems to be "magical." Keep your accounts safe while shopping online! Never give anyone your credit card number. You wouldn't hand your flight bag over to some stranger in the airport just because he asked — in the same way, you don't want to reveal your personal or credit card information to anyone who has the audacity to ask for it.

Not too long ago I actually received a scam phone call. The caller "identified" herself as being with some kind of security agency dedicated to making sure that my credit card was safe over the Internet. She told me that the credit card companies have changed their policies about covering stolen credit cards, *which is not true.* Then she asked for my credit card number. If I clued into nothing else during the conversation, asking for the number outright was a red flag.

No reputable company will call you on the phone or contact you via e-mail and ask for your credit card number. A reputable company waits for you to come to them, unless you've purchased something and agreed to complete the transaction some other way. After purchasing a book from England, and finding the secure server unresponsive over a weekend, the company and I agreed to complete the credit card transaction via e-mail, which we did. It required several e-mail messages back and forth, however, and a rather creative method of sending the number. That transaction increased my appreciation for web sites and their secure servers.

Secure Shopping

Keeping your credit card information safe while you shop online has become a major concern — not only to the shoppers, but to the vendors as well. Although scams abound that would try to convince you otherwise, shopping on the Web is probably as safe as handing your credit card to a clerk in a store.

Not long after the first big rush to the Internet in the mid '90s, vendors and customers alike wanted a safe online shopping experience. In response, online stores began to install software that created *secure servers*. When you shop online, and select the items you want to buy, the browser talks to the site in its normal way. When you get ready to purchase, you click the checkout button. At some point during the checkout process, your browser displays a dialog box that tells you that you're about to view pages over a *secure connection*.

It sounds rather James Bondish, and the first few times you see the warning box you might be tempted to grab your darkest sunglasses to complete the spy illusion. However, you (and your browser) really aren't going anywhere. When you click OK to make the dialog box disappear and continue your shopping experience, the web site and your browser agree to transmit the rest of the information in code so that no one else can intercept and read it.

Find It Online

For more information on keeping your credit card safe, visit VISA's web site (www.visa.com).

30

Shopping from Your Favorite Chair

Because it's an encrypted transmission (sent encoded), it takes a bit longer for the information to go from your browser to the site and back again. That's why the very last part of your online shopping may seem to drag a bit (plus the fact that actually paying for purchases is always a little painful anyway). When you type in your name, address, credit card, and other information, your browser scrambles the information according to the agreed-upon code and then the Web site unscrambles it when it receives the information. The site and your browser, working together, get the job done and your information remains secret.

Coming Up Next

Shopping at retail works great for a lot of people, but for others there's nothing like the thrill of an auction. If that's you, then flip ahead to the next chapter for a trip deep into the world of online auctions. Whether you're a bargain hunter, antique collector, or part-time purveyor of the odd and unusual, there's an online auction waiting for you.

Chapter 31

Playing with Bucks in Online Auctions

"Sold to the highest bidder!" Winning an auction sends the thrill of victory through your heart. You don't have to wait for the next estate auction to experience that suspense and excitement once again — thanks to your online connection, auctions await you 24 hours a day.

Although bidding in an online auction works a little differently than raising your hand or wiggling your finger (depending on the bidding price range, of course), the basic premise remains the same. You find an article you like and tell the computer how much you're willing to pay for that item. And here's where it gets interesting — you can bid on anything from antiques to computers, from books to baubles. Your only limits are the depth of your purse and your interest in what someone else has to sell.

The Auction Lineup

Auctions are big business on the Internet, and AOL devotes one of its Shopping channel categories to the thrill of bargain hunting. From the largest online auction houses, like eBay, to specialty auctions such as The Sharper Image Auction, you can find practically anything to bid on. AOL Keyword: **Shopping** opens the AOL Shopping window; look for the Auctions & Outlets category to delve into AOL's offerings.

Caution

Auction bidders need to be at least 18 or 21 years of age to participate, depending on the majority laws for your particular state.

Although the online auctions function similarly among themselves, they carry a different breadth and depth of items. Some auctions specialize in electronics or collectibles, while others seem to offer everything under the sun.

Generally, the site requests that you register before you bid, so that the auction company knows who you are. When you register you need to supply the site with the credit card information you wish to use to pay for any purchases you win. The auction then applies the purchase amount to your card, unless the site states that you have a choice of credit card, money order, or check once you win a bid.

eBay

The first of the big online auctions, eBay dominates the world of online auctioneering. The sellers on eBay offer just about anything you could ever want. Interested in replacing some out-of-production technology? Somebody's probably selling it on eBay. If you want movies, jewelry, or pottery, look for those on eBay, too. Open the site with AOL Keyword: **eBay** or go to www.ebay.com.

You can browse on eBay by category (see Figure 31-1), but with thousands of entries to peruse in each section, you're probably better off conducting a search for the item you seek. Clicking on any item name brings up its information, including the current bid amount, number of bids already logged, and a description of the item. Often the screen also includes a photo of the item.

Figure 31-1. With the thousands of things available on eBay, you're sure to find something you like.

To place a bid on eBay, you first need to register:

1. Click the Register button in the Welcome New Users area at the top of the site's main page. The eBay Registration screen appears. eBay uses a secure registration system, so your personal information is safe.

2. The system asks you for your country. Select it from the list, and click Continue.

3. The site then leads you through the registration process. Fill in your personal information and click Continue until you reach the eBay User Agreement. (If a "Security Alert" dialog box pops to warn you that "you are about to view pages over a secure connection," just click OK. That box lets you know that your Web browser and the computers at eBay created a high-security corridor through the Internet to keep your personal information safe and sound.)

4. Read through the User Agreement to ensure that you are willing to abide by the terms, and click the I agree check boxes as you go.

5. Click I Accept This Agreement to continue your registration.

eBay then sends you an e-mail that confirms your registration. When you get it, use the link in the e-mail to select your password and complete your registration.

Unlike some of the other online auction houses, eBay doesn't request a credit card number when you register as a buyer. You negotiate payment for your purchases with the individual sellers — be sure to read the payment requirements in the individual listings to find out whether you can pay by check, credit card, or money order. Once you have your User ID and password handy, browse until you find something that meets your heart's desire. If, after reading the item's specifics, you decide you want to place a bid, scroll down to the bid box and type in your offer. Then click the Review Bid button and follow the instructions. Better still, use Ebay's Personal Shopper service to automatically sift through auction listings and e-mail alerts to you when interesting items become available. For more about Personal Shopper, click the Search button at the top of the Ebay screen, then click the Personal Shopper button that appears with the other Search options.

Caution

When you place a bid you promise to purchase that item if your bid is the highest at the end of the auction. Your bid is a binding contract.

Yahoo! Auctions

Although the Yahoo! Auctions (`auctions.yahoo.com`) don't include the massive numbers of items that you see on eBay (not yet anyway) you can locate a special find or two by browsing through the Yahoo! lists. If you know what you're looking for, search for it and bypass the long lists (see Figure 31-2).

Yahoo! Auctions tell you the current number of items available in each category, which helps you decide whether to dive in. You have an idea of the number of items you need to wade through if you decide to browse a category. In addition, you also know how well-represented that category is — if the Trading Cards category contains nearly half a million entries, then you either need to know *exactly* what you're looking for or you need a couple hours free time for browsing.

One of the neatest features of the Yahoo! Auctions is its Alert Me function. If you find yourself regularly searching for a specific item or term, click Alert Me and complete an alert request. Yahoo! Auctions then notifies you by e-mail when an item matching your search criteria enters the system. This helps you keep on top of the bidding wars by knowing when to check the auctions for your favorite items.

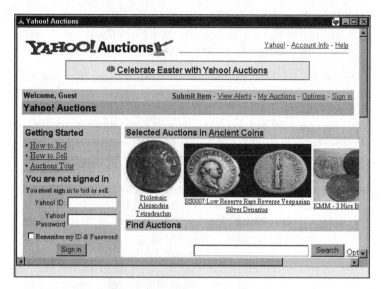

Figure 31-2. Sign in with your User ID and password, enter a search term, and see what turns up in the Yahoo Auctions.

Amazon.com Auctions

A relative newcomer to the online auctions market, Amazon.com expanded its online book empire by including an auction section. Unlike most of the other auction houses, Amazon.com doesn't post the number of items for sale next to the category listing, so each click is a bit of a wild card. You might find a few items in a particular category, or a thousand.

Searching for an item in Amazon.com Auctions may save you a lot of clicking time — subcategories are conveniently nested under category headings. But you might click down three or four levels only to find that a particular subcategory contains no offerings. (Note to Amazon: Numbers next to the categories and subcategories would be really helpful so that you would know how many items actually reside in each category *before* you begin clicking.)

When searching for something, remember to try different descriptions. If you want canes, for instance, try searching for *cane, walking stick,* and *antique cane.* Because everybody writes ad subjects differently, a little creativity and persistance when searching often uncovers a gem that everyone else overlooked.

Amazon.com Auctions also offers a search e-mail notification feature. Search for an item, and then click Sign up for Amazon.com Alerts. The site then sends you an e-mail when any item appears in the listings that matches your search criteria.

When you register at the Amazon.com Auctions site, Amazon.com asks you for a current credit card, address, and phone number to ensure that you are who you say you are. Individual auctions, however, might take credit cards, personal checks, cashier's checks, or money orders for payment.

Once you've entered your registration information, however, bidding on an individual item is incredibly easy. Sign in with your user name and password, and then search for an item. When you find it, enter your maximum bid into the text box, and click Bid Now. The site calculates your bid and a confirmation appears on-screen.

Tip

Use Amazon.com Alerts to tell you when an item matching your search criteria hits the system.

General Dos and Don'ts

Knowing a few tricks of the online auction trade eases your introduction into the bidding wars. Like everything else on-line, auctions operate under their own set of rules, formalities, and etiquette. Keeping within the perimeters of good taste and good sense takes you a long way when you're bidding on-line, but here are a few extra pointers you might find helpful:

▶ Check the seller's references and rating before you place a large bid.

▶ E-mail the seller with any questions about the item *before* bidding.

▶ Caveat emptor — if the deal sounds too good to be true, it probably is.

▶ Use automatic bidding and let the site do the work for you. Almost all of the auction sites allow automatic bidding, which means that you enter a maximum bid and the site increases your bid as necessary up to the maximum amount. Your other option is to place a bid for a specific dollar amount.

▶ Place a bid only if you're willing to purchase that item. A bid in an auction is a legally binding contract.

▶ Read the offering information carefully. You might find an unusually high shipping charge that makes the item unappealing to you. If, for example, the item currently resides in a country halfway around the world, shipping will be pricey — no matter what the item is.

▶ If you want to sell an item online but you think your offering might fall into a "gray" area for an auction site, check the site's *unacceptable item list*. This is particularly true for sites which focus on a particular genre, like antiques, computer gear, or collectibles.

Write an Ad That Sells

Online auctions give everybody the opportunity to join in the fun. You don't have to run an antique store to place items in the auction lineups. If your closets are overflowing or you want to liquidate a treasured collection, you might want to give an auction a try.

To sell an item online, you first need to catch the eye of a qualified and interested buyer. Buyers who browse tune into unique and exciting words in your item's description line. On the other hand, buyers who use the search engine need to find your item on the first search through. To do that, your product description needs to use explanatory words like "1911 novel" rather than "cool old book."

Give the one-line item description a lot of thought; this description is how your buyers will attempt to locate your merchandise. Knowing your products well always helps to write a good ad. You aren't limited to one line of information — those 45 characters or so are the words the search engine uses to categorize your item. The submission information that you supply also includes a larger text box that allows you to go into more detail.

Here's where you gush. If this product is wonderful, tell your audience so. Include a photo if you have a digital camera or can scan a good snapshot. Let's face it — good pictures sell stuff. Use that to your advantage.

If you're selling something you're not too well versed on, include as much descriptive information as you can. Not every antiques dealer is an expert in needlework books, but a good shot of the book's cover, a publication date, and the entire title tell a collector a great deal.

Coming Up Next

Chat with your friends, family, and even total strangers through ICQ, the world's most-used interactive messaging system. The next chapter takes you on a romp through ICQ, including an overview of the software, a look at your options, and tips for enjoying your conversations to the fullest.

Chapter 32

Instant Messages and More Through ICQ

You can find a number of instant-messaging software programs on the market today; AOL Instant Messenger (otherwise known as AIM) isn't the only one. ICQ (www.icq.com), a leader in the instant-messaging software field, has many of the same features as AIM — and more to boot. This chapter fills you in on the loads of options ICQ offers its users.

Defining ICQ

ICQ is a play-on-letters that sounds just like the phrase *I seek you* when you say it aloud. ICQ is also the name of an instant-messaging program of choice for millions of individuals, letting users chat, leave messages, and more. Part of ICQ's popularity can be traced to the fact that it is simply loaded with communication tools that give you great flexibility when you want to communicate with others. ICQ provides four different ways to get your message across — though ICQ messaging, through ICQ-based e-mail, through Web-based ICQ chat, or through a personal ICQ Web page.

Cross-Reference

For more about AOL Instant Messenger (AIM), see Chapter 5.

ICQ Versus AIM

AOL members are probably already familiar with the Instant Messenger that came with their AOL software. Non-AOL members may know Instant Messenger as AIM, a standalone program they may have downloaded from the Web. Regardless of how they first get acquainted with the program, Instant Messenger enthusiasts value the convenience of letting software keep track of when friends, family, and associates are actively online and available for a chat in real time.

ICQ provides that same convenience — and then some. Not only can you fire off online messages to individuals in the blink of an eye, but you can also select a group from the pool of individuals currently online and include them in a chat (AIM-style). ICQ also has long had a feature that Instant Messenger has only recently adopted: sending files directly to the individuals you are chatting with. In addition, ICQ has its own version of Instant Messenger's Buddy List — a listing you set up so the program can keep track of when particular individuals are online. In ICQ, the Buddy List becomes the Contact List, reproducing all the basic features of Instant Messenger's service. ICQ, however, gives you greater control over how you appear (if at all) in the Contact Lists of other ICQ users. If you prefer not to hear from a certain someone for a few days or weeks, you can set it up so you no longer appear to be online in that individual's Contact List, even if you *are* online at the time.

The following table outlines some other differences and similarities between ICQ and Instant Messenger. Keep in mind that the table only covers some major options, but those listed here can get you started.

Note

You can find ICQ on the latest Platinum AOL client CD. When you install this version of AOL, an icon appears on your desktop, labeled *FREE! ICQ Click Here.* Clicking that icon enables you to install ICQ on your computer right from the disc, without having to download a single file. Otherwise, download the software from the ICQ Web site at www.icq.com.

32

Instant Messages and More Through ICQ

AIM uses unique names to identify each account; ICQ uses numbers. To chat with someone using ICQ, you have to know the number (a little bit like having to know someone's phone number in order to place a call).

When the ICQ client is running, a little flower appears in your system tray (next to the time). A green flower indicates that you are online; red indicates that you are offline. Double-clicking the flower opens the client.

ICQ has more options than AIM; navigating those options can be confusing. You may need to poke around in the menus to find what you are looking for. Don't forget to use the handy Help feature, accessed from the ICQ Main menu.

Feature	AIM	ICQ
Buddy List	Yes	Yes
Buddies Online Status	Yes	Yes
Single Chat	Yes	Yes
Group Chat	Yes	Yes
File Transfer	Yes	Yes
Plug-ins	No	Yes
Leave Offline Message	No	Yes
Random Chat	No	Yes
Chat Communities (Active List)	No	Yes

Using ICQ

Although ICQ has far more capabilities than one (short) chapter can cover, even its basic features are impressive. The following list gives you a taste of what ICQ can do for you:

▶ **Sending messages to your online friends.** Sending messages in real time (or close to it) is the biggest reason to use ICQ. After you gather the names and ICQ addresses of the people you want to trade messages with — and put them on your ICQ Contact List — sending a message is easy: Double-click the name in the Contact List, type a message in the Send Online Message dialog box when it appears (see Figure 32-1), and then click the Send button. Your message is now off to the recipient. You can use the same method to send a message to someone who is offline at the moment; your message is available to read once the person is back online.

The message box has more features than what you initially see. Clicking the More button in the lower-left corner of the Send Online Message dialog box reveals three checkboxes and a button. (See Figure 32-1.) The checkboxes enable you to send the message based on their online status, send to their e-mail address, and/or minimize this window during sending.

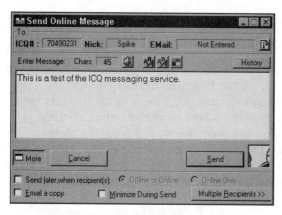

Figure 32-1. Additional hidden options for sending messages to friends.

The Multiple Recipients button in the lower-right corner of the Send Online Message dialog box enables you to send this message to more than one person at the same time. The right side of the dialog box expands to show your Contact List. You can then check the boxes of those you want the message sent to.

▶ **Participating in chats with your friends.** Because chats take place in real time, you can only talk to people who are currently online. Luckily, your Contact List keeps track of that information for you. After you have picked a potential chat partner from your Contact List, click the person's name and choose Chat from the menu that appears. A request to chat goes out to your prospective partner. When he or she clicks the Accept button, the chat session starts.

If you want to meet someone new, take advantage of the Find Random Chat button in the ICQ window to let ICQ choose a chat partner for you. Clicking that button opens the Random dialog box, where you can narrow down the search for an appropriate random-chat partner by choosing from a category list that ICQ provides. You can specify a particular age range, gender, or even a particular subject (such as games or romance). It has never been easier to meet someone.

▶ **Sending files to friends with ICQ.** Sending a file may not be an everyday occurrence, but it is a nice feature. To send a file to another ICQ member, you must be in the Advanced Mode, which makes more options

Tip

As you open various dialog boxes, messages appear that warn and inform you as needed. If you no longer want to receive these messages, check the box in the lower-left corner labeled *Don't show this message again.*

available to you. Click the To Advanced Mode button on the ICQ window. After the Simple/Advanced Mode Selection dialog box opens, click the Switch to Advanced Mode button.

Now you have all the functions available to you — including instant file transfer. To send a file to someone on your Contact List who's currently online, click the person's name and then choose File from the menu that appears. Locate and open the file(s) you want to send. (If you're sending more than one file, hold down the Ctrl key as you select the files.) Enter a little note about what you are sending; then click the Send button (as shown in Figure 32-2). Poof! The files are on their way to the recipient.

Figure 32-2. Sending files through ICQ to online friends, family, and contacts.

The recipient hears an audible "Incoming file transfer" message, sees that you are sending a file, and double-clicks your account name to accept the file(s) you just sent.

Sending messages, chatting and sending files are the bread and butter of ICQ. The rest of this chapter covers some of the secondary features of ICQ.

Settings

ICQ has a number of settings to enable you to set up the software just the way you like it. These preferences cover everything from sorting contacts to security to plug-ins. Every time a new version of the software comes out, even more improvements crop up. Given the limited space available here, I'll touch on the highlights of the settings.

Mode

The client operates in two modes — Simple and Advanced. You can easily switch between modes by using the To Advanced Mode or the To Simple Mode buttons in the ICQ window. Simple mode gives you just the basics, whereas advanced mode gives you all the features of ICQ. Which one is right for you? Let the following list help you decide:

▶ Simple mode is good for the beginner. This mode is the most basic mode, offering only a limited number of features. It gets you started using ICQ, without overloading you with options. Using simple mode, you can send messages, go to Web pages, and chat. If you want to go beyond the basics, you switch to advanced mode.

▶ Advanced mode adds the more difficult tasks — such as transferring files, using plug-ins, controlling security, and more. These advanced features are important when working with the preferences, setting your online status, or accessing available services. For instance, the general preferences are available in either mode, but the security settings are available only in advanced mode.

Preferences

When it come to preferences, ICQ enables you to change three distinct sets: application preferences, security preferences, and e-mail preferences. You will need to be in advanced mode to reach all the preferences within each set. To access Preferences, double-click the flower icon in the tray, then click the ICQ button in the lower-left corner of the open dialog box. This brings up a menu where you will find Preferences (simple) or Preferences & Security (advanced). In advanced mode, you will need to take it one more step to Preferences (here you also have access to security and e-mail preferences). Each bullet represents a tab (see Figure 32-3) on the Owner Prefs dialog box.

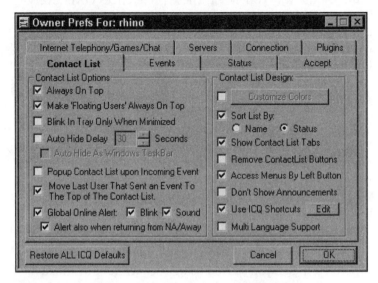

Figure 32-3. Adjust the settings in ICQ to your own preferences.

▶ **Contact List:** This tab controls your general preferences for the Contact List. You can change the way your Contact List is set up to notify you when you receive a message from someone, set the colors for the names, their sort order, and more.

▶ **Events:** The Events tab gives you access to customize four *events,* ICQ's way of referring to certain actions you can undertake with their program. The four events are ICQ Chat, Web Page Address, File Transfer, and Internet Telephony/Games/Chat. Selecting each event from the drop-down menu changes the available options to the specific event.

▶ **Status:** Imagine that while you are away from your keyboard, someone on ICQ sends you a chat request. Their Contact List tells them that you are online, but they're getting no response from you. How do you let them know that you're not being rude and ignoring them? Using the Status tab, you can have ICQ inform people that you are temporarily unavailable (or maybe just too busy to accept any chat requests). You can choose from a variety of status levels with a predefined message for each one. You can even customize these messages to suit your taste.

▶ **Accept:** The Accept tab enables you to set up the destination on your hard drive for incoming file transfers. You can set the default path that a file is sent upon receiving it. ICQ's default path may not be the most convenient to find after a file has been sent to you, so the Accept tab enables you choose your own default path.

▶ **Internet Telephony/Games/Chat:** This tab enables you to view the list of the twenty-three registered external applications supported by ICQ. This list may be updated from time to time by ICQ.

▶ **Servers:** Because each client must connect to a server, this tab shows the server(s) available for connection. You don't really have to be concerned about this tab. ICQ takes care of the settings for you.

▶ **Connection:** In order to use ICQ, you must be connected to the Internet. The settings found on this tab are the same settings you provided when you first installed ICQ. If your Internet service changes for some reason, you will need to enter the new information for your provider here.

▶ **Plug-ins:** The Plug-ins tab shows all the special add-in program features and any settings associated with them. Some of the plug-ins allow only the sound file to be changed.

Security

ICQ's security features are only available in advanced mode. To access these settings, open the ICQ panel by double-clicking the ICQ flower in the system tray on the taskbar. Then click the main menu; the ICQ button in the lower left corner. With your mouse, go to Preferences & Security, and then to Security & Privacy. From the Security Preferences dialog box (see Figure 32-4) you can use various tabs to set passwords for your account, control who can add your name to their Contact List (by first requiring your authorization), and define your control access with passwords, require authorization for your name to be added to someone else's contact

I would suggest changing the default path to C:\My Documents, which is much easier to remember.

I generally stick with the default settings in the beginning. As I use ICQ, I adjust the preferences a little at a time. If I like a change, I keep it; otherwise I set it back to default. If you get carried away and would like to reset everything back to the way it was, click the Restore All ICQ Defaults button at the bottom of the preferences dialog box.

When ICQ is running in advanced mode, right-clicking the flower opens the Services menu, which gives you access to e-mail, contacts, history, and more options that you don't find in simple mode.

list, and password-security levels. A high level of security may be important to you. If so, the ICQ maximum-security setting can require a password just to open the application.

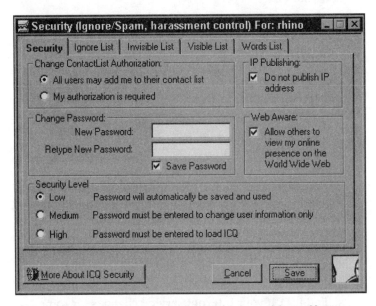

Figure 32-4. Security settings give you control of access, visibility, and language.

Given how many types of people are in the world, inevitably some have found ways to abuse a good thing. ICQ provides you with four tabs on the Security Preferences dialog box that can help shield you from such abuse.

Three of these tabs are for sorting people into (in effect) the good, the bad, and the ugly. The Visible List tab is for the good folks — the people you trust, the ones who should always be allowed to know when you are online. Enter their names and ICQ addresses here. The Invisible List tab is for the (sometimes) bad folks, the ones you don't mind contacting on your own terms but would never want to have hassle you when you're online and available. Putting them on the Invisible List means you are invisible to them at those times; they can never "see" your name listed on their Contact Lists. Finally, the Ignore List tab is for the truly ugly folks out there — the ones who start arguments online, send harassing messages, or clog your e-mail with multiple-recipient messages (better known as *spam*). Putting the ugly ones on your Ignore List means that nothing they send will ever make its way to you.

The last tab, the Words List tab, doesn't target individuals at all; it acts as a word filter. Enabling this feature filters any messages coming to you, replacing or deleting any words you have told ICQ to remove as objectionable. You are free to remove words from the ICQ list or add a few of your own.

Status

The *status* feature in simple mode only lets people know whether you are online or offline. When online, you are available to receive chat, message, and other requests. When offline, you are logged out — disconnected from the ICQ world.

Advanced mode, on the other hand, lets people in the ICQ community know in much greater detail the particulars of your online status. You can control what appears next to your name in the Contact Lists of your friends and acquaintances when you are online. The following list outlines the various status messages you can use:

Find It Online

If you have a question about a feature and would like more help, use the Help included with ICQ. Open the contact list and click the ICQ button in the lower-left corner to reveal a menu. From the menu go to Help and choose any option from the list. (The tutorials are excellent.)

Available/Connect	Connects to the server and lets people know you are available for any ICQ event, be it messaging, chatting, or file transfers.
Free for Chat	Lets all those who have your name on their lists know that you are available to chat.
Away	Lets others know that you are temporarily unavailable.
N/A (Extended Away)	Indicates that you are definitely away from your computer (and your screen saver is probably on).
Occupied (Urgent Messages)	Indicates that you are available, but only for urgent messages.
DND (Do Not Disturb)	Just as it sounds ("I'm online; but don't bother me.")
Privacy (Invisible)	You are connected, but no one can see you.
Offline/Disconnect	Disconnects you from the server, making you completely unavailable.

Add-ons

ICQ has added plug-ins to its chat client to enhance it with amazing advantages. Two plug-ins are included in the latest downloadable version. The other two can be downloaded from the ICQ Web site at www.icq.com/plugins.

▶ Voice Messaging gives you the capability to communicate verbally with others by instant message (see Figure 32-5). It packages an audio message that you record and sends it to the person you have selected. (This built-in plug-in for version 99b is listed among the Advanced Choices for the Contact List.)

Figure 32-5. Speak into the mic to record your own voice message.

The round, red button shown in Figure 32-5 starts the recording process, the square one stops it, and the triangle plays the message you just made. When you are satisfied with the message, just click the Send button to ship it off to the recipient.

▶ Another intriguing plug-in included in version 99b is Greeting Cards. Send a special thank-you to one of your contacts for talking you through a problem. Or send a little love note to that special someone.

▶ IrCQ-Net Invitation (for version 99b only) enables you to invite your ICQ friends to join you in a chat room. You can pick an established chat room or create a new one. (This plug-in must be downloaded and installed before you can use it.)

To invite one or more friends, click one person in your Contact List. From the menu that appears, select More Services (Plug-ins) and click the IrCQ-Net Invitation item. The dialog box shown in Figure 32-6 opens. To add more people to the list, click the More button at the bottom of the dialog box, click the Multiple Recipients button, and then check the boxes next to the names of the people you want to add.

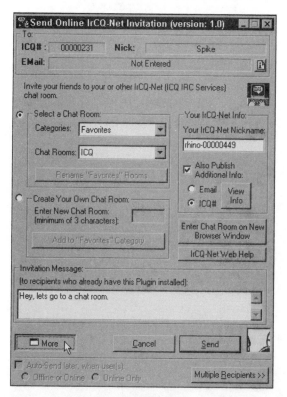

Figure 32-6. Use this dialog box to invite more people to your chat room.

▶ ICQmail Notification (for version 99a only) plug-in sends you an indicator each time a new message arrives in your free ICQ e-mail account. A special icon appears in your Contact List. (This plug-in already exists in the 99b version of ICQ, so you don't have to install it.)

Coming Up Next

Chatting by computer and sending messages back and forth does get the job done, but if you prefer talking on the phone, you can combine the two. In the next chapter, you find out about the different ways computers can handle voice communication. You might be surprised to find out how easy it is to talk to others with your computer.

Chapter 33

Move Over Phones: New Ways to Chat Over the Net

The Internet grows more and more each year. With each passing year of its short life, more people have joined in the unending stream of conversations and correspondence. Not all conversations use the phone; more take the form of e-mails, Instant Messages, and chats. This chapter covers the massive chat world, including chat basics and the tools you can use to chat. It also covers applications that allow you to talk on the Internet using your real voice for a live conversation.

What Is IRC?

In our high-tech world, "chatting" has taken on new meaning. Before, chatting was something individuals did around the kitchen table, in a corner bar, or on the front porch — casual conversation that had a feel-good feel to it. Above all, it was *verbal* conversation — live and face-to-face, with all the give and take that implies.

People still do chat around the kitchen table, but now chatting has also entered into the vocabulary of computer users. It still implies the give-and-take of conversation in real time (something e-mail really can't provide), but it is generally text-based rather than spoken conversation. Practically speaking, that means a typical computer user who's set up to chat with others must type out messages with the keyboard, send them off to appear in a recipient's on-screen chat window, and wait for the response (at best, instantaneous and friendly) to appear in a chat window on the home screen.

Chatting has long been a mainstay of the AOL community, but as big as that community is, the chatting pool for AOL members is still limited to those who have access to the AOL chatting software. Internet Relay Chat (commonly known as IRC) was designed to let you chat with (potentially) anyone on the Internet. IRC does not limit itself to one particular chatting pool, whether that be one based in the chatting features of AOL, CompuServe, ICQ or any other online service or messaging/chat program. In that sense, IRC is truly universal, for it lets you chat with people from around the globe. The Internet component of *Internet Relay Chat* traverses the world, it allows you to chat with literally anyone on the planet who has IRC up and running. Far-flung family and friends can chat with each other, even from halfway around the world.

Find It Online

You can find whatever topic you want to chat about in the AOL chat area (AOL Keyword: **Chat**). Topics cover religion, parenting, romance, hobbies, and opinions on everything. If you want to talk about it, someone else wants to talk about it too — sometimes a crowd of someones. You can be in a chat session with just a few people (where the conversation moves very slowly), or enter a session where hundreds of people try to have a conversation at the same time (good luck).

IRC Clients

AOL members don't have to bother with any additional software when they chat within the AOL community. To venture out into the world of IRC chat, however, one does need to download a separate program (known as *client software*) in order to connect to the chat service. Every IRC client offers something different, so it pays to look around for a client that has the the features that fit your desires. The following examples of IRC clients will give you an idea of the types of clients available. These clients range from the very basic, chat-only client to ones that have e-mail, voice, and collaborative features. Be aware that IRC clients only work with the same client, which means everyone you want to chat with must be using the same client you are.

AIM

If you're interested in a full-featured, easy-to-use IRC client, look no farther than America Online's own Instant Messenger, also known as AIM. (For the full-length version of the AIM story, flip back to Chapter 5; for the abridged version, read on.)

AIM is a *stand-alone* IRC client — a software program separate and distinct from your regular AOL software. To use AIM, first you download the program, either from within AOL (AOL Keyword: **Download AIM**) or from the Web (www.aol.com). Then install the downloaded program on your computer. With that behind you, you can start chatting — "instant messaging" — with thousands of other AIM users, inside and outside the AOL community. Using AIM, you can send friends and family a quick hello, a birthday photo, even sound files and text files. In addition, AIM provides a handy Mail alert window so you can keep tabs on incoming e-mail as it arrives in your AOL account (or another e-mail account). If you have a microphone connected to your computer, you can even talk with buddies over the Net, just as if you were using the telephone. For such a compact software program, AIM has lots to offer.

mIRC

mIRC (www.mirc.com) is recognized as one of the most popular of the chat clients, with literally thousands of channels to hang out in (and if none suit your fancy, you can create your own channel devoted to the topic of your choice). mIRC sets up easily, letting you start chatting in minutes. As you can see from Figure 33-1, you can keep track of conversations in the main window — and the people having them in the right column.

Find It Online

A number of IRC clients are available for download from the Internet — some for free, others for a small fee. A good source for downloading IRC clients is at www.download.com. Once there, search on **IRC** and pick a client from the list.

Cross-Reference

For more information on AIM, AOL's own IRC client, see Chapter 5.

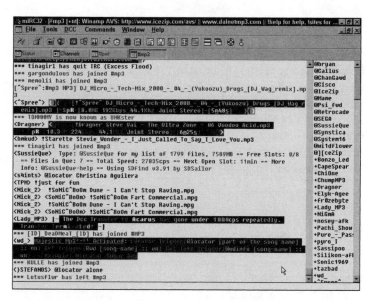

Figure 33-1. Keeping track of a conversation becomes difficult if you're chatting with several people at once; this screen, for example, shows pieces of simultaneous conversations among 28 people in the same chat room.

Pirch

The Pirch client (www.pirchat.com) lets you chat with others in thousands of communities spread across several different servers around the globe. In addition to providing a plethora of available chat rooms, Pirch also lets you send file attachments directly to another Pirch user. You can even view live Webcam broadcasts using Pirch's built-in video player. Pirch definitely broadens your chat horizons to include sending sound files (great for birthday greetings), text files, and video images.

PeerChat

Although PeerChat (www.peerchat.com) uses the Internet to set up chats (as does any IRC), it takes a different approach to Internet chatting. It has no interest in the thousands of chat communities out there on the Internet and therefore doesn't even bother to connect to a server to handle chatting. Rather, it is a separate chat client meant for *peer-to-peer* (from person

Note

Conversation can be chaotic in chat rooms with more than 20 people; it's like sitting in a crowded room with everyone talking at once.

Cross-Reference

For more on Webcam broadcasting, including descriptions of the hardware available, see Chapter 23. For more on sending sound files as attachments, see Chapter 9.

to person without connecting to a server on the Internet) use, which means you can have private, one-on-one chat sessions over a secure connection with anyone who also has PeerChat installed and running. Other than the lack of any listings of chat communities, PeerChat has all the features of other basic chat clients, including e-mail and file transfers. You can even share sketches with your chat partner (with the help of a drawing pad available as a plug-in). If your idea of chatting means private conversations with friends and family, PeerChat may be the chat client for you.

Talking on the Net

Clearly one drawback of text-based chatting clients is that you have to be pretty good at the keyboard to make the most of your chat experience. If you're a hunt-and-peck typist, you may find it hard to keep up with the rapid pace of speedier typists in many chat rooms. And what about when your hands are busy playing an online game with a buddy? Chatting gets in the way during the hot action. Speech-recognition software (described in Chapter 9) may offer a solution for some, but others still yearn for the sound of a living, breathing human voice. The PowWow chat client (more about that in a minute) has helped make voice capabilities a popular feature to look for in chat clients — indicating demand for an easy way to transmit the human voice over the Internet. Technology is always driven by demand, and the technology developed to meet the demand for "talking" through your computer is now available: Voice over IP.

Voice over IP

Voice over Internet Protocol (VoIP), a technology still in its infancy, is set to expand into areas far beyond Internet chatting. The motivation behind the move toward VoIP is purely economic — in the long run, its cheaper. Businesses traditionally have had to keep two separate and distinct communications infrastructures in place: a circuit-switched network for voice and fax communications and a data network for data communications. The promise of VoIP is that it would allow businesses to rely on just one network — the data network — for all their communication needs. That's the promise, but it will still be some time before your home phones get replaced with VoIP phones. VoIP works by simultaneously recording the conversation, dividing it into small pieces called packets, and sending it to the recipient. The recipient then gets the re-assembled message, a few fractions-of-a-second later.

VoIP voice quality is slightly lower when using the public Internet networks compared to a privately managed network. However, the quality problems caused by the delay in reassembling voice packets at the receiving end are being dealt with effectively by improved Internet access speeds though broadband services, and voice packet prioritization on the networks. This may all sound impressive, but shows the improvement yet to be made with this technology.

To use your computer to talk over the Internet, you must have a *sound-enabled* machine, meaning it must have a working sound card, speakers, and a microphone. (Optionally, you might prefer using a headset. Headsets give you a little more privacy; using one feels more like talking on the phone. A headset fits on your head, provides an earpiece speaker, and puts a microphone close to your mouth.) After you have the hardware it takes to start talking through your computer, you have to decide on a software program to use for VoIP. The following sections cover some of the more popular programs available.

Cross-Reference

To see how AIM, AOL's own IRC client, uses Voice over IP technology, see Chapter 5.

NetMeeting

Microsoft's NetMeeting, covered in Chapter 23 as part of our Webcam discussion, is the easiest way to test out VoIP. In addition to its ease of use for voice communication, it also offers the capability to use text-based chatting and share programs. Throw in a whiteboard to draw on and the ability to use a Web camera and you have a highly versatile program. To communicate with another person, one person must "host" a session, then the other person(s) connect by having their computer dial up the Internet Protocol, or IP, number of the host computer. Once the call is accepted, you can talk to your heart's content.

Roger Wilco

Hear your friends while you play online with Roger Wilco (www.rogerwilco.com). This free program works with most games allowing you to voice chat with your friends during intense multiplayer battles. You can download it for free, but you must register it for full functionality; fortunately, registration is also free.

Roger Wilco works just like a walkie-talkie on the battlefield. You have choices, such as Push-to-Talk and Voice Activated, that give you full control of your communications. You can create channels based on IP numbers — meaning that, for team games like StarSiege Tribes, each team can be on a different channel. You can also password-protect your team's channel to prevent eavesdroppers from listening in on your top-secret strategies.

Net2Phone

Imagine using your own computer to make both domestic and international phone calls through the Internet. Net2Phone does just that, allowing you to carry on a conversation over the Internet from your computer to a telephone, another personal computer, or even a fax machine. The free Net2Phone software even gives you voicemail. Portions of the service are free of charge (for example, PC-to-PC calls and voicemail); the rest charge a small fee for usage. The Net2Phone site (www.net2phone.com) advertises one cent per minute phone rates inside the U.S.

The process of making a phone call is as simple, as Figure 33-2 illustrates. A computer with a sound system initiates a phone call, using the Net2Phone software. The information then goes to Net2Phone's telephone switches, which relay the call to its destination. When the person receiving the call answers, both parties can talk to each other just as they would if it were a normal phone call.

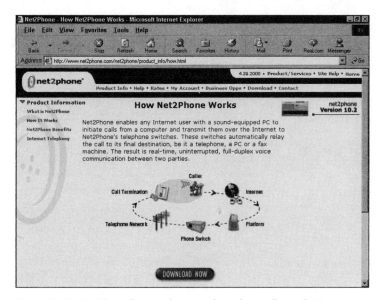

Figure 33-2. Net2Phone illustrates how to make a phone call over the Internet.

Coming Up Next

As you have been reading along in this book, you may have come across software programs of interest to you. The natural next step is downloading them. The next chapter covers some useful tools that can assist you in the downloading process, offers some facts about FTP, and more. Go to the next chapter and you can start downloading today.

Chapter 34

Downloading the Net,
One File at a Time

Ever lie awake at night, dreamily wishing you could transfer files through FTP from servers across the country, just like the pros? No? Well, even if you haven't, you still may want to check out FTP to see how it could be useful to you.

Why, you may ask? Ever since the rise in popularity of the Internet, the use of Web browsers has most people focused on looking around all those graphical Web sites, surfing from site to site, and — that's about all. Although transferring files from Web sites to your local computer is relatively easy, *sending* files to create (or update) a site doesn't even appear on the mental radar screens of most computer users. Thus an ability to work the Internet to full potential has receded just beyond the reach of most Net surfers — when actually using the services available by FTP isn't that hard; you don't have to become a techno-supergeek. This chapter introduces the potential and the power of FTP. This new power can make keeping a Web site of your own a snap as you transfer updates back and forth.

Making Life Simpler with FTP Applications

As you surf the Net, you're certain to come across files that you want to download. Unfortunately, some of those files may prove troublesome to download if you rely just on your standard Web browser to get them. For instance, downloading multiple files at once from a site can take a noticeable amount of time as you click and wait. In addition, sometimes the download fails halfway through the transfer of a large file (for example, your modem may hiccup), and you have to start all over again. The list goes on.

Encountering such inconveniences, you may find yourself thinking, *I wish someone would make downloading easier.* If so, let me make your day by introducing a couple of FTP applications that can do just that — and they're only two examples of what is available. (Come to think of it, making life easier on you when you're hanging around the Internet is what this book is all about.) Meet Go!zilla and Cute FTP.

Definition

File Transfer Protocol (FTP): The standard method for transferring files from one computer to another. This method allows a local computer to manipulate the files on a remote computer, transferring one or many, as needed. Before you can use FTP, however, the computer you want to connect to must have an FTP server program up and running.

34

Downloading the Net, One File at a Time

Go!zilla (www.gozilla.com)

Don't you hate waiting, crossing your fingers, hoping that your modem will behave and the file you're downloading will make it all the way to your computer without failing? Want a wonderful application to help you download your files? Go!zilla is just the application you need. Go!zilla runs as an FTP client for Web browsers. As you are surfing Web sites and you come across a file to download, Go!zilla will do the work for you. It looks up any alternate sites that have the same file. It will keep attempting to download the file and supports Smart Restart sites. You can even queue several files to download and have Go!zilla pull them down for you.

Getting Go!zilla is easy, and you're sure to like the price: It's free. Simply go to the Go!zilla Web site as `www.gozilla.com`, click the download button on the left, and then click the link labeled *Click here to download Go!zilla.* Then follow the simple on-screen instructions.

Definition

Smart Restart: If a download fails in the middle of a transfer, Smart Restart sites allow the transfer to continue from the point at which the download failed. The idea is to save time downloading files.

How does this wonderful program work? After you install Go!zilla, the next time you launch a Web browser and try to download a file from the Internet, Go!zilla starts, asks you when (now or later) you would like to download the file and then takes care of the rest. The following features (see Figure 34-1) make Go!zilla handy when you are downloading several files:

▶ Go!zilla queues multiple files.

▶ You can schedule when to download the file.

▶ Go!zilla keeps trying to download files from problem sites.

▶ It keeps a history of the files you've downloaded.

▶ Go!zilla shows the status of files being downloaded.

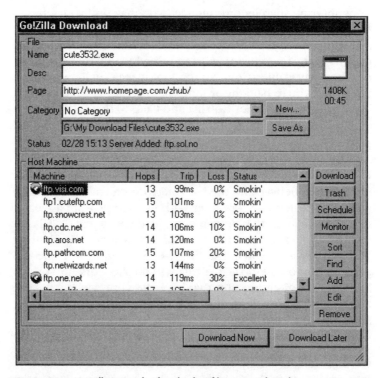

Figure 34-1. Go!zilla can make downloading files easy and painless.

Cute FTP (www.cuteftp.com)

How can I download files without the use of a Web browser? With an FTP client you can download to your heart's content.

Several FTP clients are available. Some are free for the taking; others are available for purchase for a nominal fee. The Cute FTP client, found at www.cuteftp.com, falls in the nominal fee category. You can download a functional application from their Web site to check out for yourself. When you purchase your own copy, the banner ads are removed.

If you would like a straightforward FTP client application, then look no farther. Cute FTP has an abundance of features:

▶ A full-featured Site Manager to keep track of your fa-vorite sites (see Figure 34-2).

▶ A site wizard helps you configure a site connection.

▶ You can schedule when you want your downloads to take place.

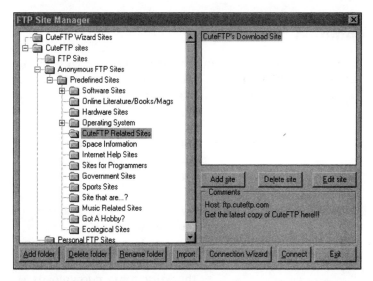

Figure 34-2. The Cute FTP program's Site Manager gives you a hand with keeping your site list organized.

Both of the above applications have helpful Web sites in the event that you have trouble with their respective programs. You can keep an eye on these Web sites for updates to their programs. Updates are not a frequent event, but the updates are worth the wait.

FTP Sites

Searching for Sites

You can make use of the Internet search engines (such as Excite or Alta Vista) to search for FTP sites. It may take some work to find some that have worthwhile applications. One method you could use would include searching on the keywords, such as **anonymous FTP**. You then have to filter through the search results to get to Web sites that might have what you are looking for. Anonymous FTP sites don't require that you have an account to access their files. Therefore, use "anonymous" as the user ID and your e-mail for the password at these sites.

Common Sites

Caution

If you thought that surfing the Web consumes hours of your time, wait until you start snooping through FTP archives looking for bits of treasure. (Hint: Don't forget to eat.)

Here are a few sites that you can view and search with a standard Web browser. Each site has interface features that can help you find what you are looking for.

www.download.com	This site is operated by C-Net.
www.shareware.com	Another C-Net site with the same information as download.com.
www.winfiles.com	This site was originally called www.windows95.com and has changed to winfiles.com to cover all Windows applications.
www.tucows.com	This site has locations around the world for fast downloads and includes files for Macs, PCs, and other systems.

Following are some additional no-frills public anonymous FTP sites. These sites are easiest to access if you use an FTP client; they contain collections of programs of all types, from calculator programs to Web tools and more.

ftp.uml.edu	University of Massachusetts
ftp.download.com	A version of download.com by C-Net

papa.indstate.edu	Indiana State University
oak.oakland.edu	Oak Archives
wuarchive.wustl.edu	Washington University Archives
ftp.cdrom.com	Walnut Creek CD-ROM Archives

The common FTP sites listed here are by no means all that exist. You can add to this list yourself by doing your own searches. Also, FTP sites aren't limited to .COMs and .EDUs — or even limited to the U.S.A. The Internet does not recognize the boundaries of countries. You might find interesting applications from around the world at some sites you end up connected with.

AOL has its own FTP area that offers downloadable shareware programs. Use AOL Keyword: **Download Center** to find the goodies you're looking for.

General Downloading Tips

This section of the chapter cuts to the chase, summarizing some resources and techniques to get you downloading with FTP in record time.

The Special Download Directory

When you're downloading several files of different types, the locations to which you saved the files can get confusing — so it makes sense to create a single directory where you can drop everything you download. Having one directory for downloads at least gives you a consistent place to find them. If you want to put graphics with graphics and .wav files with other .wav files later on, you can. After you spend some time collecting files, you may notice that you have the beginnings of your own archive.

If you prefer to have things neat and tidy, you might want to create subcategory directories to sort your new downloads into (see Figure 34-3). This will come in handy when you want to look up an application that you downloaded a month ago.

Downloaded files can fill up your hard drive in no time. Go to Chapter 36 for tips and suggestions on storing your newfound files.

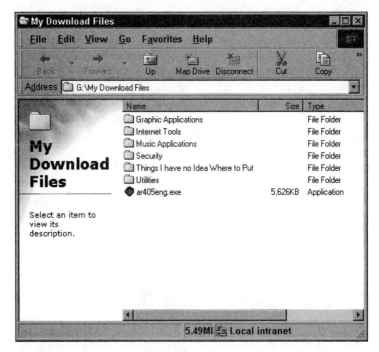

Figure 34-3. Sample of a download directory with topical subdirectories for those who like organization.

Finding the Best Files to Download

How and where do I find the best files to download? This question is common among even the most experienced Internet downloaders. Sometimes you simply have to cruise sites and snoop around until you find what you need. Many Web sites that have large archives of downloadable files also have a rating scheme to show what's hot and what's not. (Normally the FTP sites themselves take the forms of simple lists, without offering ratings.)

The rating schemes vary from site to site. Some sites rate by the number of download requests; others rate according to evaluations of the software. Even if a site has rated the files it offers, however, don't rely on someone else's ratings too heavily. In the end, you are the best judge of how useful a piece of software is to you.

Additional Tips

Here's a grab-bag of FTP hints that may come in handy:

- ▶ Most FTP applications allow you to download or up-load entire branches of directories — including all the files and folders contained in a particular folder — which can save time if you want to move a big batch of related files.

- ▶ FTP sites generally have time-outs set. If you take too long to choose files to download, you may get disconnected.

- ▶ If you have a fast Internet connection, you can open multiple sessions of your FTP program and have all of them search for that special file — which can get speedier results.

- ▶ Some FTP sites have a limited number of available con-nections. If all of them are in use when you try to reach a site, it means someone else must disconnect before you can connect.

- ▶ Many FTP applications have a feature that you can set to retry your connection several times if a particular FTP site is busy.

Coming Up Next

There you have it — the basics of transferring files using FTP. Besides outright usefulness for downloading files from anony-mous FTP sites, an FTP client is invaluable for uploading your Web-page creations to your personal Web site for the world to see. If you want to check out your new creation with a Web browser, the next chapter tells how.

AOL has a built-in FTP capa-bility. To find out more — or to use this feature — click the Internet button on the main menu; then choose FTP (File Transfer) from the menu that appears. In the AOL FTP win-dow, click one of the five visi-ble folders to learn more (or click the Go to FTP button). You also have your own FTP site available at members.aol.com.

When collecting programs found on public FTP sites, re-member to run your virus checker, like McAfee VirusScan or Norton AntiVirus, to prevent any viruses from infecting your computer. Nothing worse than a computer with a cold.

34

Downloading the Net, One File at a Time

Chapter 35

Switching Web Browsers

Surfing the World Wide Web has become a pastime for young and old alike. This phenomenon fuels not only the demand for Internet access, but also advancements in connection technology and further development of the tools we use to surf. Clearly, the Web browser we use is critical to getting the most from the Web. AOL not only provides an excellent browser of its own, but also works with other popular browsers. This chapter takes a look at some of those browsers, where you can get them, and how to install them.

Using Other Browsers with AOL

When you use AOL to connect to the Internet, more likely than not you use the browser built into the AOL software. You may not need to go beyond this browser client program for an Internet-roaming application; the software engineers at AOL have worked hard to incorporate features that anticipate your browsing needs. In fact, with the integration of AOL and Internet connect you can pass seamlessly between AOL and the Web. Just use the AOL toolbar navigation buttons as you would with any browser.

If, however, you have reason to use another browser, then you have every freedom to do so if you want to. The AOL software easily accommodates other browser applications. Simply connect to AOL as you would normally, minimize the AOL client window after you have completely connected, and then start your browser of choice.

Browser Options

If you want to take advantage of the AOL software's flexibility, many different Web browsers are possible options. Although Netscape Navigator and Internet Explorer make up the vast majority of the world's browsers, a myriad of other browsers are just waiting for your patronage.

Netscape

Netscape (www.netscape.com) is one of the founding members of the browser community; you would be hard-pressed to find a browser with an older pedigree. Although it was developed soon after the birth of the World Wide Web (in Internet terms, relatively ancient history), Netscape is in no way mired in the past. Fully aware that the requirements, complexities, and demands for browsers have grown as the Internet's popularity has grown, the folks at Netscape have kept up with changing times, continuously pushing the envelope with enhancements of browser technology.

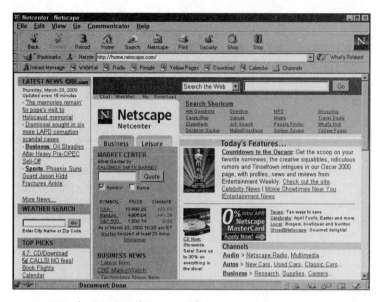

Figure 35-1. The Netscape 6 browser interface.

Figure 35-1 shows you the features available with Netscape 6 browser. With Netscape Navigator, you have Back and Forward navigation buttons to quickly return to previously viewed Web pages, a quick-launch bar that you can customize for your most frequented Web sites, easy access to your bookmarks, and much more.

Netscape Communicator is an attractive package that bundles together the Netscape Navigator browser with e-mail, newsgroup, and Web-page-creation tools. The package even includes AOL's own Instant Messenger clients — making Netscape Communicator an all-in-one application. Not bad for something that won't cost you a penny (beyond ISP charges, that is) — downloads are free.

Internet Explorer

Seeing that Netscape had beaten it to the punch with the Navigator browser, software giant Microsoft (www.microsoft.com) felt compelled to come up with its own free Web browser — and fast. Their answer to Netscape Navigator — Internet Explorer (known simply as IE) — quickly became the Netscape browser's leading competition.

Definition

The term *newsgroups* refers to the online news-listing service offered by Internet service providers. Currently there are more than twenty thousand news topics ranging from hobbies to computers to movies. Most of the time these groups are used as discussion forums to share information, opinions, and advice.

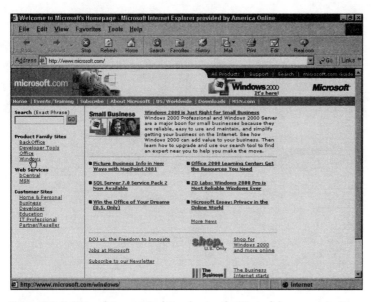

Figure 35-2. Microsoft Internet Explorer, showing the Microsoft home page in the browser window.

IE, as seen in Figure 35-2, has all the standard features to be found in browsers today, including large control buttons and customizable toolbars. Microsoft now bundles IE with its Windows operating system, along with the Outlook Express program for handling e-mail and newsgroups. Both programs are available to download for free at the Microsoft Web site.

Other Browsers

In addition to the two most popular Internet browsers, Netscape Navigator and Internet Explorer, you can choose any of several shareware and freeware browsers. One such shareware browser is Opera (www.opera.com), which includes all the features found in the Big Browsers (navigation buttons, e-mail, and newsgroup capabilities), but prides itself on being small, fast, and customizable. Figure 35-3 gives you an idea of Opera's appearance. To try it out, go to Opera's Web site and locate the Try It - Buy It area to find the download locations. After you have it downloaded, install the program to give it a test run; if you decide you like it, just send the company $35.

Note

Microsoft Internet Explorer is *cobranded* with AOL, which means Microsoft allows AOL to change the browser's logo (in the upper-right corner) and title bar to reflect AOL. This in no way changes the funtion of the browser, only its on-screen appearance.

35

Switching Web Browsers

Definition

Shareware: Software that you can download, install, and try out for a limited time period before you buy it at a nominal fee.

Definition

Freeware: Software that you can download for free and install for free. Nobody expects you to pay a thing for a freeware download, ever. Often, however, these programs come with little or no technical support.

Definition

Open-source: Software created when a community of programmers not only work collectively on a piece of software and distribute it for free, but also make the *source code* (the raw computer code that makes the software work) available to other programmers to develop, subject to certain licensing restrictions.

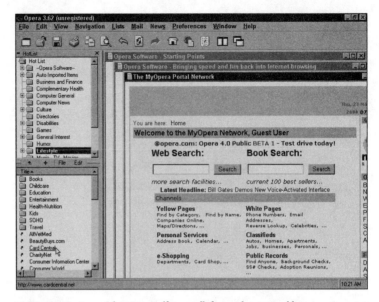

Figure 35-3. Opera advertises itself as small, fast and customizable.

Mozilla falls in the category of *open-source* software (see the Definition), and is therefore freely available. Mozilla was originally modeled after Netscape because Netscape released their software code to the programming public. The overall appearance of Mozilla now differs significantly from its original model, and now has returned the favor to Netscape 6.0 (which is modeled on the Mozilla browser interface). Innovative features, such as a My Sidebar for quick access to anything from searches to bookmarks, add to the appeal of this program. Note, however, that the makeup of just about any open-source program is always changing; Mozilla is not set in stone. Programmers are always adding new bits and pieces to the program, so updates take place often.

Where to Download

Here's a summary of where you can download the browsers mentioned in this chapter:

Netscape   www.netscape.com

Internet Explorer   www.microsoft.com/windows/ie

Opera	www.opera.com
Mozilla	www.mozilla.com

If none of the browsers listed here coincides fully with your idea of what makes a perfect browser, don't give up hope. Many programmers have created browsers for their own enjoyment, to meet a challenge, or to satisfy a need for something different; one of those browsers may be just what you're looking for. You can keep up with new developments in the browser field by visiting CNET Download.com (www.download.com) and searching for browsers.

You can find more shareware browsers at www.download.com. Search for Internet Browsers and you will find leads to several.

Installation and Use

If you've seen one browser download and installation, you've probably seen them all. The following sections show how a download and installation works for Netscape Navigator. Downloads and installations for any other browser will likely follow the same pattern.

Netscape Installation

Not only is Netscape 6 free of charge, it's also fairly straightforward to install, as the following steps show:

You can have multiple browsers loaded on your computer at the same time. You can even have them all running simultaneously, too.

1. Load your current browser and access the download page for Netscape 6 at www.netscape.com/download.

2. Choose the operating system for your computer (Windows 95/98/NT or Mac PowerPC) and the desired language (English, Japanese, French or German).

   A small program downloads to your computer. Be sure to note what folder its file was saved to for the next step.

3. Locate the file you just downloaded by using My Computer on your desktop.

   Make sure you're connected to the Internet before you do the next step.

4. After you find the downloaded file, execute (run) it by double-clicking it.

5. The Netscape 6 Setup program begins with a welcome window. Click the Next button to continue.

6. The next window is the Software License Agreement. You are asked to read the agreement and respond by clicking a button. Clicking the No button cancels the setup program; clicking Accept continues the setup process.

7. You have four installation options, as shown in Figure 35-4:

> **Typical** (8 MB) installs all the preset application components that are added to the Netscape browser (such as Netscape Instant Messenger, Net2Phone, and Shockwave Flash), minus Java.

> **Complete** (16 MB) includes all the Typical choices, plus Java.

> **Custom** (varies from 5 MB to 16 MB) gives you your choice of which components you want installed.

> **Netscape** (5 MB) installs only the browser.

You can also choose where to put the files. Click the Next button to proceed.

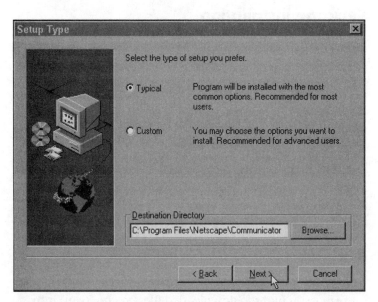

Figure 35-4. This Netscape setup shows Typical as the selected choice.

8. The Program Folder dialog box gives you the option of how to identify the program from the Start menu. Click the Next button to use the default name.

9. The final dialog box confirms what you will be installing. Look it over, and then click the Install button if everything looks fine.

   The setup program starts to download the needed files for the option you chose. Depending on your Internet connection speed and the option you select, this process could take some time. When all the files have been downloaded, the setup program continues installing the Netscape program where it belongs. When that process is finished, all you have to do is use Netscape as your browser.

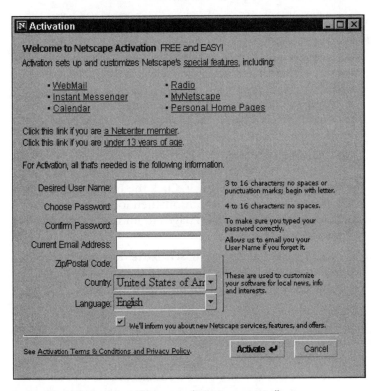

Figure 35-5. Netscape 6 sets browser preferences automatically.

35

Switching Web Browsers

When you use another browser with the AOL client, its browsing function is all you can use with AOL. If your browser comes with e-mail and news clients, they are usable only with Internet service providers (ISPs) outside AOL.

Internet Explorer downloads in two stages: the ie5setup.exe file, and then the installation files themselves.

10. When the Setup program finishes, an Activation dialog box appears (as in Figure 35-5) to help you set up and customize Netscape features such as WebMail, Calendar, and Instant Messenger (or you can cancel and go right to the browser).

Netscape 6 includes a Profile Manager feature you can use to set up multiple people to use the same machine. Adding a new person is as easy as opening the Profile Manager, adding a new name, and then double clicking the new name to activate it.

There you have it. With installation, setup, and configuration completed you are now set to surf the net with Netscape.

Internet Explorer Installation

Microsoft has made Internet Explorer easy to get and install; follow these steps:

1. Load your current browser and access the download page for Internet Explorer at www.microsoft.com/windows/ie.

2. Click the Download Now button on the Web page to open the Internet Explorer Products Download page.

3. Locate the version of Windows that you have on your computer. The Windows version, listed in red, shows a list of applications below it. Click the Internet Explorer 5.01 and Internet Tools button; then follow the instructions on subsequent Web pages to initiate the download to your computer.

4. After a small file named *ie5setup.exe* downloads to your computer, locate the file and then double-click it to begin the installation of Internet Explorer.

5. After the ie5setup.exe program begins, you see the License Agreement dialog box. Click the radio button next to *I accept the agreement* and then click the Next button to continue.

6. The next dialog box lets you choose the type of installation you want. As Figure 35-6 shows, you have two choices: You can install now or download the files for future installation. Either way, you still have to download the rest of the files for the installation, which will take some time. Choose Install Now and click the Next button.

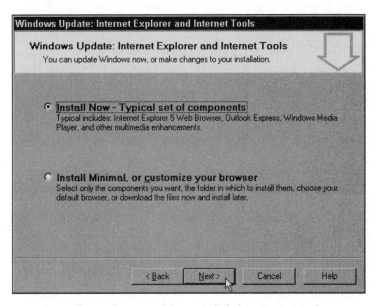

Figure 35-6. Choosing between installation methods during Internet Explorer's setup.

A window appears, showing the status of the installation process. When the download is complete and all the files are installed, a dialog box appears, indicating that the installation is finished and you should restart your computer to establish the new program.

7. Click the Finished button and restart.

After you have restarted the computer, Internet Explorer customizes your preferences for you. If you currently use another browser as your default, IE lets you know and asks whether you want to set the default to IE. You can make that choice yourself.

Note

If you choose to install and use Mozilla, it comes as a zip file; no separate installation procedure is necessary. You simply extract the files from the zip into a directory and then double-click the mozilla.exe file to run the browser.

Coming Up Next

In your virtual travels browsing the World Wide Web, you are sure to come across files, pictures, and such that you want to keep. The longer you surf, the more stuff you collect. Eventually you have to consider whether to delete the much-loved collection, save it to floppy disks, or add hard-drive space. The next chapter describes the hardware options available to you, and shows where to look for more information.

PART

XI

WE CAN REBUILD IT!
MAKING YOUR PC NEWER,
FASTER, AND BETTER

Chapter 36

Downloading the Net Takes Lots of Space

As computers get more capable, software gets more complex and files get bigger — which means system storage has always been a concern. This chapter covers the basics of data storage, checks out the equipment available, and offers pointers on how to find the information you need — all of which should help you make informed decisions about your storage needs. Technologies change quickly in the computer field, so it makes sense that data-storage technologies change with equal rapidity. This chapter helps you keep pace with this changing world.

Adding Space on Your System

Back in the days when you could fit more than one software program on a 1.44MB floppy disk, hard drive space was not an issue (at least it didn't seem like much of one). A 40MB hard drive could fit tons of applications with room to spare. Today, however, drive space is a concern. Software continues to get larger, taking up more space on the hard drive. Now, with access to the Internet, you have even more opportunity to fill the space you have left with more programs, updates, music, and images.

Just to let you know how quickly your hard drive can fill up these days, consider this: An average MP3 song takes up 5MB of space on your hard drive. A CD worth of songs (10 to 15) can take between 30MB and 50MB of space (more than the total capacity of some hard drives in use ten years ago). If you saved that single 5MB MP3 song as a .WAV file, suddenly it would take up — all by itself — 50MB of precious space. If you use a scanner to create digital images, a single 8.5 x 11 photo can take up to 30MB, depending on the quality of the scanning. In addition to housing the existing programs, additional downloaded content, and valuable data files, your hard drive has to allow Windows *some* free disk space to use for itself.

Removing unused programs, data, and files might not be an option for you. Removing files randomly might cause you to delete something you should have kept. Not a good idea. A much better option involves fixes that let you keep your digital data while still making space so you can add more data as time goes on.

Checking Out Your Hard Drive

Hard drives contain the program data for your computer. When you open the My Computer icon on your desktop, you see a listing of drives. The C: drive is the primary storage device for your system. Having enough space for all your programs and data files helps to ensure that your system works smoothly. Performance can vary, depending on your drive's current size, available space, and used space. The more you edge up into the upper limits of your storage capacity, the less efficiently your system runs.

To check the available space on your hard drive, double-click the My Computer icon on your desktop to access a listing of available drives; then right-click the drive you want to check.

Caution

Never randomly delete files from your computer — especially if you're not sure what they're for. Windows and other programs use many of the files on your computer; some of those look pretty obscure. If you happen to delete a needed file, your programs may not function properly.

Find It Online

You can find products for all the categories listed in the chapter in the AOL Store. Use AOL Keyword: **AOL Store** and go to Hardware, then Storage and Drives.

36

Downloading the Net
Takes Lots of Space

The Drive Properties dialog box appears (as shown in Figure 36-1), showing you all the information you need to know about your drive — used space, free space, total capacity, and some details of your drive's specifications. You can even see a graphical pie chart that illustrates how much usable space you still have on your drive.

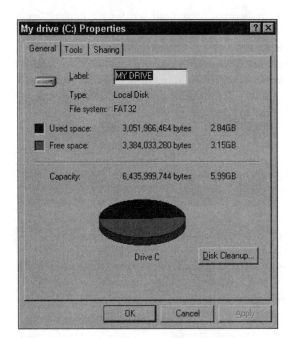

Figure 36-1. Drive Properties — all the details you're likely to need.

If the Drive Properties dialog box informs you that your present hard drive is working at near capacity, it's time to consider adding some space. You may want to install a second hard drive (or upgrade to one with more storage space) to keep pace with your storage needs.

Digesting the Alphabet Soup of Hard Drives

When you shop for hard drives, you may find yourself adrift in a vat of alphabet-soup abbreviations. The following guide to the arcane abbreviations of hard-drive terminology may come in handy on your quest for more disk storage space:

Note

After installation, your system names any additional hard drive by using the next available drive letter — which may also change the letter associated with your CD-ROM drive. The effects of this change may vary, but some programs assume that the CD drive letter *never* changes — and they may complain (or lose track of the CD drive altogether) after the drive letters change. Then you have to identify the new CD drive letter manually when asked by the computer.

Tip

Deleting files in Windows (95, 98, and later) sends the trashed files to the Recycle Bin. Right-clicking the Recycle Bin on the desktop gives you the option to empty it immediately, which frees up the space used by those files.

IDE   Most of the hard drives on the market today use an older technology known as *Integrated Drive Electronics* (IDE); the electronics needed to run the drive are integrated into the drive itself. One disk controller can handle no more than two disk drives (master and slave). The controller acts as the middleman between the disk and the computer, handling the transfer of data. You usually find two controllers in most computers, allowing a total of four IDE devices. Newer IDE hard drives are generally less expensive, can hold huge volumes of data, and are usable in nearly every personal computer made.

SCSI   A *Small Computer System Interface* (SCSI) links up to six (on newer controllers, fourteen) drives or devices to one controller. The controller handles the transfer of the data between the drive and the computer.

ATA   *Advanced Technology Attachment* (ATA), another term for IDE.

UDMA   *Ultra Direct Memory Access* (also known as Ultra ATA or Ultra ATA/33) sets the next standard in drive speeds: up to 33.3 Mbps. The even speedier ATA/66 drive processes data at 66.6 Mbps. Faster drive speeds means better access.

Installing and Configuring a New Hard Drive

Installing or replacing the hard drive in your computer *may not* be a task for everyone to attempt. If you have worked on your own computer before, have read (and understand) the drive-installation intructions, and you're williling to try the procedure yourself, then installing a new hard drive may be a valuable and money-saving experience for you to try. Otherwise have a professional install the drive for you. Installation should only take less than an hour if you choose to do it yourself. The basic steps for adding a drive consist of opening the computer case, finding an open bay where the other drives are installed, configuring the drive as *master* (first drive of two) or *slave* (second drive of two), physically installing the drive in the open bay, and connecting the cables.

Note

Computer hard drives using older versions of Windows 95 uses partitions no bigger than 2GB at a time. All versions of Windows use the fdisk program to divide drives larger than 2GB in a way that uses all the available space. (Windows 98, NT, and 2000 can use all of it at once.)

Find It Online

As you search for computer parts and come across a word you would like more information on, look it up in Webopaedia at www.pcwebopaedia.com.

Find It Online

Western Digital (www.wdc.com), Maxtor (www.maxtor.com), Seagate (www.seagate.com), and others produce quality hard drives in a variety of sizes. Each of their Web sites shows their products, provides online technical help, and (in some cases) marketing promotions for dealers.

Caution

Working on your own computer exposes you and your computer to possible electrical shock — which can be as damaging to a computer as it is dangerous to the person working on the computer. Follow the instructions that accompany any new device you plan to install in your computer. If you are unsure of how to do the installation safely, err on the safe side; take the computer to a professional to have the components installed.

When you have a hard drive and have it physically installed, you have to set it up for Windows to use. Every drive out of the box needs to be set up for the operating system. Think of it like a blank piece of paper. First it needs to be partitioned which is determining how much of the paper we are going to use. Then it must be formatted, which would be similar to drawing lines on the paper as the guide for when we write the data. (If you had a professional install the drive, this should have been done by them.) The following instructions assume that you have just installed a second hard drive and that you are using Windows 98.

1. Select Start⇨Run from your Windows taskbar.

   This command brings up the Run dialog box for launching applications manually.

2. Type **fdisk** in the Run dialog box, replacing any words that might have been there previously.

   This command opens a window with the DOS fdisk program running inside. (Click the top of the window to make sure it is the active window.)

3. The fdisk program asks whether you want to enable large disk support. Press Y for Yes; then press Enter.

   The five menu options for the Start menu of the fdisk program appear.

4. Press the **5** key for option number 5 which reads "Change current fixed disk drive" and then press Enter to choose the drive you want to set up.

   The screen displays all the hard drives on your computer, each showing the drive letters assigned to it.

5. Press the number **2**, for drive two, which should not have any letters assigned to it. (This is the drive you just installed.)

6. Press Enter to let the fdisk program know that this is the drive on which you want to make the changes.

   The Start window for the fdisk program reappears.

7. Choose the number **1** and press Enter to begin the configuration process.

   The fdisk program checks the drive and asks whether you want to use the maximum available size for the partition.

8. Press Y to indicate Yes (you do want the maximum available size for the partition); press Enter to proceed.

   The program then creates the partition, letting you know when it's finished.

9. Press Esc three times to exit the program. (If you use an antivirus program, you may get a warning that something is trying to write to the Master Boot Record, or MBR. In this case, change the MBR so your computer can recognize the new drive. Specify that you want to continue.)

10. Reboot the computer to complete the change.

11. If necessary, format the new hard drive for use by opening My Computer, right-clicking the newly created drive letter, selecting Format from the menu, and clicking Start.

If your computer has room for only one hard drive (or you don't feel comfortable adding something inside your computer), try one of the other options for increasing your storage capacity. This chapter introduces you to some storage devices that may fill the bill.

Note

The MBR is crucial to the operation of your computer; some virus programs are designed to attack it specifically. If you are running an antivirus program to help protect the MBR, it may mistake your changes for an attack. You may want to temporarily disable your antivirus program before you make a change in the Master Boot Record.

CD-R

Almost everyone who listens to music these days listens to a Compact Disc (CD), but CDs are not limited to the music world anymore. They have also become mainstays of the computer world. Older technology made writing to a CD-ROM drive a pricey option for the home computer user, but recent advances have made so-called *CD-R drives* (CD-ROM drives that allow you to save data to them) more affordable for computer applications. Currently recordable CD drives are available for under $200.

A CD-R disc can hold 650MB of information, becoming a permanent copy. (Sorry, this medium does not allow re-recording over the same space on the disc.) You can use the CD-R drive to store anything you'd usually store on a regular hard drive. Because the CD technology mirrors the technology found in your home stereo system's CD player, any audio files you move from your computer to a CD in your CD-R drive can be played on your home stereo. (A great option if your computer speakers can't compare with those in your stereo system.)

CD-RW

In addition to creating read-only CDs, a newer type of CD has been developed that allows you to copy over data previously saved to the CD. Such a reusable CD requires a special CD-ROM drive know as a *CD-RW drive.*(CD-RW drives usually aren't choosy about the kinds of CDs you put in them. You can use either the once-only or the reusable variety.) Most current drives that allow you to record to CDs are CD-RWs. The reusable CDs can be found for around $10; the once-only kind usually cost around $1 per disc. Although reusable CDs can't hold any more information than the once-only kind (about 650MB of data), they do allow up to 1000 erasures and rewrites.

Because you can reuse this medium, you can save your work, graphic artwork, and even keep your projects together on a single disc, knowing that your updates can write over the existing files on the disc.

DVD-R

Although you mainly hear about Digital Video Disc (DVD) technology as a high-capacity storage option for movies, DVD has also begun to find its way into the consumer computer market. DVD-RAM drives vary in price from around $250 to $600, but as the technology develops, you are sure to see prices dropping. The DVD discs themselves presently go for around $25 for 2.6GB and $50 for 5.2GB.

DVD discs can handle 100,000 read/write cycles (that's a lot of erasing!) and come in two types. A 5.2GB disc uses both sides of the disc (2.6GB for each side) and comes sealed in its own cartridge. The 2.6GB disc uses only one side of the disc, but it does have one advantage over the larger-capacity discs: You can remove a 2.6GB disc from its cartridge and use it in some DVD video players.

DVD offers a great deal of storage capacity, probably more than the average user needs. But if you work regularly with very large files (digitized home movies, high-resolution photos or other digitized artwork) a DVD drive may be for you. DVD drives are especially popular in the graphics industry, precisely because of their ability to handle the storage of large files with ease.

Creative Labs (www. americas.creative. com/mmuk/cdrw-8432) makes the CD-RW Blaster 8432, a complete kit for turning out CDs on your computer. Creative Labs also offers a number of other multimedia products.

To get more information on DVD-RAM for your home computer system, check out HiVal on the Web at hival.com/products/ hdvdr-00r1.7.htm. Creative Labs, at www.creative.com/ destinations/pcdvd, specializes in 5.2GB drive kits.

Zip Drives

DVDs are not the only storage option that uses cartridges. The Iomega Zip drive also takes advantage of the higher storage capacity cartridges can offer. When Iomega first introduced the Zip drive, the cartridges used for storage had a capacity of 100MB; newer cartridges can now hold 250MB.

The Zip drive comes in external or internal versions that are compatible with a variety of connections (USB, parallel port, and SCSI). The parallel version of the Zip drive, shown in Figure 36-2, works on the same port as your printer. This drive is an excellent way to store, move, or save a few files to a location off the computer.

Figure 36-2. You can purchase your parts directly through AOL Shops. Check out the offer on this Zip drive.

Jaz

Jaz drives (also developed by Iomega) function like removable hard drives. Jaz-drive cartridges hold either 1GB or 2GB (more than enough storage for most situations). The Jaz drive only comes with a SCSI connection. Using SCSI gives you near-hard drive speeds with the flexibility of changing cartridges within seconds. Jaz drives allow you to access files, programs or video directly from the drive, in effect giving you the luxury of an extra hard disk without the bother of installing an actual new hard drive.

Clik!

If you need a little extra space for your laptop, you can turn to the Clik! disk. These little disks hold 40MB of data, but the drive is the size of a PCMCIA card. In fact, this PCMCIA card fits in a Type II card slot, which makes it convenient for travelers to use in laptops, handheld devices, or even some digital cameras. These are the same Type-II card slots that accommodate PCMCIA modems, Ethernet cards and such. Simply insert the drive into the slot, follow the provided driver installation instructions, and you have more space. It's that easy.

Be careful with these disks; they are very thin and potentially fragile. Use the carrying case that comes with the drive to store your extra disks (don't just stick 'em in your pocket). Inserting the disks into the drive is just as easy. Make sure the disk is oriented properly, per the instructions, then push it in gently until you hear it go *clik!*

SuperDisk

The SuperDisk drive is produced by a number of different firms, including Imation and Mitsubishi. The SuperDisk drive comes in both internal and external versions; both can handle the specially designed 120MB SuperDisk diskettes as well as your standard 1.44MB 3.5-inch floppies. Many PC manufacturers, including Gateway and Compaq, have slowly started to replace their traditional 3.5-inch floppy-disk drives with SuperDisk drives in order to give customers the storage flexibility that comes with increased capacity. The internal version looks much like a standard disk drive; the external version utilizes a parallel port, SCSI or USB connector to link up with your computer.

Other Media

Desktop computers are not the only electronic equipment with data-storage needs. Digital cameras, handheld devices such as PalmPilots, and laptop computers may also need some form of removable storage. Memory cards such as the CompactFlash and MultiMediaCard (both made by SanDisk Corporation, www.sandisk.com/cons) have storage capacities ranging from 4MB to 192MB. That's a lot of storage for a digital camera.

Find It Online

Iomega produces Zip, Jaz, and Clik! Drives. You can find out more about the Iomega line of drives at their web site at www.iomega.com. You can also purchase some of these drives in the AOL Store (AOL Keyword: **AOL Store**) under Hardware — Storage and Drives.

Find It Online

Imation, the trademark holder of SuperDisk, touts its own products (and offers roundups of industry news concerning SuperDisk) at www.superdisk.com. Mitsubishi offers an overview of its own products at www.superdiskdrive.com.

Another device, called FlashDrive (also developed by the SanDisk Corporation), can replace a small hard drive. The memory capacity of this device can reach 440MB for around $1100. With no moving parts, FlashDrive might be an excellent candidate for a laptop that experiences high levels of physical stress, vibration, or shock.

Coming Up Next

After you've increased the available storage space for your computer system, what about protecting the data that changes? Data, such as the letters to Aunt Jane, the Civil War report for school, or the latest copy of tax records, must be backed up. The next chapter shows you different ways to protect your valuable data from corruption, accidental loss, natural catastrophes, or human-made calamities.

Chapter 37

Protecting Your Dearly Downloaded Data

Have you ever lost information from your computer by accidentally overwriting it, having a hard drive fail beyond repair, or watching the fireworks as a lightning strike damaged your system? If you have, then you understand the frustration of losing data. Data lost means time lost, and time (especially for a small business) is money. This chapter will help you prevent that frustration by showing you how to protect your files — a step toward ensuring that the time you spent creating those files will remain time well spent.

Something About Backups

As you work along, you may be so focused on the task at hand that a particularly sobering thought never occurs to you: You may, in an instant, lose your entire collection of files, pictures, and general data, and have to start accumulating them all over again. These losses can occur in several ways — through equipment failure (nothing lasts forever), accidental deletion or overwriting (accidents do happen), catastrophic acts of God (an insurance-industry term for earthquakes, tornadoes, or floods) or fire (including smoke damage from a fire). These *accidents* can cost an unprepared company more than it can afford (in time, money, and lost effort) to replace just the data that was lost. As an individual, you may not incur the same huge replacement costs, but the time lost can be just as frustrating. Fortunately, you can protect yourself against the worst effects of this loss by the most traditional of approaches to saving data — doing regular backups.

The homey-sounding term *backup* refers to a procedure that creates a duplicate copy of vital data — and then stores the copy elsewhere for safekeeping. The backup can use various media — including tape drives (discussed later in this chapter), floppies, CDs, additional hard drives (see Chapter 36), and even remote computers. Later in this chapter, you get an introductory tour of the devices and software used to do a successful backup.

Tape Drives and Media

What should the files be backed up on? Most big-time system administrators prefer tape. Administrators generally deal with big operations, and therefore choose the most reliable, cost-effective media to hold the great quantities of data they have to deal with. For their particular situation (which is definitely quite different from that of the private computer owner), using backup tapes (in conjunction with a backup drive designed to record data to the tapes) makes the most sense.

Tapes come in a variety of styles and forms. Although similar to the familiar medium associated with VHS, camcorders and audio cassettes, backup tapes are specially designed to hold computer data reliably. Popular types are listed in the table included here. Choosing a type of tape does not lock you into buying products from only one maker; various manufacturers (such as Hewlett-Packard, Sony, and others) make a range of tapes and drives.

Type	Capacity Range	Average Cost per Tape	Average Drive Cost
Travan-4	4GB-8GB	$35	$250
ADR50	25GB-50GB	$50	$650
DDS-2	4GB-8GB	$15	$700
DDS-3	12GB-24GB	$25	$1000
DDS-4	20GB-40GB	$40	$1000
AIT-2	50GB	$126	$4000
DLT-III	15GB-30GB	$40	$1500

Choosing a tape format (and accompanying drive) according to capacity quickly narrows the search. Choose a tape capacity that can accommodate the amount of data you intend to back up. If you have a 20GB hard drive, but only 5GB of data, then an 8GB tape is sufficient. However, if you expect to fill up the entire 20GB of space on your hard drive, you can still use the same tape capacity — but expect to change tapes several times during the process; the backup software continues the operation across as many tapes as needed to get the job done.

Another consideration is backup *speed*. For instance, a Seagate (www.seagate.com) internal ATA Travan drive has an average transfer rate of 600Kbps; by comparison, a product from OnStream (www.onstream.com) — the Internal SCSI-3 ADR50 drive — has a rate of 4Mbps, Translation: The ADR50 drive is over six times faster than the Travan drive.

The tape drive itself has an effect on backup strategy. Normally a data tape works only in a drive designed specifically for that tape. A particular tape won't work in just any drive (and vice versa), just as an audio cassette won't work in a VCR. Drives and the media they use are part of the same system, and should be considered that way.

Tip

Test the backup by trying to restore a file: After a successful backup, make a small change to an expendable copy of an existing file (for example, delete one word from the title of a document). Then restore the original file from the backup copy. The modified file should revert to its original condition, indicating a successful backup-and-restore operation.

A number of manufactures produce quality tape drives that match any available tapes. The Travan-4 (TR-4) tape drive, also known as QIC, is the most popular and economical. Hewlett-Packard, Seagate, and Compaq offer Travan tape drives. Hewlett-Packard has the widest selection of drive types, including models designed for home and business (see Figure 37-1).

Tip

After completely backing up your system to tape, remove the tape and take it to another site for safekeeping. Doing so can help prevent the loss of both tape and computer from the same catastrophe.

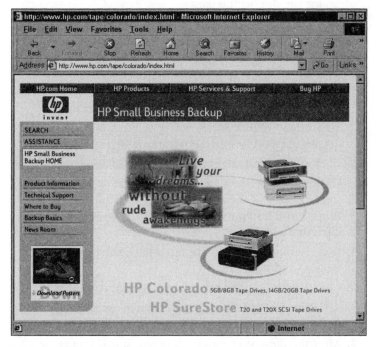

Figure 37-1. Hewlett-Packard offers all types of tape drives. Travan is the most economical.

Tip

If you don't have much data to lose (or do not want the expense), all you need do for an effective backup is to save a copy of your data to some other source. Diskettes are a good medium for storing backup files for small projects, as are the drives mentioned in Chapter 36. For somewhat larger projects, Zip drives are an excellent alternative. Zip drives have storage sizes of 100 MB and 250 MB, which means you can hold larger size and amounts of files than conventional diskettes.

To back up your data to a tape drive, you must have the software to perform the operation. Such software is designed to access the drive, compress the data, and manage the backup session while it's in progress. Each time you back up to a tape, the software records the event as a session, marking it with the time and date. This way you can have more than one backup on one tape, as well as an indication of which is most recent. The software usually has a built-in feature to allow automated backups, freeing your time for other activities.

Cross-Reference

Computers on a network can share drives, which means you can easily back up your data from one computer to another computer on the network. Chapters 11, 12, and 13 talk about setting up a network and show how to share drives.

Backup/Recovery Software

Some software can back up your data by using other drives. The built-in Backup feature of Microsoft Windows, for example uses either a tape drive or an alternate disk drive as a destination for the duplicated data.

You can normally access the Backup program in Windows by choosing Start⇨Programs⇨Accessories⇨System Tools⇨ Backup. If Backup is not installed on your computer, the following steps can remedy that situation:

1. Open the Control Panel by clicking Start and then choosing Settings⇨Control Panel.
2. Locate the Add/Remove Programs icon and click it.
3. Click the second tab at the top of the dialog box (Windows Setup).
4. In the center of the dialog box, you see a list of applications. Scroll down the list to System Tools and double-click that option.
5. When a new dialog box opens, check the box next to Backup and click OK.
6. Click the OK button twice more to load the software.

   After the software loads, shut down all open programs and reboot your computer.
7. After the computer reboots, choose Start⇨Programs⇨ Accessories⇨System Tools⇨Backup to launch the software.

Norton SystemWorks 2000

 **Find It Online**

To purchase SystemWorks 2000 online, go to the AOL Shop (AOL Keyword: **AOL Shop**), click the Software tab, and then click the Utilities link. This reasonably priced product can save you time and frustration.

Though it's not quite backup software, Norton SystemWorks 2000 (www.norton.com) does offer several valuable data-recovery features. Although this package of utilities does not replace a good backup, it can complement one; it helps stave off the need for recovering files. Using SystemWorks 2000, you can also back up specific programs. Key functions of the package are indicative of what it can do for you:

▶ Clean Sweep maintains the files on the computer. Normally, when a program uninstalls, several remnant files remain. Clean Sweep keeps track of the files as they are installed and safely removes them when they are no longer needed. It also backs up data (see Figure 37-2), does archiving procedures, and moves specific programs.

▶ Crash Guard is meant to protect the computer from the system crashes and screen freezes that can doom unsaved work in an open application that suddenly refuses to follow commands. Although designed to help you regain control of the system and save work that would otherwise be lost, this program has prompted some reviewers to remark that it causes more problems than it fixes. (If your computer suddenly becomes unstable, try removing this program to see whether it becomes more stable again.)

▶ Utilities detect problems with hardware and software, repair them, optimize the system for better performance, and can recover deleted files. The Utilities are worth every penny spent on this product.

▶ AntiVirus watches for viruses as files are opened, moved, or copied — and cleans infected files before other files become corrupted.

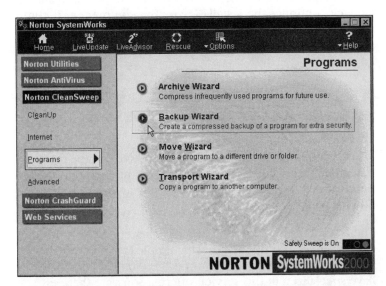

Figure 37-2. SystemWorks 2000 offers the option to back up specific programs.

Note

GoBack is currently available for Windows 95 and Windows 98 only. The WildFile Company, which manufactures GoBack, expects to have Windows NT and Windows 2000 versions released by mid-2000.

GoBack

Have you ever wished you could go back in time? Well, now you can — in a way. Using the amazing GoBack software from WildFile (www.goback.com), you can revisit earlier versions of the data on your hard drive — the next best thing to going back in time. GoBack protects you against unwanted recent changes made to your files by periodically taking "snapshots" of your hard drive. These "snapshots" reflect the state and condition of the files on your computer. Some of the benefits of this approach are immediately useful:

▶ Immediate recovery from system crashes, virus attacks, failed software installations, and file loss.

▶ Protection of your data as you work.

▶ A way to fix some of your own PC problems in seconds.

▶ Automatic repair — if the problem is one the software can handle, you don't need to know what went wrong to get your PC operating again.

Installation of GoBack takes place in two phases: The first phase takes place right away after you launch the setup program. Follow the instructions as prompted by the setup routine; be sure to restart when asked. After your system restarts, GoBack continues the installation on the computer as it completes the process. When you're up and running, you may forget you have this protection until you need it.

Internet-Based Backup Systems

What if you have no tape drives, tape archive, or tape-rotation schedule? You still need some sort of backup method. One option that may work for you involves using an Internet destination for your backups.

The Internet is based on the idea of connecting one computer to computers in other places. This simple fact is enough to make Internet-based backups appealing. Some companies have specialized in this service, offering software that performs a secure transfer of your valuable data to a specified storage area. One such company, eVault (www.evault.com) even gives you a 30-day trial. Just fill out a form, download and install the software from the eVault site, and start backing up files to a secure place on the Internet. eVault allows you to transfer up to 30MB of data per day, filling up to a total of 1GB of available space. Figure 37-3 shows eVault as a solution for the home-business desktop computer.

Figure 37-3. For a nominal fee, you can create backups with eVault software that can be accessed from anywhere through the Internet.

eVault charges a monthly fee — approximately $17 for the first 250MB plus $.07 per MB thereafter.

One drawback to using the Internet is connection speed. The slower the connection speed (for example, a 33.6-Kbps modem), the longer it takes to send a file for backing up. In effect, the file spends a longer time at risk, making this method a less palatable backup alternative, if a viable solution at all. If you use a broadband connection to the Internet, it becomes much more plausable to use this method for doing backups. On the other hand, saving to the Net makes a lot of sense for a user who needs to save data somewhere safe without having to worry about a lost, damaged, or stolen laptop. eVault also offers to create a CD or tape of your data (for $25 plus expenses) — a small price to pay for peace of mind.

Habits for Backups

Administrators of large computer systems have developed strategies and routines for backing up data. Over time, these processes have been refined, proven and implemented in the largest computing systems in the country. Although designed for large networks, the principles behind such strategies and routines work just as well for the private computer user.

Any computer user generally has to deal with two specific types of backups: full and incremental. A *full backup* does just what you'd expect — it makes a complete copy of all the files that reside on a particular machine, drive, or directory. Because this complete backup includes everything (including the kitchen sink), it can take considerable time. Nevertheless, one good full backup on your system is excellent insurance when performed at reasonable and regular intervals. Between those occasions comes the *incremental backup* — which includes only the files that have changed since the last full backup. This procedure requires less time (fewer files get modified on a daily basis), so it can be done more frequently.

Strategies for creating your backups should be simple. A typical example would include a combination of full and incremental backups over the course of a week or month. For instance, a weekly backup schedule may look like the following; you would use tapes as the medium and rotate the tapes over the course of the whole backup cycle:

Monday	Full backup of the C drive (Tape 1).
Tuesday	Incremental backup of the C drive (Tape 2).
Wednesday	Incremental backup of the C drive (Tape 2).
Thursday	Incremental backup of the C drive (Tape 2).
Friday	Incremental backup of the C drive (Tape 2).
Monday	Full backup of the C drive (Tape 3).
Tuesday	Incremental backup of the C drive (Tape 1).

This approach typifies an effective backup strategy. You vary the strategy by expanding its interval to two weeks, three weeks, and so on.

Regardless of tape capacity, you need enough tapes available to complete a *tape rotation* — staggering the tapes so you never overwrite the only backup copy of your files. In the example given here, Tape 1 would contain only the full backup; Tape 2 contains only the files that have changed. When you use Tape 3, the unchanged files (still on Tape 1) do not get overwritten and are therefore kept safe.

This routine of making backups should become a part of your daily activities. Many backup programs can be set up to automate the process, leaving the changing of the media as the only required human intervention.

Power Protection

In addition to protecting data by creating backup copies, keeping the source of the files safe from damage is also important. A *power spike* — the flooding of an electrical system caused by lightning strikes and power surges — is a major source of computer failure. *Surge protectors,* little devices you can attach between the wall outlet and the computer, can help protect your computer system from such spikes. These gems keep computers happily humming along — deflecting most electrical disasters from the delicate electronics inside the computer.

In addition to surge protectors, designers have come up with another handy device known as a *UPS.* (In the computer world, UPS stands for Uninterruptible Power Supply, not for the package delivery service called United Parcel Service.) The UPS takes its place between the wall outlet and the computer, much like a surge suppressor. Under normal conditions, the UPS acts like an extension cord, passing the electricity from the wall outlet to the computer. When the power fails, however the UPS does its main job: providing enough power to the computer to keep it running, giving you the time needed to save data, close programs, and safely turn the computer off.

Tip

For the duration of the backup cycle, the total space used by the incremental backups should not exceed the space used by the full backup. In other words, don't extend your strategy too far out in time.

Note

It's actually healthy to become compulsive about backups. Work under the assumption that the next time you sit down at your computer, you may discover that all the data on your computer has been destroyed. With that scenario as a starting point, you will have the incentive to back up regularly — and thus be prepared for the day when the assumption comes true.

Caution

A surge protector is not the same thing as a power strip. Both extend to the wall outlet, but only a surge protector offers any kind of protection to electronic equipment from incoming power surges.

Note

Many manufacturers refer to surge protectors by different names — *surge protector, surge arrest, surge suppressor,* but never *power strip.*

Find It Online

Other popular UPS manufacturers include Best (www.bestpower.com) and Tripp Lite (www.tripplite.com). Each company site includes assistance in helping you choose a product that will fit your needs.

Tip

Outside of using a good UPS with your computer, you should protect valuable equipment with some form of surge protecting power strip with a phone port. They can protect your computer and other electronics from lightning strikes, even when the strike comes through the phone line.

The UPS contains a rechargeable battery and the electronic circuitry to charge the battery when the electricity is on. Thus the power from the battery is available to keep any devices working when the power goes out. Several UPS devices include software (and a serial connection) that can tell your computer when the power goes out and shut down the machine unattended.

American Power Conversion (www.apcc.com) leads the industry with UPS devices and surge protectors. Their models range from small, take-it-with-you devices for laptops to systems that could power a house (for use with industrial computer systems). APC provides a form on their Web site (seen in Figure 37-4) that asks you questions about your computer, and then recommends a suitable UPS for your computer.

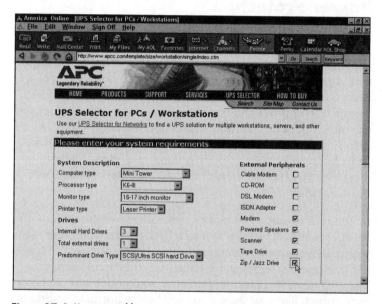

Figure 37-4. You can quickly size up an appropriate UPS for your system by using the form on APC's Web site.

Coming Up Next

Knowing how to do and schedule backups can radically reduce your worry about losing data. With your data protected,
you can turn your attention to the visual aspects of presenting
it. The next chapter discusses the improvements that you can
make to the video components of your computer, such as special monitors, video cards, DVD players and even color printers. These components have a large effect on the look of
games, graphic design programs, and movies. Find out how
you can improve your system in these areas; it's in the next
chapter.

Chapter 38

Visual Beauty through Better Technology

Just to show you how long I've been hanging around computers, I can remember when monitors were one color (usually green or amber) and when looking at so-called "graphics" meant looking at text characters meticulously lined up to make up a picture — when observed from ten feet away. High-resolution, high-color monitors that display photo-quality graphics and movies are commonplace today, with more innovations coming out every day. This chapter covers some newer products in the visual computing arena.

LCD Panel Monitor

A major improvement in the current crop of peripherals is a replacement for the standard cathode-ray-tube monitor. Traditionally, such monitors take up the most room on the desk, consume more power, and are heavy (especially the larger ones). To help combat the negatives of the traditional tube monitor, the Liquid Crystal Display (LCD) panel adapts for the desktop. LCDs have long been used in laptops, but only recently has the technology improved to the point where their size, clarity, and affordability are ready for the desktop.

A major advantage of the LCD panel is its small *footprint,* the amount of space it takes up on actual office furniture. Because the panel itself is no more than three inches deep, it needs only a small base to support it (see Figure 38-1). LCD panels are also immune to the effects of *electromagnetic interference (EMI)* — disruptions of picture quality arising from the electrical fields that surround large electrical motors, overhead lighting, speakers, or even a desk lamp. For businesses that depend on constant, high picture quality, a monitor unaffected by EMI is an added plus.

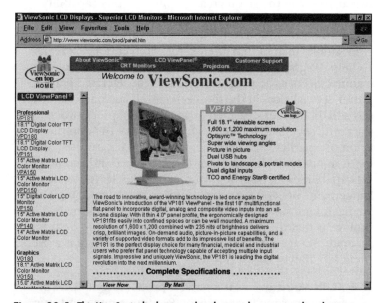

Figure 38-1. This ViewSonic display is so thin that you have to wonder where it puts its loads of features.

Find It Online

To find the best price on LCD monitors, look at PriceWatch (www.pricewatch.com). To navigate to the LCD panels, click the word Monitors under the Output category. Then click the monitor size you are looking for.

Tip

Some people get headaches from conventional cathode-ray-tube monitors because the scan pattern creates a subtle, but annoying, flicker. Changing to an LCD panel monitor removes the flicker and makes work more comfortable.

One of the largest drawbacks to LCD panels is cost. The prices are dropping, but it will take a while before LCD panel prices match traditional tube-monitor prices. For instance, a 15-inch and an 18-inch LCD monitor cost around $900 and $3000, respectively, compared to comparable 17-inch and 21-inch tube monitors coming in at $250 and $800, respectively. LCD panels are really nice, but — given the huge price difference — you may have some difficulty convincing yourself (or whoever controls the family checkbook) that an LCD panel is absolutely crucial for your computer system.

3D Video Cards

Even though *3D video acceleration* is something of a buzzword in the computer world these days, average computer users probably don't think much about it as they browse Web sites, read e-mail, and play Solitaire. Most earlier video cards that come with computers use 2D technology that does a wonderful job of displaying those programs. For some users, however — computer gamers, DVD movie watchers, and visual artists who thrive on great graphics — this capability means everything. 3D cards render computer images faster, giving smooth motion to the animation (in contrast to the jerky, clunky images that lurch across conventional screens). To help 3D graphic cards smooth out the bumps, computer manufacturers added specialized AGPs (accelerated graphic ports), special slots in the motherboard to accommodate various add-on devices designed to speed up graphics processing. Currently, several 2D/3D cards that go inside the computer exist on the market; choosing one from the pack can be confusing, if not overwhelming. Since these combo cards combine 2D capabilities for your regular applications with the 3D enhancements needed for games, movies, and such, 2D/3D cards are becoming standard in recent computers. Their main advantage is that they eliminate the need for an additional, but separate, 3D accelerator card in the computer. Here is a list of some top-drawer cards:

▶ **3Dfx Voodoo5** — the newest product from 3Dfx, offering amazing image quality, fast frame rates, and stunning effects for 3D games (as well as 2D image viewing and MPEG movies). Available for about $300.

▶ **ATI All-in-Wonder 128** — this mixed card offers the renowned ATI Rage 128 technology plus a TV tuner, S-video (super-video) input for capturing video and outputs for using a TV as a monitor. S-video produces a better video signal than does the standard video in/out that we see on VCRs, camcorder, and such. Available for about $200.

▶ **Matrox Millennium G400** — offers excellent viewing of 2D, 3D, and DVD applications. Some versions of this card have dual ports for viewing two monitors (available in Windows98). This comes in handy for sophisticated graphic artists (as an example) who need to view a different program in each monitor. Available for about $150.

▶ **Matrox Marvel G400-TV** — this card has all the functions of the Millennium G400, plus a programmable TV tuner, video capture, and video editing capabilities. Available for about $300.

▶ **Creative 3D Blaster® Annihilator** — using the GeForce256 chipset, this card's performance is in its own class for 2D, 3D, and video acceleration. Available for about $300.

Driver Updates

Regardless of the video card installed in your computer, you may have to update the drivers periodically; they too are subject to revision, improvement, and replacement. Over time, improvements to the driver increase the hardware's performance, eliminate compatibility problems, and decrease video troubles. Driver updates are important to prevent display problems in applications, especially for newer video cards. You can download these drivers from your video card manufacturer's Web site. Because everyone's Web site looks a little different, let me just tell you what to look for on the site to find the downloadable drivers. Look for a Support area on the site, then look for a reference to the type of card you own (have its model number handy). The site should offer some download directions, as well as any special installation instructions for the driver.

 Find It Online

You can find video cards from the AOL Shop. Use AOL Keyword: **AOL Shop** to open the storefront. Click the Hardware button, then the More button, and then Video & Sound Cards to see what's available.

 Definition

Accelerated Graphics Port (AGP) — a special port in computers, especially designed to handle the large amounts of data transferred to and from 3D graphic cards.

Caution

Be sure to download the correct driver for the hardware you own. The wrong driver can cause the device to stop working properly, possibly damaging the hardware.

To find the current driver information about the video card you currently have installed, follow these steps (these instructions are for Windows 98; Windows NT and 2000 require a slightly different procedure).

1. Use the right mouse button to click My Computer on your desktop.
2. Select Properties from the menu that appears.
3. From the System Properties dialog box, click the Device Manager tab.
4. Double-click the Display Adapters item.
5. Select your video card's maker and model from the list; then click the Properties button.

For Windows NT and 2000, follow these instructions:

1. Right-click the desktop background and choose Properties from the menu that appears.
2. Click the Settings tab of the Display Properties dialog box.
3. Near the bottom of this window is a button labeled Display Type. Click this button.
4. From the Display Type dialog box, you can find the current driver information and have the opportunity to change it (or update the driver) if need be.

From here you can see the device's General information and Drivers tabs; the Drivers tab tells you more (as you may expect) about the drivers — such as manufacturer release dates, revision codes, and version numbers. All such numbers can help you determine whether you need to update your drivers. (My video driver, as seen in Figure 38-2, shows a date of 11-3-98; the Web site shows a date of 8-27-99 — time for an update.)

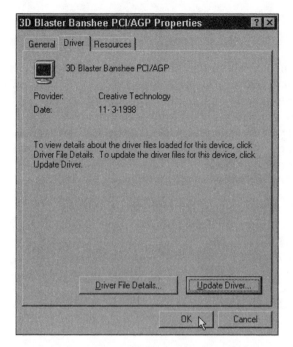

Figure 38-2. You can get the details about drivers from System Properties.

Pairing 3Dfx Cards for Maximum Beauty

When 3D video cards first came out, I wasn't completely sure what the hype was about. I had an excellent 2D graphics card and could not have been happier with it — until I saw a 3D card in action. My solution was to use a 3D accelerator in conjunction with my existing video card. I could have my cake and eat it too. I found a 3Dfx Voodoo card to add to my system. My monitor plugged into the Voodoo card, which then plugged into my video card. Normal graphics just passed through the Voodoo card without a hitch; 3D graphics from games got processed by the Voodoo card.

Although that particular model of Voodoo card has long been obsolete, the Voodoo2 can still be found on some store shelves or through mail order. Most video-card manufacturers combine the standard 2D with the 3D to make *2D/3D graphics cards* like the Voodoo2.

DVD

DVD entertainment is not just for the home theater system; you can enjoy it at your computer as well. DVD drives built for your computer look just like CD-ROM drives, but they can read DVD movies and put them on your monitor screen. The catch with DVD drives is that the video card must be fast enough to process the images without errors. The majority of 3D video cards make provisions to process MPEG-2 images (the format of DVD movies).

Nearly all DVD players can read normal data and music CDs. Technically, that means you need only one drive to read music CDs, data CDs, and DVDs. DVD-ROM drives sell for around $150 to $250; you can pick one up at your favorite computer store. Creative sells a kit called PC-DVD Encore 8X (for around $250) which includes the required MPEG-2 encoder board to process the images for you to enjoy.

Color Printers

Recent advances in color printers have resulted in the development of three separate kinds of color printers: inkjet, laser, and photo (a special inkjet printer for photos). Most of the affordable color printers are *inkjet*, which means a kind of high-tech squirt gun in the moving print head places tiny drops of color on the paper as it moves, creating the picture one multi-colored line at a time. Inkjet printers cost between $150 and $300, and are made by a number of different manufacturers. Hewlett-Packard carries a long line of inkjet printers; too many to list. They do have an tool on their Web site to help you to narrow the choices. Go to www.hp.com and select the dark gray HP Products button at the top of the page. Then click the Color Printers choice from the Printing and Digital Imaging section of the next page. You see a blue button labeled *Help Me Choose a Product ... Click Here* (which you can then do to start narrowing the printer selections).

The more expensive color laser printers do an awesome job, but are *much* more expensive — in the neighborhood of $3000. These printers are primarily for commercial environments, but could work well for individuals with high-volume printing needs (and deep pockets). The Hewlett-Packard Color LaserJet 4500, for example, prints color, connects directly to a network, and can handle huge volumes of print jobs.

For those who take digital pictures, creating paper copies of photographic quality can be a challenge. Photo printers fit that need well, and are popping up all over the market. The Lexmark Photo Jetprinter 5770 ($300) is an example. Though it prints like any other inkjet printer (see Figure 38-3), this printer accepts memory cards from digital cameras without requiring the aid of a computer. Thus you can use this model as a dedicated printout device for a digital camera — or as the family color printer. You can find a long list of cameras and memory cards at the Lexmark Web site: www.lexmark.com/printers/inkjet/5770/cameras.html.

Find It Online

To find AOL's list of color printers, visit the AOL Shop at AOL Keyword: **AOL Shop**, choose Hardware⇨Printers. A host of Lexmark and Hewlett-Packard DeskJet color printers appears on-screen.

38

Visual Beauty through
Better Technology

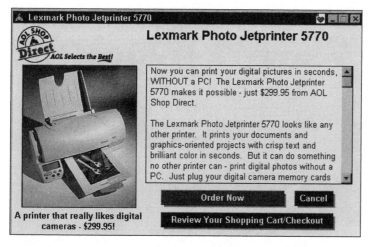

Figure 38-3. Print photos from a digital camera without turning on the PC.

Coming Up Next

To complete your mighty Internet-cruising system, the next chapter shows you the wonders of three-dimensional sound, the sound cards that make it happen, and the speakers that give new meaning to *Wow!*

CHAPTER

39

SOUND THAT ROCKS
YOUR SOCKS

Chapter 39

Sound That Rocks Your Socks

Visual enhancements to your computer system, dazzling as they are, still aren't the complete story. To get the full effect of what the modern Internet makes available, your system needs sound enhancement. Amazingly, tremendous improvements in computer sound systems could *almost* replace the home stereo system. (Almost, but not quite! Yet.)

Sound Upgrades

The sound system you can find on most computers repro-
duces sounds adequately. You can tell a train wreck from a
heavy-metal band, even if the sound quality is nothing to get
excited about. When I bought my first desktop computer personal computer, even a pair of cheap external speakers
sounded much better than the little speaker inside the computer. The sound system on my latest computer really rocks
for listening to music, playing games, or watching DVD
movies; I'm spoiled. It's okay to be completely satisfied with
your current setup. I thought I was with mine until I heard a
favorite game being played on a friend's system; it was outfitted with a subwoofer. Thus began my sound-system upgrade.

Because the sound system has only two real components —
sound card and speakers — I first changed the speakers,
which produced the largest audible improvement in music
and games. With that done, I changed the sound card to improve the system's compatibility with the speakers — which
improved the sound quality another notch or two. Why? Well,
you could say that the sound card is the first key to a better
understanding of the whole sound system.

3D Sound

Many improvements have taken place in computer sound
cards in recent years, the greatest change being in 3D sound
technology. Movie theaters, home stereo systems — and now
computers — all try to recreate a three-dimensional (3D) listening experience.

Having 3D sound coming from your computer while playing
your favorite games adds to the total gaming experience. Even
listening to your favorite music CD through your computer
can be amazing. And if you can watch DVD movies through
your computer, you may want to strap yourself into the seat.

 Note

Replacing an older sound
card with a new, powerful
one and keeping the same
cheap $5 speakers you had
before, would be like putting
a lawnmower engine in your
shiny new sports car. It might
look nice, but it won't sound
very good.

39

Sound That Rocks Your Socks

Aureal

Cross-Reference

QSound and SRS Labs have worked out ways to split up the sound for the 3D effect. For more information about these company's products, check out Chapter 25.

Aureal (www.aureal.com), a leader in sound technology, produces a sound-processing chipset that many other manufacturers (such as Diamond Multimedia, Hi-Val, and Turtle Beach) use in their products. Aureal's sound cards, the Vortex SQ1500 and Vortex2 SQ2500, use the A3D technology that they developed. This technology makes two speakers mimic the 3D sound that the human ear hears in the real world. The listener gets the impression that the sounds are coming from any 3D position — up/down, left/right, front/back.

The Vortex SQ2500 (see Figure 39-1) uses the Vortex 2 chipset in combination with A3D technology to produce one of the best sound cards on the market today. Features of this card include two sets of speaker jacks for front and rear pairs of speakers, professional 576-voice wavetable synthesizer, DirectSound 3D acceleration, and more. Basically, this sound card is loaded for the game and music enthusiast.

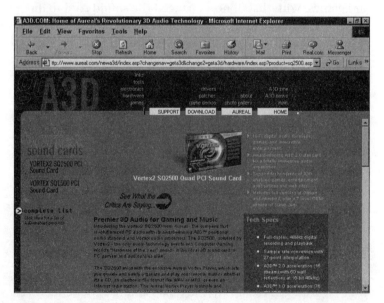

Figure 39-1. The Vortex is Aureal's top-of-the-line sound card.

Creative

Creative has made a name for themselves with the Sound Blaster (www.soundblaster.com) line of sound cards. This line starts with Sound Blaster 16, which is their baseline sound card. In the middle would be the Sound Blaster Live! Platinum. This card's software bundle combines those from the XGamer edition and the MP3+ version into a single package. At the top of its long list of products, you'll find the Sound Blaster AWE64 Gold (see Figure 39-2), available in the AOL Store at AOL Keyword: **AOL Shop Direct**.

Note

Reviewers links from Aureal's Web site shows that the SQ2500 is getting very high marks and winning awards — for example, *GameSpot* (www.gamespot .com) gave it a 4.5 out of 5 in their review; and *PC Gamer* gave it the Editors' Choice award.

Note

In my humble opinion, only the Sound Blaster AWE64 Gold card can begin to compete with the Aureal Vortex2 SQ2500 in the area of 3D spatial sound.

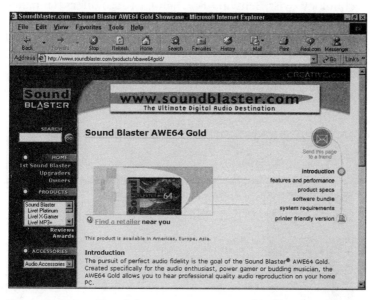

Figure 39-2. One of Sound Blaster's newest generation of sound cards — AWE64 Gold.

The Sound Blaster AWE64 Gold was created for the serious game and music buff. Creative's 3D Stereo Enhancement technology works with just two speakers to give games 3D sound for the ultimate gaming experience. Likewise, the true-sound hardware wave-table synthesis gives a budding musician professional quality sound along with the flexibility of specialized sound equipment, such as track mixers, synthesizers, and such.

39

Sound That Rocks Your Socks

Speakers

Speakers complete the other half of your sound system. You may have the best sound card ever made, but cheap speakers still sound weak. Therefore, to get the most out of your system, find the speakers that complement your sound card.

Benwin

If you are looking for versatile speakers with a new-technology twist, Benwin (www.benwin.com) offers flat-panel speakers that provide excellent sound quality. They use a 0.25-mm-thick panel instead of a cone to vibrate, giving a full 360-degree sound projection throughout the room. These speakers can be mounted on either side of the monitor, on free-resting stands, or on the wall. They include a subwoofer to catch the low bass sounds.

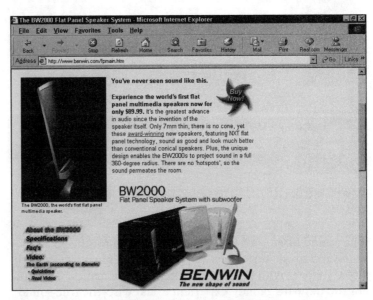

Figure 39-3. The Benwin BW2000 speakers are only 7mm thick.

Note

Benwin also carries a full line of traditional speakers for your multimedia needs, including both two- and three-speaker systems.

I like these speakers for their versatility as well as for their performance. The power, volume, tone, and 3D controls are mounted on the subwoofer, designed to sit on top of the desk for easy access. As you can see from Figure 39-3, the speakers are as thin as they claim.

Altec Lansing

The name Altec Lansing (www.alteclansing.com) is to computer speakers as Goodyear is to car tires. You cannot find a company with a better reputation and product line for computer speakers. Their product line ranges from simple, two-speaker systems to extensive 3- and 5-speaker systems for gaming and home-theater experiences. I've owned a few of their speakers and have found them superb.

For a full-sounding set of speakers, I'd recommend the AC56 5-speaker gaming system seen in Figure 39-4, also available at the AOL Store (AOL Keyword: **AOL Shop Direct**). It includes four satellite speakers and a subwoofer. The speakers and the power line feed into the subwoofer, which also includes a S/PDIF (Sony/Philips digital interface format) connection for the new sound cards that support this capability. The volume, bass, and treble controls for the speakers are in the front right speaker. A mode button enables 3D sound (when it's off, only the front speakers are active). Even though this system is advertised as a game speaker system, the sound quality is perfect for anything you listen to on your computer.

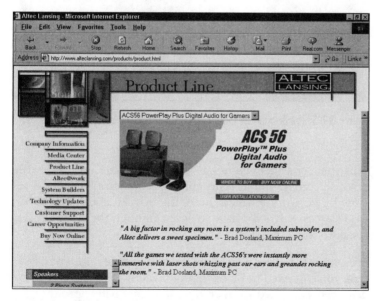

Figure 39-4. The Altec Lansing AC56 speaker system makes the perfect gaming speakers.

39

Sound That Rocks Your Socks

Definition

THX, developed by LucasFilm for the *Return of the Jedi* movie, is the three-dimensional sound technology found in more than 2000 cinemas. To find out more about THX, visit www.thx.com.

Klipsch

Klipsch (www.klipsch.com) is a name well known in the entertainment industry for cinema speakers, DJ rigs, stage monitors, and corporate-intercom speakers. They are now branching out into the computer/multimedia area. The ProMedia v.2-400 is the first THX-certified, 5-speaker sound experience (see Figure 39-5). The controls for the speakers appear on the front satellite speaker; the power line is connected to the subwoofer.

Figure 39-5. The demand for these THX-certified speakers caused major back orders.

This speaker system comes as an option from Compaq or can be ordered over the Internet through Klipsch's Web site. A review by *PC Gamer* called these "the best PC speakers on God's green earth." I'd have to agree (though the Altec Lansing speakers are a close second).

Caution

Because the demand is high, don't be surprised if these speakers are on back order. If you choose to wait for them, you won't be sorry.

Even after you have purchased a set of speakers for your system, you still need to place them correctly for them to work as designed. For a two-speaker system to adequately produce three-dimensional sound, they need to be lined up on either side of the monitor in front of you. They also need to be at an equal distance from you. With a four speaker system, the

remaining two speakers should be placed on either side of
you approximately the same distance away as the first two
speakers. These second speakers will sit on tables or stands.
Figure 39-6 illustrates the proper placement of a four-speaker
setup.

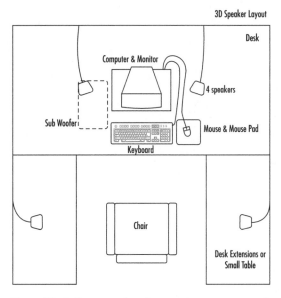

Figure 39-6. Proper speaker placement is as important as the speaker quality to get
the greatest-sounding results.

Coming Up Next

You've finished a hard day and you want to take a little time to
relax playing a computer game. Great! The next chapter covers the controllers you may need to improve your gaming
skills. The chapter covers the different types of controllers
and pairs the controller with the types of games most appropriate for them.

Chapter 40

Taking Control of Your Games

This chapter introduces you to a variety of game controllers — which can add tremendously to the gaming experience, though they can't win the games for you. If you suspect that your interest in gaming is more than just a passing fancy, check out the various types of controllers described in this chapter — as well as the games they're best for — and get tips on using the controllers. Before you know it, you'll be ready to take the gaming experience to the extreme. (Now all you may need is the leisure time to enjoy it.)

Game Controllers

A *game controller* is any control device used to play a game —
from a keyboard to a game pad. Controllers actually designed
for games can improve your performance, make the game
simpler to play, and show your opponent that you reign
supreme. Who could resist?

The quest for the perfect controller has spawned quite a range
of different types, so matching the controller with the game is
a good move. Each type has its place — often within a specific
game genre. For instance, you'd use a joystick in a game that
uses flight as the primary activity; a steering wheel would be
the natural choice for a driving game. Diehard gamers tend to
be very particular about game controllers; they take the time
to visit stores to look at, touch, and try out various game controllers in an attempt to find the one that they feel most comfortable using. I suggest you do the same. Finding the one that
works best for you is a lot easier than trying to invent the perfect controller.

The following lists the three major types of controllers and
the associated game genres (including some popular representatives of the genre).

Controller	Game Type (Genre)	Examples
Joystick	First-person shooters	Quake, DukeNukem2, StarSiege Tribes, Half-Life, Unreal
	Flight	Microsoft Flight Simulator, Apache, Gunship, Descent
	Mechine	Mech Warrior, HeavyGear, StarSeige
Steering Wheel	Racing	Need for Speed, IndyCar Racing, NASCAR racing, Sega Rally, Test Drive
Game Pad	Sports	NBA Basketball, NFL Championship

Tip

Some real-time strategy games (such as Red Alert, Dark Reign, and StarCraft) are best played with an old-fashioned keyboard and mouse.

Another recent feature of game controllers is the addition of *force-feedback* to increase the realism in a game. A force-feedback controller includes a device that moves the controller in response to the action in the game. For instance, if you are using a force-feedback steering wheel with an off-road racing game, you will feel the wheel respond to road conditions — jerky for a rough road, jumpy when you hit a pothole, and so on. Having a game controller with force-feedback capability doesn't mean that the effect will be equally dramatic with all games. The game itself must be *force-feedback-capable* or the controller will work like a conventional controller.

Joysticks

For most people, a game controller means a joystick. As one of the most versatile gaming instruments, the joystick crosses a couple of the game genres, though it is most useful with flight games. You can also use the joystick in first-person shooter games, Mech games, and other combat games where a weapon trigger, precise targeting, and multiple controls are important. The accompanying table lists a few joysticks with price, manufacturer, and Web site.

Controller	Price	Manufacturer	Web site
Sidewinder	$129	Microsoft	www.microsoft.com/sidewinder
SP550	$30	Saitek	www.saitekusa.com
F16 CombatStick	$80	CH Products	www.chproducts.com
Wingman Force	$80	Logitech	www.logitech.com
TopGun USB	$40	ThrustMaster	www.thrustmaster.com

Note

Many manufacturers of game controllers make more than one model; some even produce controllers geared to a particular genre. Saitek, for example, makes its X36 controller specifically for flight and Mech games.

Joysticks have become much more complex than when I first started gaming. One of my first joysticks had a handle to control and two trigger buttons. The latest joysticks have so many controls that I'm not sure that I'd ever be able to use them all. Figure 40-1 shows some of the controls available on a joystick, though these are by no means all the possible variations. Recent models of controller feature four trigger buttons *and* a four-way (hat) switch — and that's just on the handle — as well as additional controls on the base (such as a throttle control) for your other hand to manage. These days you've got your hands full.

Figure 40-1. Saitek's AP550 joystick is loaded with buttons, triggers, and switches for maximum firepower.

Another change in controllers is the way they connect to the computer. With earlier models, you had to make sure that you had a sound card with an available game port (which they usually had anyway). Many controller companies today are using USB as the preferred means of connecting the controller to the computer.

Steering Wheels

Steering wheels work really well for racing games (no surprise there), especially force-feedback steering wheels. I use a force-feedback steering wheel with off-road-racing games; it contributes to both the realism and the challenge. Most wheels also come with foot controls for the throttle and brake. The accompanying table provides a sample.

Cross-Reference

To learn more about getting more USB devices on your computer, look at Chapter 6 for USB hubs.

Controller	Price	Manufacturer	Web site
Sidewinder	$160	Microsoft	www.microsoft.com/sidewinder
R4	$50	Saitek	www.saitekusa.com
Wingman Formula	$160	Logitech	www.logitech.com
NASCAR Charger	$40	ThrustMaster	www.thrustmaster.com

The best wheel controller of all is the NASCAR Charger by ThrustMaster (see Figure 40-2). This wheel also has buttons on the wheel for games that have power-boost and other controllable functions. Engage the nitro, grab hold of the wheel, and hang on as you speed to victory (with some required skill).

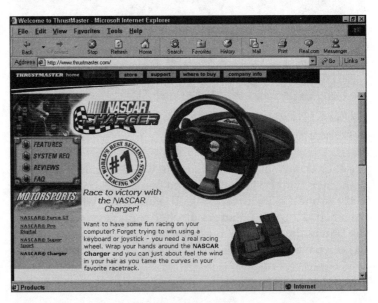

Figure 40-2. ThrustMaster takes the checkered flag for racing wheels.

Game Pads

Game pad controllers can be used in most games; however, they are not always the best choice. For instance, games that require control, like aiming in war/battle games or for flight games, a joystick or mouse would be a better choice. They have handles for gripping by both hands with buttons accessible for one hand and a four-way control switch for the other hand. These controllers are great for sports games where only a few controls are needed. Here are a few of the manufacturers of game pad controllers.

Controller	Price	Manufacturer	Web site
Sidewinder DualStrike	$45	Microsoft	www.microsoft.com/sidewinder
P2000	$50	Saitek	www.saitekusa.com
USB GamePad	$30	CH Products	www.chproducts.com
Thunderpad Digital	$10	Logitech	www.logitech.com

The exception being the Microsoft Sidewinder DualStrike (see Figure 40-3) which combines the game pad with the joystick. Although the player holds it with two hands like a regular game pad, it swivels in the middle — giving the player joystick-like control. This controller works well for first-person shooters because the split function lets you use the swivel and look to better aim.

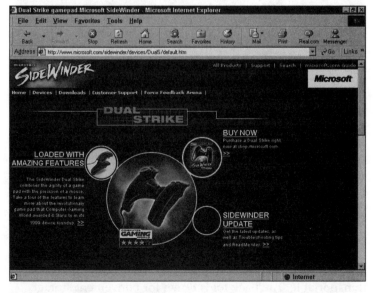

Figure 40-3. Microsoft's DualStrike game pad can also be used with first-person shooter games.

Alternative Game Devices

When you're tired of using the keyboard and you don't want to use any of the other controllers, you might consider ActLab's ArcadeREX shown in Figure 40-4. ActLab (www.actlab.com) has three controllers that put arcade-style gaming within reach. These controllers are customizable for the game controls you desire. This type works well for the arcade-style games such as Mortal Kombat, so you can have the same controls as the machines in the local arcade.

Figure 40-4. Get arcade-like action with this controller from ActLab.

Gaming Chairs

Taking games to the ultimate extreme is what Intensor (www.intensor.com) has done with their gaming chair. This chair plugs into the sound system, turning audio into blasts felt throughout your body. You see, hear, and now feel the explosions from your favorite games. The chair also can plug into your home entertainment system, stereo, TV, or Nintendo for "feeling" some arcade action. The chair is designed to be transportable. The back folds down for convenient storage and a handle is modeled into the chair to make carrying easy.

Tip

Remember that to win at a computer game, you need lots of practice, patience, and every advantage you can get. Pick a controller that you feel most comfortable handling, with all the features you want to give you the added edge to win.

You can see from Figure 40-5 that the Intensor LX Gaming chair looks like a normal desk chair with roll-around wheels, but don't let appearances fool you. This wasn't made just for sitting! You can purchase it online from the AOL Shop (using AOL Keyword: **AOL Shop**). When you see the storefront, click the Hardware tab. A new window appears, from which you can click the Keyboards, Mice, Etc. option. Included in the list that appears is the Intensor LX Gaming Chair.

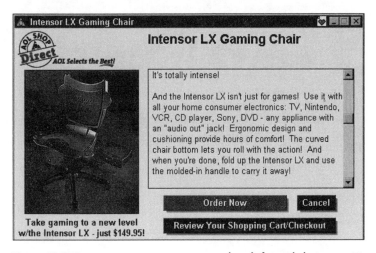

Figure 40-5. Experience games in ways you never have before with the Intensor LX Gaming Chair.

Coming Up Next

Using a computer at home or at work comes with its own set of challenges, but computing on the road changes things a bit. Traveling with a laptop comes with the challenge of carrying everything you need with you as you travel, planning ahead for the unforeseen circumstances, and not leaving anything behind. The next chapter will help give you some useful tips when planning your next trip with your laptop.

Chapter 41

Road Warrior's Tools and Tips

IN THIS CHAPTER

Traveling with your laptop computer

Gathering the right tools and accessories

Rarely would people consider picking up a desktop computer, tucking it under an arm, and running off to the airport on a trip. However, people don't think twice about traveling with their laptop computers. Anyone who has done extensive traveling keeps a list of must-have computer-related items. In this chapter, we tell you about some of these essentials and give you tips to help make your next trip with your laptop a pleasant one. Or . . .

Imagine sitting in the airport terminal, half drifting in thought, half listening to the drone of conversations, and a haunting feeling overwhelms you. You start going through a mental checklist of all the things you need for this trip. Toothbrush.

Check. Suit. Check. Presentation handouts. Check. You finally get to your computer and accessories and realize that you are missing something. But what is it? Then it hits you: Your computer power supply is sitting on your desk in your office. If this sounds familiar, then you need to read this chapter.

Your Bag of Tricks: Essential Computer Travel Accessories

Experienced travelers always have a number of items that they keep handy in a travel bag. These items range from rubber bands to extra power supplies for the trusty laptop. You probably already have your own list of items you want to keep around, but this chapter shows you exactly which items you simply must take when you travel with your computer.

Most travelers (I include myself) arrive at a destination, secure the room, then set up camp. Part of my ritual camp setup includes unpacking the laptop, recharging the batteries, and dialing up to check on the latest e-mail. Included in this laptop configuration is the surge protector (power and phone), phone-line tester, and just-in-case tool kit (which I rarely need). True, the extra stuff I carry around makes the overall weight go up slightly, but the peace of mind is worth it. The rest of this chapter explains the importance of these items and how they are used.

Surge Protector

The most popular and recognized form of surge protection is the kind of protection you find on a power strip. Yes, that kind of power surge protection is important, but don't rest easy just because your power supply is safe. If you plan to hook up your laptop computer to any phone line while on the road, you should know that phone lines are just as susceptible as power lines to line spikes and over-voltages. Lightning has destroyed more than one computer over a phone line, even when the power was unplugged from the wall, so you need to take steps to protect your computer against any such eventuality. American Power Conversion (www.apc.com) carries all types of "power" products, including surge-protection devices for desktops and laptops. Figure 41-1 shows a compact power-line surge protector that incorporates phone-line protection. Other companies that provide surge devices include Tripp Lite (www.tripplite.com), RoadWarrior (www.roadwarrior.com), and Panamax (www.panamax.com). This is a good lesson for the home desktop owner as well.

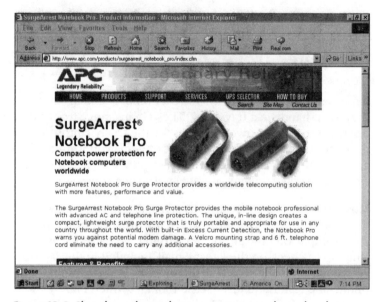

Figure 41-1. Phone-line and power-line surge protection can be purchased at a reasonable price for laptop computers. Better safe than sorry.

Modem-line Testers

A modem-line tester may not seem necessary to a home user, but to a traveler, it can mean the difference between making a successful call and destroying a modem. Modems use analog phone lines for communication. Hotels and even larger business offices, however, often use digital phone lines. Digital phone lines are incompatible with analog modems. Kind of the way matches are with gasoline. A modem-line tester, such as the one shown in Figure 41-2, can let you know immediately which phone jacks in a room are safe (analog) and which phone jacks will make you sorry you used them (digital).

Figure 41-2. Phone-line testers check to see whether connecting in is safe.

Tool Kits

You never know when you may need a tool while you're on the road. Even the type of tool you may need is anybody's guess. For example, once (when I was traveling) a paper clip slipped out of my hands and fell between the keys of my keyboard. My fingering for it only managed to make the clip slip farther into the keyboard. I happened to have a Swiss Army knife with tweezers, which allowed me to successfully remove the paper clip from the keyboard. But one thing is sure — you should always be prepared for whatever situation you may find yourself in when traveling.

A couple of tools available on the market today make being prepared for anything a bit easier. One such tool is the Leatherman Micra, shown in Figure 41-3, complete with scissors, tweezers, and multiple flathead and phillips screwdrivers. Another tool you may want to consider always having around would be a screwdriver with replaceable tips, available at any hardware store. Unconventional screw types may prove resistant to your standard flathead or phillips screwdriver, so if you have funny-looking screws in the things you use and don't want frustration (or stripped screws), be sure to keep a replaceable-tip screwdriver handy (with a set of tips to fit the types of screws that you have around you).

To give you an example of the delight that comes from having the right tools along, let me describe an experience I shared. A business meeting was to take place several hundred miles from the home office, which required the attendance of several individuals from this company. Upon arrival, one of the laptops would not start. Everyone from the home office had the same model laptop, so I borrowed one of the other laptops to help track down what the problem might be. After trying the batteries, I wanted to see whether the hard drive from the bad laptop would work in the good one (only because they were identical laptops). The hard drives were held in by a special screw that came with the laptops; they weren't designed to be opened with anything but one special tool (for security). Had I not had one of those tools with me, I would not have found that the hard drive had loosened during the flight; it worked fine in the "good" computer, and then worked in the "bad" one after I replaced it and tightened that screw.

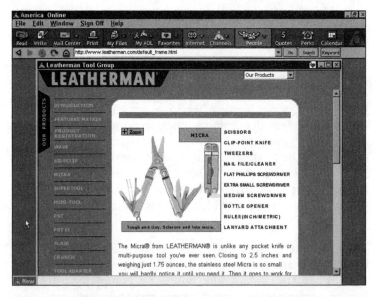

Figure 41-3. The small size of the Leatherman Micra can be deceiving.

Extension Cords and Cables

Stores offer more cables and accessories available on the market today than you can shake a stick at. And making sure that everything is hooked up correctly and has power running to it can be a chore — even in the safety of your own home. When you travel, your troubles can multiply because you can never really know what the environment will provide.

Will the phone jack be near a power outlet? Will there be a data jack in the room? If the phone jack and the power outlet are near each other, will I have to sit on the floor to work? These are good questions to ask yourself before starting your journey so that you can prepare for a few worst case scenarios. To come to terms with such scenarios, the following table lists a few items that may make the difference between an enjoyable on-the-road experience and an uncomfortable one.

Accessory	How It Helps You
25 foot phone cable	Most modems include a 6-foot cable. A longer one will allow you to sit comfortably across the room.
Phone coupler	In some hotel rooms, the phone cable is wired directly into the wall. A phone coupler will allow you to connect two male-ended phone lines together.
Phone-line splitter	This little adapter will let you connect both your modem and the phone at the same time. It will save you from plugging and unplugging your modem and phone when you want to switch between the two.
Standard power extension cable	A simple extension cord is handy to allow your laptop power supply to reach a wall outlet. You can work and charge at the same time.

Mobile Tips

The following collection of travel tips and tricks are for when you travel with your laptop. These time-saving and data-saving ideas will make your next trip a pleasant one. You can even jot down notes for some new ideas that come to you as you read through this list.

▶ **Always check with the concierge or the front desk to make sure that data lines are available.** You can also look on the hotel room phones for a data port labeled "DATA."

▶ **Don't forget the power of improvising.** You may not always be able to use that creative brainpower and improvise when on the road with your computer. But when the batteries fail and the screen goes black, there are always a pen and paper to write that letter.

▶ **Make a backup of your critical files before you leave on your trip.** As a rule of thumb, think of your data with a dollar figure. How much would it cost to recreate the data if you lost it? With that dollar figure in mind, ask yourself, "Can I afford to replace this file?" Back up your files!

▶ **Never leave you laptop case unattended.** According to one listing, there are over 2,000 laptops stolen everyday. Don't let yours be counted among the statistics.

▶ **Power supply: Don't leave home without it!** What more can I say? Batteries last only so long without being recharged. If, by chance, you do leave your power supply behind, you will either need to shell out the clams for a new one or wait to recharge until you return home again.

▶ **Consider the difference in power and phone-line requirements that you find when you travel to other countries.** The U.S. uses 120 volts for electrical power. Other countries will vary from 120 volts to 240 volts. Most laptop power supplies are designed to automatically switch between voltages, but the plugs on the end will require an adapter to fit into wall outlets.

When traveling internationally, you will need to bring along a phone adapter designed to work in the country of destination. Different countries may have different phone plugs, so do your research before you get on the plane.

▶ **Use your computer equipment for pleasure as well as work.** At some point during your travels, you'll want a break from the drone of work. Take along a pair of headphones and some CDs to listen to during breaks.

Note

International travel: Office supply stores are a good resource for travel adapters for both your power supply and for the phone.

▶ **Engage the battery-saving features found in your operating system to extend your battery life.** The following instructions show you how to enable those settings in Windows 98.

Feel free to follow these instructions for optimal energy-saving performance.

1. Click the Start button and choose Settings⇨Control Panel from the extended menu that appears.

2. When the Control Panel window is open, double-click on the Power Management button. The Power Management Properties dialog box appears, as shown in Figure 41-4.

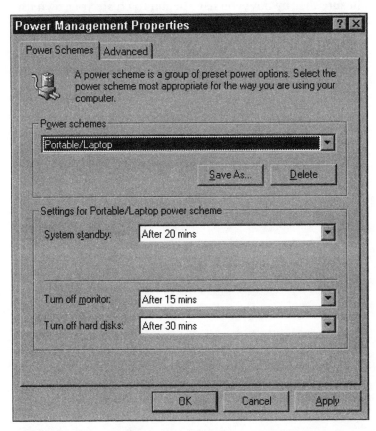

Figure 41-4. Power Management control panel for your systems settings.

Note

You can adjust the settings to fit your preferences. However, the System Standby setting has to be set to a few minutes before the Turn Off Hard Disks setting, or the hard drive will not be running to capture the system settings for standby mode.

3. Select Portable/Laptop from the Power Schemes drop-down menu. New settings will appear in the remaining boxes. These new values are inactivity times limits. The default values for the remaining functions are as follows:

   ▶ System Standby: After 20 min.
   ▶ Turn off monitor: After 15 min.
   ▶ Turn off hard disks: After 30 min.

4. To take monitoring your system power one more step, select the Advanced tab and check the box for Always Show Icon on the Taskbar. This will allow you to see how much battery life you have left as you work.

I'm sure that, by now, you have begun to create your own list of "must have" items for your next trip. Just don't forget to incorporate the times I've discussed here. Now you can pack for your trips, using your new list and rest assured that you have everything you need. Got the airline tickets? Have a good trip and thank you for flying with us.

Index

Continued

Rio 600 Digital Audio Player!

The Diamond Rio 600 Digital Audio Player shatters the personal sound barrier with customizable features and high-end audio you simply cannot get anywhere else! Capture and playback up to 1 hour of digital-quality music from AOL, the Internet and your CDs.

Seize your audio, master your mix, re-tool your memory, even select your cover color - it's radical freedom of choice. Whether you passion is alternative, hi-hop or the fringes of spoken word, Rio 600 delivers a listening experience beyond mainstream electronics.

- 32MB built-in memory with option to upgrade your memory via Snap-on memory pacs in 32MB, 64MB or 340MB capacities - so you have endless opportunities of listening power.

- Supports MP3 and WMA digital formats

- PC & Macintosh compatible - USB

- Lightweight & skip-free design - no moving parts!

$149.95 (s&h $8.95) #0014739N00012805

your personal audio player

AMERICA *Online.*

So easy to use, no wonder it's #1

Includes: Rio 600 audio player, high-quality ear-phones with over-the-ear sport clip design, USB cable, AA battery, getting started guide and audio management software for PC and Mac.

Please allow 1-3 weeks for delivery. Prices and availability are subject to change without notice.

AOL Selects the Best!

Enhancing Your Online & Computing Experience

The Fast, Easy Way to Share Your Photos Online!

Order Today!
1-888-299-0329

AOL's PhotoCam

Everything you need in one great package to get you started with digital imaging. Just point, click, connect and send! Save money and time. There is no film or developing costs. It is easy to share your photos with family and friends through your e-mail or view pictures on your TV/VCR with the video output connector. AOL's PhotoCam includes an easy to use manual, MGI's PhotoSuite III SE, 8MB of built-in memory to shoot and store up to 128 pictures, beautiful black vinyl carrying case, 4AA batteries, USB and serial Connectors, and more. Available for PC.

$199.95 (s&h $8.95)   #0014740N0012828

Just Point, Click, Connect and Send!

So easy to use,
no wonder it's #1

AOL Selects the Best!

Enhancing Your Online & Computing Experience

Get the Most Out of Your Computing Experience!

Go to AOL Keyword: Shop Direct

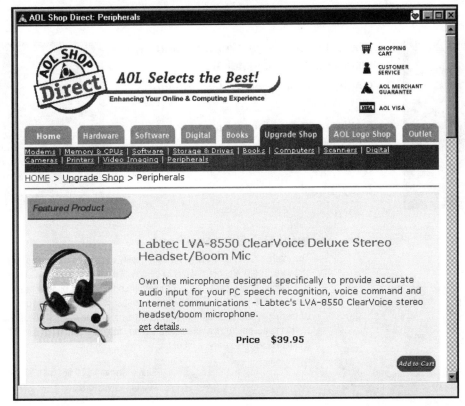

AOL Shop Direct: Peripherals

AOL Selects the Best!

Enhancing Your Online & Computing Experience

SHOPPING CART

CUSTOMER SERVICE

AOL MERCHANT GUARANTEE

AOL VISA

Home | Hardware | Software | Digital | Books | Upgrade Shop | AOL Logo Shop | Outlet

Modems | Memory & CPUs | Software | Storage & Drives | Books | Computers | Scanners | Digital Cameras | Printers | Video Imaging | Peripherals

HOME > Upgrade Shop > Peripherals

Featured Product

Labtec LVA-8550 ClearVoice Deluxe Stereo Headset/Boom Mic

Own the microphone designed specifically to provide accurate audio input for your PC speech recognition, voice command and Internet communications – Labtec's LVA-8550 ClearVoice stereo headset/boom microphone.

get details...

Price $39.95

Add to Cart

AOL Shop Direct Upgrade Shop

AOL is dedicated to help you have the best online and computing experience. In AOL Shop Direct's Upgrade Shop we have devoted an entire area to assist you in finding products that will help you get the most out of your time online!

Visit us today and check out our:

- Video Conferencing equipment
- Digital Cameras
- Digital MP3 Audio Players
- Multi-function Printer/Scanner/Copier/Fax Machines

All these products and more are available at Keyword: AOL Shop Direct

AMERICA Online.

So easy to use, no wonder it's #1

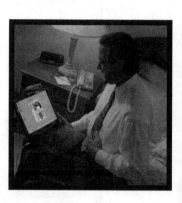
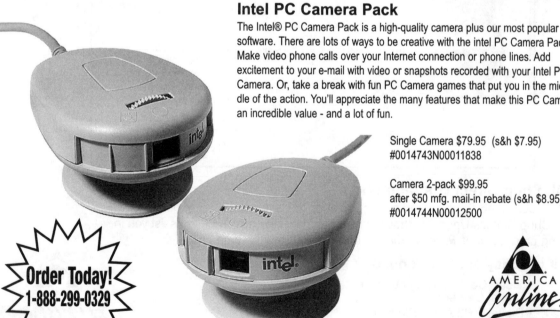

Get Your AOL Mail Anywhere, Anytime!

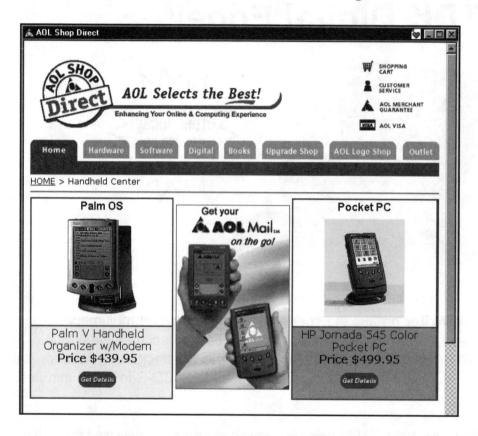

Go to AOL Keyword: Handheld Center

AOL Mail for Palm™ Organizers and Windows CE Palm-Size PCs

Your AOL Mail is not just on your computer anymore! Now you can get the power to send and receive AOL e-mail messages in the palm of your hand! All you need is a hand-held device/modem and an AOL account!

Using AOL Mail is similar to using AOL's desktop software - with "tabs" that display New Mail, Read Mail and Sent Mail. Members can easily read, delete, forward and reply to messages - all on-the-go!

Find all the products you need to get your AOL mail anywhere at Keyword: Handheld Center

So easy to use, no wonder it's #1